Strength Training for Young Athletes

Second Edition

William J. Kraemer, PhD
Steven J. Fleck, PhD

Human Kinetics

Library of Congress Cataloging-in-Publication Data

Kraemer, William J., 1953-
   Strength training for young athletes / William Kraemer and Steven Fleck--2nd ed.
    p. cm.
   Includes bibliographical references and index.
   ISBN 0-7360-5103-1 (soft cover)
   1. Exercise for children. 2. Isometric exercise. I. Fleck, Steven J., 1951- II. Title.
   GV443.K687 2004
   613.7'042--dc22

                                       2004009980

ISBN: 0-7360-5103-1

The Web addresses cited in this text were current as of August 1, 2004, unless otherwise noted.

Acquisitions Editor: Edward McNeely; **Managing Editor:** Wendy McLaughlin; **Assistant Editor:** Kim Thoren; **Copyeditor:** Cheryl Ossola; **Proofreader:** Erin Cler; **Indexer:** Betty Frizzéll; **Permission Manager:** Toni Harte; **Graphic Designer:** Nancy Rasmus; **Graphic Artist:** Sandra Meier; **Photo Manager:** Dan Wendt; **Cover Designer:** Keith Blomberg; **Photographer (cover):** Carlos Ortiz; **Photographer (interior):** All photos by Carlos Ortiz, unless otherwise noted. Photos on pages 128, 140, 179, 183, 195, 196, 198, 199, 210, 215, and 225-227 provided by Gerard Martin; photos on page 216 courtesy of Dr. William Kraemer; **Art Manager:** Kareema McLendon; **Illustrators:** Kareema McLendon, Human Kinetics, and Mic Greenberg; **Printer:** United Graphics

Other credits: We thank Life Fitness Academy, 10601 W. Belmont Avenue, Franklin Park, IL 60131, for their assistance in providing the location and many of the photos used in this book, and Tom Proffitt for his help and support in this effort. Life Fitness is part of the Life Fitness World Headquarters, 5100 N. River Road, Schiller Park, IL 61076. For more information, visit their Web site at www.lifefitness.com, or call 800-634-8637.

Human Kinetics books are available at special discounts for bulk purchase. Special editions or book excerpts can also be created to specification. For details, contact the Special Sales Manager at Human Kinetics.

Printed in the United States of America   10 9 8 7 6 5 4 3 2 1

Human Kinetics
Web site: www.HumanKinetics.com

United States: Human Kinetics
P.O. Box 5076
Champaign, IL 61825-5076
800-747-4457
e-mail: humank@hkusa.com

Canada: Human Kinetics
475 Devonshire Road Unit 100
Windsor, ON N8Y 2L5
800-465-7301 (in Canada only)
e-mail: orders@hkcanada.com

Europe: Human Kinetics
107 Bradford Road, Stanningley
Leeds LS28 6AT, United Kingdom
+44 (0) 113 255 5665
e-mail: hk@hkeurope.com

Australia: Human Kinetics
57A Price Avenue
Lower Mitcham, South Australia 5062
08 8277 1555
e-mail: liaw@hkaustralia.com

New Zealand: Human Kinetics
Division of Sports Distributors NZ Ltd.
P.O. Box 300 226 Albany
North Shore City
Auckland
0064 9 448 1207
e-mail: blairc@hknewz.com

To my wife, Joan, and my children, Daniel, Anna, and Maria. And to my sister, Judy, my mother, Jewell, and my late father, Raymond, for their support and love in my life.

William J. Kraemer

To my wife, Maelu, for allowing me the time and freedom to pursue my interests; and to my parents, Marv and Elda, for their support and love throughout my life.

Steven J. Fleck

Contents

Preface

Over the past 10 years it has become painfully obvious that most children in the United States have become less physically active because of fundamental changes in what they do for leisure-time activities. Now, at the start of the 21st century, we are living what Disneyland's "Future World" of the 1950s yearned for in the next century: a life of ease with few physical demands! This has influenced how children entertain themselves. For most children, entertainment has an inherent technology base; in only a few instances has this translated to promoting physical activity and making it fun (for example, video games and TVs on steppers and exercise bikes). A more sedentary lifestyle has become entrenched by the widespread use of home computers, the Internet, computer games with virtual reality, cable television, videos, and DVDs.

In the United States inactivity, obesity, and type 2 diabetes have grown to epidemic proportions in children. Inactivity is fueled by many factors, including drastic fiscal cutbacks in school physical education classes and after-school activity programs as well as limited opportunities for widespread sport participation. Resistance training, however, is a popular form of exercise for children of all fitness levels. Interestingly, it is perceived as less threatening to children who are overweight and allows feelings of success and achievement in an area of conditioning that has real health and fitness benefits.

An appropriately designed resistance-training program can yield these benefits:

- Increased muscular *strength and power*
- Increased local muscular *endurance* (the ability of a muscle to perform multiple repetitions against a given *resistance)*
- Prevention of injury during sports and recreational activities
- Enhanced status of tissues other than muscle (especially bone), which has great importance in the aging process
- Improved performance capacity in sports and recreational activities
- Development of proper behaviors for an active lifestyle
- Improved health and fitness profile
- Behavioral habituation to a lifelong pattern of physical activity
- Alternative activities for successfully coping with and avoiding negative behaviors, which promote productive time use
- Social and personal benefits such as self-esteem, improved body image, and self-confidence

In fact, as we learn more about strength training for children the benefits appear to increase each year. In this second edition of *Strength Training for Young Athletes*, we give our readers the latest information on strength training for children of all ages. With the resurgence in interest in physical activity for children, many people are finding that resistance training is a major conditioning tool that can successfully address some of the problems with youth health and fitness in the United States and around the world.

Acknowledgments

We want to thank the many people who have contributed to the completion of this book. The professionals at Human Kinetics Publishers made this second edition possible and we thank the total team at HKP for their professionalism and excellence. Special thanks for the needed persistence to make this happen goes to Ed McNeely and Dr. Mike Bahrke during the early development of this second edition. We thank Wendy McLaughlin for her exhaustive efforts in producing this book and to Kim Thoren for taking the baton on the last leg of the effort.

We thank our friends, Greg Bahnfleth and Christine "CC" Cunningham, at the Life Fitness Academy, part of the Life Fitness World Headquarters, for the majority of the exercise and equipment photos used in this book. We also thank Tom Proffitt from Life Fitness for his help and support in this effort. For more information on their equipment, see the Life Fitness website at www.lifefitness.com or inquire at 800-735-3867 for more information.

Special thanks to Gerard Martin, head strength and conditioning coach at the University of Connecticut for his support and for helping to fill in some of the needed photos.

To all of the young athletes who participated in the photo shoots and gave of their valuable time and efforts to the success of this book for the benefit of their peers, we give you a hearty "Thank You"!

Strength Training and Your Child

Strength is the ability to produce maximal force. It is a key factor in every sport, not only for physical performance but for prevention of injury. For many years few people believed that resistance training could improve a child's strength; coaches and teachers believed that children got stronger as they got older and that strength training was only for older athletes. Surprisingly, some initial scientific studies even confirmed this misconceived idea.[1] But in fact children can benefit from a properly designed, age-appropriate resistance-training program.

The fear of resistance training started to subside as the weight of scientific evidence in the late 1980s showed that our earlier ideas were truly misconceptions and that young athletes could make significant gains in muscle strength without injury.[2] This concept gained further support when professional and medical societies began endorsing the use of resistance training by young athletes to better prepare them for the rigors of sport.

BENEFITS OF STRENGTH TRAINING

A properly designed and implemented resistance-training program not only provides important health benefits, prevents injury, and prepares athletes for competition, it's also fun! In today's world we have to look at the health benefits of activity as well as physical performance gains in sport. The evidence that resistance training is effective in youth is convincing: Scientific studies, review papers, and clinical observations have all reported that properly designed resistance-training programs can improve the strength development of prepubescent children and adolescents beyond the gains of normal growth and development.[2, 3] Children as young as 6 years of age have benefited from resistance training in studies lasting as long as nine months.

To date, selected strength tests reveal no major differences in strength gains between prepubescent boys and girls as a result of weight training. Programs for both genders can utilize similar designs that eventually lead to programs intended for adults.[4] During childhood, many physiological changes related to growth and development occur dynamically and rapidly. For example, muscular strength—defined as the maximal force a muscle or muscle group can generate—normally increases from childhood through the early teenage years, at which time there is a striking acceleration of strength in boys and a general plateau of strength in girls.[5]

Strength gains can be dramatic, with children demonstrating improvements as great as 74 percent following eight weeks of progressive resistance training.[6] On average, short-term (8- to 20-week-long) resistance-training programs in children typically result in gains of roughly 30 to 50 percent. How much of this improvement is related to motor learning effects that occur in the early phase of training remains to be determined. Some reports indicate that relative (percent of improvement) strength gains achieved during prepubescence can be equal to if not greater than the relative gains observed during adolescence. Obviously, the absolute strength gains (i.e., the amount of weight lifted) appear to be greater in adolescents than in prepubescent youths, and adults can make even greater absolute gains than young adolescents.[7] Strength changes resulting from a low-volume (sets × repetitions × load), short-term training program may not be distinguishable from those due to normal growth and development. In order to yield results greater than those from normal growth, an adequate training stimulus is needed. One must use proper programs with heavy enough resistance and volumes of exercise (sets × reps) to create an effective training program for prolonged periods of time. In other words, to achieve above-normal strength gains an extended training period and adequate training stimulus are essential. Do not think of it as only a 6- or 12-week program: Resistance training needs to be continued, or its benefits dissipate with natural growth and you cannot maintain your level of fitness.

A wide variety of progressive resistance-training programs appear to work over short periods in untrained children. For example, a progression from 1 set of 10 repetitions to 5 sets of 15 repetitions has elicited improvements in desired training outcomes such as increased strength. How resistance-training programs differentiate over time at various ages is still not clear in children. However, in adult populations several months of training are needed to see the discrete training adaptations that result from different programs.[8] In addition, in our "electronic culture," in which children are conditioned to have short attention spans, it appears that training has to be "periodized," or varied over time, or boredom could well limit adherence to a program. Studies that show positive training adaptations use many training modalities and a wide variety of equipment, including adult weight machines, child-sized machines, free weights, hydraulic and pneumatic machines, isometric muscle actions, wrestling drills, modified pull-ups, and calisthenics.[2]

An Ounce of Prevention

Youth sports started to grow by leaps and bounds by the late 1970s and have continued to get bigger and bigger. Approximately 30 million American children (roughly 50 percent of boys and 25 percent of girls) play competitive organized sports and many others participate in community-based sport programs. Worldwide, the increase in injuries to young athletes over the last two decades is due to more intense sport participation at younger ages. With this increase in sport participation have come numerous reports of injuries to the ill-prepared or improperly trained youth athlete. Everything from Pop Warner football leagues, youth soccer leagues, basketball leagues, Little League baseball, gymnastics, and now X Games sports, such as skateboarding and BMX bicycle events, have shown tremendous growth. And young athletes are making the same mistake so many athletes did in the 1950s and '60s: They attempt to "play themselves into shape." With high sport demands and forces acting on young bones, ligaments, and tendons, sport-related injuries have started to proliferate. Often injury is due to being physically unprepared to participate. Optimal resistance-training programs may limit injuries from sport by preparing the body for the rigors of competition.[9] One report was prophetic in showing that resistance training may in fact be key to the prevention of injury in high school athletes.[10] However, in order for these programs to be effective, they must be properly designed and supervised.

By the early 1990s parents, coaches, and sports medicine professionals were starting to realize that young athletes need to prepare their bodies for the demands of a sport. Children were being injured in sport activities; obviously, their bodies were not able to meet the physical demands of the sports they were playing.[11] Resistance exercise, by making the tissues of the body stronger and more resistant to damage, is a potent tool that can reduce the severity of athletic injury and possibly prevent it. Modified games and proper sport techniques and coaching are keys to reducing sport injuries in the immature athlete.[12] However, resistance training can also help in the process of sport preparation.[13]

© Human Kinetics

Proper resistance training can help prevent injuries in high school sports.

Strength training is important in improving physical performance; in addition, resistance-trained athletes respond better to physical rehabilitation—their tissues repair themselves more quickly from injury. We even see this fact acknowledged in orthopedic surgery, where physicians instruct patients to train their muscles prior to knee surgery.

Preparing for Competition

Resistance training can help young athletes develop their physical abilities and enhance their physiological function, but will it make an elite athlete out of anyone? That depends on the many factors that go into sport performance; physical abilities are only part of the equation for success. Some young athletes do bring amazing genetic talent and physical maturity to the game early in their careers, such as basketball stars Darryl Dawkins, Kobe Bryant, and more recently LeBron James, who all entered the NBA as teenagers. Talent is paramount to elite performances.

Talent aside, an optimally designed and implemented resistance-training program can give many young athletes competitive advantages throughout their school years. Sadly, not all programs are cutting edge in design, and not everyone visualizes the same developmental timeline. The concept of the "late bloomer" has been famous in many sports; even at the college level, "walk-ons" are given the chance to train and develop for a few years prior to possibly taking on a starting role on the team. In the past such a practice had been the hallmark of the University of Nebraska football teams, which had more fifth-year starters due to their ability to develop players over a career. Today, the "win now" mentality can be seen at many major college and professional sports venues, where young athletes play as they come through the door. Development of physical abilities must match the natural pattern of physical maturation, which is different for each person. Advantages from training come only when young athletes perform optimal programs, not ones that are outdated or inappropriate and therefore ineffective in eliciting desired changes.

As former coaches, we understand the importance of sport technique, coaching strategies, and proper sport selection or position play to the success of a young athlete. In addition, psychological maturity and what many coaches call "heart" are also important. But in an age where children grow up too soon, we still need to give them the chance to develop at their own rate. Physical training does have many benefits other than the physical attributes it produces that carry over into the competitive environment. Creativity and sensitivity are essential in creating programs that enhance the psychological as well as the physical development of the young athlete.

Time spent in the weight room can teach children about the relationship between hard work and positive outcomes. In everyone—boys and girls, men and women— effective training also underscores the importance of the persistence needed to build physical abilities. As sport scientists, we both have seen many athletes demonstrate a competitive personality in the weight room; it's related to both physical and psychological maturity. Often, the way an athlete trains gives important clues to how he will compete. Attention to details, concentration, poise under conditions of fatigue, helping others, and attitude about themselves and others are just a few things revealed in the weight room. A well-designed resistance-training program can help develop positive characteristics and give children confidence in their physical abilities and performance. We are just starting to learn about the many benefits beyond the physical that occur with proper implementation of conditioning programs for both boys and girls.

Kids Just Want to Have Fun

Too often sports take on a very serious nature, and this even translates over to conditioning activities for health and fitness. But the successful programs provide an environment in which the child can have fun. Novel experiments in school fitness programs have used a "health club" model, which provides children with a multitude of high-tech fitness devices from resistance-training equipment to cardio machines. The key is to hook children on the concept of seeing their own progress and working hard to improve; however, success in meeting that goal appears to be in part due to the exciting health-club-like environment: headsets playing the children's favorite music, peer interactions, laughter, the latest equipment, and computer monitoring to track progress and training histories. In addition, competent instructors provide appropriate starting points and training progression, making these experiments a new approach in school-based health and fitness programs for the 21st-century student.

The first step in training may well be simply to go through the motions and develop an exercise habit. Over the years we have called this a "base program," or "general preparation phase," in periodization, the first three to six weeks of a resistance-training program where loads are light. This time is used to gradually develop the body's initial toleration to resistance exercise stresses and learn proper exercise techniques. The key is learning how to enjoy exercise and allowing the body to make adjustments to the initial physical changes with limited negative outcomes (e.g., muscle soreness and boredom); in other words, you must resist doing too much too soon. Although some of us may not have environments that simulate a health club, the most important factor appears to be enjoyment. A flexible schedule, high-tech equipment, music, and socializing all contribute to an enjoyable environment.

MISCONCEPTIONS ABOUT STRENGTH TRAINING

Most of the many misconceptions concerning resistance training and children result from misunderstandings and impressions gained from partial truths, stereotypes, or sport myths. One classic myth is that one can become muscle-bound or slower as a result of resistance training. Many adults think of resistance training in terms of the specific sports that use such training in the competitive arena, such as bodybuilding, power lifting, and Olympic weightlifting. In addition, many misconceptions arise from sport myths and coaching fallacies, such as resistance training in basketball players will hurt their shot, or lifting will cause injury. Even more insidious are the marketing strategies that promote myths of achieving fitness in six weeks, or that all you need to do is one set of exercises, or that using free weights produce more injuries. All this misinformation has caused confusion in the lay public that warrants some clarity: Resistance training for young athletes is a dynamic process designed to meet the ever-changing training goals of the child. Mythologies and misconceptions only hurt the child and limit a program modality that's effective in developing physical fitness and promoting a healthy body.

Injuries

Many people presume that there is a high risk of injury associated with resistance training. Data gathered in the 1970s and '80s by the National Electronic Injury Surveillance System (NEISS) of the United States Consumer Product Safety Commission (USCPSC) led to the fear of injury associated with resistance training in youths. NEISS used data from hospital and clinic emergency rooms to make nationwide projections of the total number of injuries related to exercise. In 1979 the USCPSC reported that more than half of the 35,512 weightlifting injuries requiring emergency room treatment involved 10- to 19-year-olds. In 1987 it revealed that 8,590 children ages 0 to 14 visited emergency rooms because of so-called weightlifting-related injuries. However, these reports did not distinguish between injuries associated with resistance training and those associated with the competitive sports of power lifting and weightlifting. This is an important discriminating factor because a competitive athlete whose goal is maximal performance will take greater risks in training and competition than will someone who is training for fitness. Many people confuse the risk-to-benefit ratio of resistance training for general fitness with that of competitive sports. Failing to distinguish between the two impacts understanding of both the training programs needed and the associated risks of competition in sport.

The most common resistance-training injuries in the NEISS reports are sprains and strains, although it also notes more serious injuries, such as epiphyseal fractures and lumbosacral (lower back) injuries. From 1991 to 1996, individuals under the age of 21 suffered 20,940 injuries. Muscle strains and sprains accounted for 40 to 79 percent of all injuries, with the lumbar back cited as the most commonly injured area. However, nationwide projections of emergency room visits and case reports of injured young athletes provide limited information on the predisposing factors of these injuries. In fact, improper training methods, excessive loading, poorly designed equipment, or a lack of qualified adult supervision caused many of the reported injuries. Although these findings indicate that the unsupervised use of heavy resistances during weight training or lifting competitions may lead to injuries, it is misleading to attribute them to properly designed and closely supervised youth resistance-training programs.

Generally, the risk of injury associated with resistance training is similar for children and adults. But a traditional area of concern in children is the potential for damage to the epiphyses, or growth plates, of the long bones. The epiphysis is the weak link in a young skeleton because cartilage is not as strong as bone. If not properly treated, damage to the epiphysis could cause it to ossify (become bone) prematurely, stopping limb growth or resulting in limb deformity. A few retrospective case reports have noted epiphyseal plate fractures during prepubescence and adolescence. However, most of these injuries were due to improper lifting techniques, maximal lifts, or lack of qualified adult supervision. The classic example of a young boy trying to lift a near-maximal weight in the basement of his house without supervision or proper understanding of the exercise and spotting techniques is the worst-case scenario for increasing the risk of injury.

Both prepubescent children and adolescents are susceptible to growth plate injuries, yet a prepubescent child may be less susceptible than an adolescent because his growth plates may be stronger and more resistant to sheering-type forces.[14] Significantly, growth plate fractures have not occurred in any prospective resistance-training studies that included appropriately prescribed training regimens and competent instruction.

Another concern about resistance training in children is the potential for repetitive-use soft-tissue injury. Because children with this type of injury frequently don't go to the emergency room or see a physician, the incidence of these injuries is more difficult to determine. Nevertheless, several retrospective studies involving adolescents do associate lower-back soft-tissue injuries with resistance training. In fact, lumbosacral pain was the most frequent injury in high school athletes who participated in resistance-training programs. In one report, a majority of the injuries to the lumbar spine might have been attributable to the improper use of a device designed to improve vertical jump ability.[15] A study of adolescent power lifters who presumably trained with maximal or near-maximal resistances revealed that 50 percent of reported injuries were to the lower back, 18 percent to the upper extremities, 17 percent to the lower extremities, and 14 percent to the trunk.[16] The potential for similar injuries in prepubescent children should be recognized. The available evidence and clinical observations indicate that training-induced injuries to the lower back are a noteworthy concern for clinicians and coaches.[2]

Prospective studies involving resistance training and children indicate a low risk of injury. In the vast majority of the published studies, no overt clinical injuries were reported. Although various training modalities were used, all the programs were closely supervised and appropriately prescribed to ensure that they matched the initial capacity of the child. Only two published studies report resistance-training-related injuries in children—a shoulder strain that resolved with one week of rest[17] and an undefined "minor" injury.[16] In the shoulder-strain study there was no evidence of either musculoskeletal injury or muscle damage following 14 weeks of progressive resistance training. Generally, the risk of injury in resistance training is very low when appropriate training instructions are followed and supervision is provided.

Resistance training in children, as with most physical activities, does carry some degree of inherent risk of musculoskeletal injury, but it's no greater than in many sports or recreational activities in which children participate. In the only prospective study that evaluated the incidence of sports-related injuries in children over a one-year period, resistance training resulted in .7 percent of 1,576 injuries, whereas football and basketball resulted in 19 percent and 15 percent, respectively, of all injuries.[18] When the data were evaluated in terms of injuries per 100 participants, football (28.3) and wrestling (16.4) were at the top of the list, but resistance training was not included in this final analysis.

A retrospective evaluation of resistance training and weightlifting injuries primarily incurred by 13- to 16-year-olds revealed that the aforementioned activities are markedly safer than many other sports and activities.[19] Weightlifting is defined as the Olympic lifts of the clean, jerk, and snatch lift. Resistance training is the use of external resistance of many types to create an external load for the muscle(s) to exercise against. The study indicated that the rate of injury for weightlifting was lower than for resistance training, which may be explained in part by the fact that the sport of weightlifting is characterized by knowledgeable coaching and a gradual progression of training loads. In some countries children as young as 8 years old are taught advanced multi-joint lifts, although weight is not added to the bar until age 12 or 13. The potential for injury during free-weight exercises should not be overlooked, especially from accidental dropping of weights.

Catastrophic injury can occur if safety standards (e.g., adult supervision, safe equipment, and age-specific training guidelines) for youth resistance training are not followed.[3] In one case study report a 9-year-old boy died when a barbell rolled off a bench-press support and fell on his chest.[20] This fatality underscores the importance of providing close adult supervision and safe training equipment for all youth resistance-training programs, but especially for younger children.

Any exercise or activity for children has risks as well as benefits. Although the risk of resistance-training injuries is very low, it can be further minimized by close adult supervision, proper instruction, appropriate program design, and careful selection of training equipment. No justifiable safety concerns preclude prepubescent children or adolescents from participating in a supervised program.

It is important to note that no injuries have been reported in prospective studies that utilized adequate warm-up periods, appropriate progression of loads, close and experienced supervision, and critically chosen maximal-strength tests (e.g, the maximal amount of resistance one can lift or force one can produce in a given movement) to evaluate training-induced changes in children.[2,21] Direct strength and power tests are needed in order to evaluate functional changes in children that reflect the physiological effects of training. Strength is the maximal amount of force that can be produced in a given movement and power is the how fast that force can be applied over a range of motion. The National Strength and Conditioning Association (NSCA) supports the relative safety of using supervised 1RM and power testing in laboratory settings to evaluate training-induced changes in muscular strength.[3] Most of the forces that children encounter in sports and recreational activities are greater in exposure time and magnitude than competently supervised and properly performed maximal-strength tests. Conversely, unsupervised and improperly performed 1RM testing (e.g., inadequate progression of loading and poor lifting technique) is inappropriate for children under any circumstances due to the risk of injury.

Various professional position stands express concern when children lift maximal or near-maximal weights. Maximal-strength testing—lifting as much weight as possible for one repetition, or 1RM (repetition maximum)—for clinical evaluation or research under the supervision of trained professionals has not resulted in injury. However, chronic maximal-strength training (lifting only 1- to 3RM resistances) over a training period may yield different results, especially when it is unsupervised. Therefore position stands continue to recommend that prepubescent children be limited to weights they can lift at least six repetitions or more. The age at which children can start to use heavier weights depends on their maturation and training experience.

Children who lift maximal or near-maximal resistances, especially during their developmental years, risk possible injuries related to the long bones and the back, especially if a predisposing joint, skeletal, or muscle pathology is present. This perceived risk is even greater when children are unsupervised, because they may not understand or use proper lifting techniques, safety spotting, and appropriate program design.

Resistance-Training Sports

Power lifting, Olympic weightlifting, and bodybuilding are competitive sports with goals that reflect adult training capabilities and values. In addition, the goals of bodybuilding are related to the development of muscle size and definition. Medical and scientific professionals typically discourage children from participating in such adult competitions because of the heavy training loads required. Competition in the sport of power lifting comprises three lifts: the bench press, the squat, and the dead lift. The winner of the competition is the person who can lift the most weight for one repetition in each of these lifts. Similarly, competing in the sport of weightlifting (also known as Olympic weightlifting) requires maximal-strength performance in two lifts called the snatch lift and the clean and jerk. Again, the goal is to lift the most weight for one repetition in each lift. Training for such competitions is inappropriate for children. However, the lifts used in these sports, when performed with proper supervision, correct exercise technique, and appropriate resistance, are suitable for children. Remember, prepubescent children should not lift maximal or near-maximal weights.

Model lifting programs do exist; many younger boys and girls are involved in supervised programs such as USA Weightlifting's Junior Weightlifting Program and have developed a love for the sport. Additionally, they have gained significant physical benefits, including enhanced bone development and an increased ability to grow and repair from the rigors of exercise training.[22-24] In working with young lifters from 14 to 17 years old, we have observed that programs for this age group need to utilize proper training progression (see table 1.1), meaning that more advanced training techniques are gradually introduced as the child matures. The keys to any sport-training program are individualization, monitoring of physical demands, recovery, specificity of training, appropriate design for the age group, and competent supervision and coaching.

The sport of bodybuilding consists of a competition in which judges score an individual competitor on a variety of physical attributes including muscular size and definition, symmetrical muscular development, and the ability to perform various muscular poses. Because children typically do not make large gains in muscle size, bodybuilding can represent unrealistic, if not physiologically unattainable, competitive goals for the prepubescent child. Conversely, the principles used in bodybuilding, which emphasize the importance of exercising all of the muscle groups, symmetrical development of the upper- and lower-body musculature, and a disciplined diet and lifestyle, are positive aspects of the sport that should be part of any good training program. You must identify whether specific aspects of any training program or goal are appropriate for a child. In addition, remember that exercise programs need to demonstrate an overall balance in total fitness, including not only strength but flexibility and cardiovascular development.

Historically, people involved in power lifting, weightlifting, or bodybuilding have been consulted to help develop programs for resistance training. These lifters and ex-lifters have been the source of empirical and anecdotal information for many years in the world of the strength and conditioning profession. Thus many resistance-training programs reflect a strong influence from the competitive lifting sports. Even today, most of the experts have backgrounds in various forms of competitive lifting or are former athletes who engaged in serious resistance training to enhance their athletic performances. Personal lifting experiences and sound scientific principles can positively influence the development of a resistance-training program, but optimal program designs carefully translate these into what is needed by each child.

INTRODUCING A STRENGTH-TRAINING PROGRAM

A resistance-training workout can create anxiety, fear, and even anger if the program variables are combined in a specific manner.[25] For example, short rest periods between sets and exercises produce high amounts of lactic acid and greater metabolic demands. If an athlete does not gradually progress toward this type of workout protocol, it can be very demanding and psychologically painful due to extreme exertion demands. Dizziness, nausea, and at an extreme level, vomiting can occur, which means the protocol is too physically and psychologically demanding. The "puke index," as some coaches call it, is not a sign of a good workout; this is where proper design comes in so that workouts are neither too demanding nor inappropriate for a particular athlete. Such demanding programs, although they have their place in preparing certain athletes for competition (e.g., wrestling, 400-meter sprint), need to include proper progression and, more important, the athlete's understanding of what will happen and why. If the athletes, young or old, understand what is happening to them, they can more readily focus on the positive benefits of their hard work. A good strength-training program relies on preparation (ask yourself if your child is really ready to begin strength training), continuation (understanding the importance of continuing the program throughout your child's growing years), and comprehension (knowing the anatomical and physiological components associated with a strength-training program).

Preparation

The old days of seeing conditioning activities as derivative of a militaristic discipline filled with rebuke, guilt, and punishment are over; such an attitude is not a part of any successful program in the evolution of youth fitness today. The new grand experiments in school-based, health-club approaches to fitness have shown that children are most successful when the environment is enjoyable and familiar and allows them to see that the reward of hard work is progress. Ultimately it is the idea of the children competing with themselves that makes the process work optimally. Human nature, in both children and adults, directs us to seek pleasure and avoid pain. So we must redefine the rigors of physical exercise in the context of "good pain," fun, the release provided by exertion and letting off steam, and the feelings of pleasure and satisfaction after a workout.

Today's world exposes children to the concept of resistance training in many ways. Almost every school in the United States has some form of weight room, and many communities have gyms, health clubs, or YMCA/YWCAs, often with classes for children. Television, movies, the Internet, and magazines also acquaint children with the concepts of resistance training or weightlifting. Unfortunately, due to the mixed messages these information sources generate, along with a lack of factual information about resistance training and children, many misconceptions and fears concerning resistance training for children still exist. In addition, many people bring prejudices from their own resistance-training experiences, which do not optimally serve a child. Only in the past 10 years have concerns about resistance training by children been tempered, both in the mainstream of the coaching profession and the lay public. Yet now we are challenged the correct the misinformation about resistance training for children, because now the public is ready to listen.

Coaches, parents, and instructors should carefully think about whether a young person is ready to participate in a resistance-training program. They must answer and address various questions and considerations:

- Is the child psychologically and physically ready to participate?
- Which program should the child follow?
- Are the goals and objectives of the program clear, and do they match the program's design?
- How is the program individualized and what is the progression plan over time?
- Do the child and the supervisor understand proper lifting techniques for each exercise?
- Do the child and the supervisor understand the safety spotting techniques for each lift?
- Does the child understand safety considerations for each piece of equipment used in the program?
- Does the resistance-training equipment fit the child properly?
- Does the child have a balanced physical exercise program that addresses other fitness components (e.g., cardiovascular and flexibility training)?
- Have all of the child's fears and misconceptions about resistance training been addressed?

- Is the child genuinely interested in participating in such a conditioning program?

All of these factors need to be considered before a child begins a resistance-training program.

Basic Guidelines
for a Children's Resistance-Training Program

The possible dangers involved in resistance training are related to inappropriate exercise demands placed on the child. Although there are general training guidelines, you must consider the special needs of each individual. In essence this means you must design a program for each child's needs that employs proper exercise techniques and safety considerations. If implemented properly, resistance training is one of the safest physical activities, and the benefits to the young athlete far outweigh the risks. The following points are essential to having a safe and successful program for your child.

1. **Proper program design.** Do not impose a program designed for adults on a child. Work with a professional to design a program that fits the individual needs of your child within her own lifting abilities.

2. **Supervision by a knowledgeable adult.** Supervision is required at all times, by either a parent or coach, to help prevent injury and overexertion.

3. **Better physical preparation to prevent sports-related injuries.** All athletes should participate in a general strength-training program. Athletes who are 14 to 16 years old should also include training based on their individual sport. (See chapter 13 for sport-specific training examples.)

4. **Physical and emotional maturity.** When you introduce resistance training to a child, keep in mind her physical and emotional maturity; she must be mentally and emotionally ready to undergo the stress of exercise training. As with any sport or exercise program, the child should have a thorough physical exam by a physician. There is no standard age at which a child can start resistance training. Typically, if she is able to participate in sports, she is ready for some type of resistance-training program (see table 1.1).

5. **Ability to follow directions and perform exercises safely and with proper form.** Children with physical and mental disabilities can also participate in resistance training as long as they receive appropriate teaching and necessary equipment adaptations. Programs for all children should provide proper instruction and gradual progression in exercise stress (see chapters 3 and 4). Remember, children need about three to six weeks to get used to the stresses (i.e., base program or general preparation phase). It is important to teach them the difference between "good pain" and "bad pain. Good pain is the natural feelings related to fatigue and being tired in your muscles and body. Bad pain is the sharp pain related to injury or trauma to the joints, bones, or muscles.

6. **Realistic goals.** People engage in resistance training for a variety of reasons. Select the goals that are most appropriate to your child's situation and focus on long- and short-term plans for obtaining them.
   - Improved muscular strength and power
   - Muscle-size change (little or none in younger children)
   - Improved local muscular endurance
   - Positive influence on body composition
   - Improved strength balance around joints
   - Improved total-body strength
   - Prevention of injuries in sports
   - Positive influence on sport performance
   - Improved self-confidence

Table 1.1 Basic Guidelines for Resistance-Exercise Progression

Age	Program Design
7 years or younger	Introduce child to basic exercises using little or no weight; develop the concept of a training session; teach exercise technique; progress from body-weight calisthenics, partner exercises, and lightly resisted exercises; keep volume low.
8-10 years	Gradually increase the number of exercises; practice exercise technique in all lifts; start gradual progressive loading of exercises; keep exercises simple; gradually increase training volume; carefully monitor tolerance of the exercise stress.
11-13 years	Teach all basic exercise techniques; continue progressive loading of each exercise; emphasize exercise techniques; introduce more advanced exercises with little or no resistance. Progress to more advanced youth programs in resistance exercise; add sport-specific components; emphasize exercise techniques; increase volume.
14-15 years	Progress to more advanced youth programs in resistance exercise; add sport-specific components; emphasize exercise techniques; increase volume.
16 years or older	Move child to entry-level adult programs after all background knowledge has been mastered and a basic level of training experience has been gained.

Note: If a child of any age begins a program with no previous experience, start him at previous levels and move him to more advanced levels as exercise tolerance, skill, amount of training time, and understanding permit.

Continuation

One fact that has become obvious is the need for continual training in youth, especially during preadolescence and the adolescent years up to about age16, to maintain an advantage over what normal growth can produce.[26] In other words, if a child stops training, "detraining" occurs and his strength will eventually revert back to a normal growth level. One report observed that children doing strength training during a school year were significantly stronger than their matched controls, but when neither group trained over the summer vacation months, there were no differences in strength when they returned to school in the fall.[27, 28] This report underscored the importance of continuity in resistance training for children.[28, 29] The precise mechanisms of the detraining response and the physiological adaptations that occur as a result remain to be fully elucidated, although changes in neuromuscular functioning appear to play a significant role, at least during the prepubescent years.

Comprehension

Strength improvements are created by the exercise stimuli, which change several physiological functions. The nervous system is one of the first systems to adapt to a resistance-training program. Then, over the course of the training program, the quality and quantity of proteins in muscle change. Thus, improved strength is the end result of many physiological changes that occur in response to a specific resistance-training program. The following factors are integral to producing strength gains with training.

Neural Factors

The cause of strength improvements in children is a complicated question that is of great scientific interest. The key to understanding improvements in muscle strength in younger athletes is the nervous system. It is the nervous system that sends the electrical impulses down the spinal cord and out to the muscles to stimulate them, and improvements in its function can dramatically increase the body's ability to produce force. Scientific evidence points to the important role the nervous system plays in producing strength gains in children, at least during training periods of less than six months.[30] Both boys and girls gain strength by improving the functional ability of their nervous systems rather than by markedly increasing the size of their muscles. Hypertrophy, or an increase in muscle size, is more difficult for children, especially prepubescent ones, to achieve than for adults over short training periods. In addition, changes in the quality of the muscle proteins (e.g., type of muscle proteins) could also explain improvements in force production in children. Several training studies report significant improvements in strength during prepubescence without corresponding increases in muscle size and shape, as compared to a similar control group, which indicates that neural mechanisms caused the majority of the strength improvement.

We've established that the improvement in muscle strength that results from proper resistance training is a product of a trained nervous system, not large increases in muscle size. The trained nervous system is capable of better stimulation of muscle to produce force. Because large increases in muscle mass beyond normal growth are not possible in younger children, they should not participate in resistance training only in the hope of getting big muscles. This can be a problem for young boys who see older (16- to 17-year-old) boys with defined, larger muscles. Don't allow any young child, especially a boy, to believe that a few months of lifting weights will give him the muscle size and look of older children. However, as children (especially males) go through puberty, they become able to increase muscle size. At this point, muscle size gains become a viable training goal.

Muscle Hypertrophy

Even without increases in size beyond normal growth, a child's muscles can still benefit from resistance training because it improves and enhances muscular function, thus improving performance and physical fitness. Prepubescent children generally lack adequate concentrations of circulating growth factors and androgens to stimulate hypertrophy, thus they experience more difficulty increasing their muscle mass through resistance training as compared to older populations. However, studies do show the potential for hypertrophy in younger children, so this remains a topic of research that attempts to identify physiological conditions or program types that cause muscle size increases in children.[31, 32]

Testosterone and Growth Hormones

During puberty testicular testosterone secretion in boys is associated with considerable increases in fat-free mass (e.g., muscle and bone), and hormonal influences on muscle hypertrophy become possible. Training-induced strength gains during and after puberty in boys may therefore be associated with dramatic changes in hypertrophic factors. Lower levels of androgens in girls may limit the absolute magnitude of training-induced increases in muscle hypertrophy; however, other hormones and growth factors (growth hormone and insulin-like growth factors) may be at least partly responsible for muscle development in younger women. The growth hormone/insulin-like growth factor-1 secretions from the brain and liver, respectively, are quite complex and play multiple roles in both men and women. These hormones no doubt are a central mechanism in the interplay between exercise and tissue growth during development. This interplay's relationship to strength training and youth is currently the topic of intense scientific study.

In boys, clear-cut changes in muscle size and mass occur with the dramatic growth during adolescence when testosterone surges; not only does it develop the young boy into a man, it also enhances his muscle size and strength. This is especially true for the upper-body musculature and is an important gender difference when compared to changes observed in the physical development in young girls during puberty. Figure 1.1 shows the relationship between the magnitude of testosterone surges with growth in boys and girls.

In all children, but especially girls, physical development of muscles and bones is related to important anabolic hormones other than testosterone. Growth hormone and the insulin-like growth factors are vital in the physical development of muscle and bones in both boys and girls. For girls and women these hormones are thought

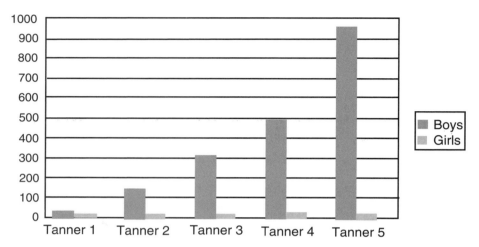

Figure 1.1 Size and testosterone surges in growth for boys and girls.

to compensate for the lower amounts of testosterone (10 to 30 times lower in concentration) circulating in their bodies when compared to boys and men.

Growth hormone is secreted from the pituitary gland, and growth factors (most notably insulin-like growth factor-1) are secreted from the liver and also produced in small quantities in the muscles. Like testosterone, these hormones are anabolic, meaning "to build"; they help stimulate the growth and strengthening of tissues such as muscle and bone.

Organization Position Stands for Children and Strength Training

Interestingly, remarkable similarities exist between the various professional societies' and associations' guidelines for strength training in children. The key issues are safety, medical clearance to participate, proper programming, and competent supervision. With physical inactivity reaching epidemic proportions in this country, encouragement of exercise activities has become a focus of all of the major sports-medicine and science groups. Any differences in position stands are related to the various expertise levels of the organizations: medical groups emphasize the medical concerns and exercise professionals focus on exercise design and program elements. Nevertheless, all of the major organizations support resistance training in children.

For more details, readers can examine the Web sites and references for each of the organizations' position stands on strength training for children. The American Academy of Pediatrics (www.aap.org/policy/pprgtoc.cfm); National Strength and Conditioning Association (www.nsca-lift.org), which is endorsed by the American College of Sports Medicine (www.acsm.org); and American Orthopaedic Society for Sports Medicine (www.sportsmed.org) all support strength training for the young athlete. Each organization promotes the following major concepts:

1. Proper exercise and spotting techniques need to be used.
2. Proper supervision should be provided for all training sessions.
3. Training should be individualized for each child.
4. Resistance should be limited to a 6-repetition maximum, and maximal lifting should be used only for research purposes.
5. Warm-up and cool-down periods should be utilized.
6. Proper progression in frequency, intensity, and duration should be used.
7. Resistance training should be one part of a total conditioning program that also includes aerobic training, flexibility training, and nutritional counseling.
8. Children should have a physical exam by a physician before engaging in a strength-training program.
9. Children should not use adult resistance-training programs but should have programs specifically designed for their age and needs.
10. Children should be voluntary participants in their exercise program. They should have the emotional maturity to be able to understand what they are doing and why.

SUMMING UP AND LOOKING AHEAD

Training with weights can be fun, safe, and appropriate for a child. Resistance training should be part of a total fitness program that changes as the child's goals and needs change throughout life. Adults should stress the need for adherence to and consistency in training, which requires discipline and hard work in order for the child to achieve positive gains through resistance training. At the same time, they should not impose adult definitions of hard work on a child. Since each child grows, matures, and thus adapts to resistance training at an individual rate, limit comparisons to other children and allow him to gain satisfaction in his own progress. Programs must be very progressive in nature yet not overshoot the child's physical or emotional abilities to tolerate and recover from the exercise stress.

In the next chapter we will examine some of the basic concepts of growth and development of children. This will help shape our expectations of a resistance-exercise program for children.

2

Physical and Psychological Development

The different maturation levels of children require the trainer to match the conditioning program to the individual child. Think about it. Merely by watching a Little League baseball game or a youth soccer game you can easily see the pronounced physical and emotional differences among children. You might observe that some children are bigger than others, some are faster and more coordinated, and some are more skilled. One child may become very upset about a missed catch or a missed shot on goal while another may not seem too concerned. One child may be an intense competitor; another chases after the beautiful orange leaves falling from a big oak tree onto the soccer field during a game. Physical and psychological differences do exist and must be understood when dealing with sport or conditioning activities for children.

Physical and psychological differences result from the impact of what biologists call "nurture or nature" on a given trait or ability. In other words, are you a function of the environmental influences in which you developed or are you purely a function of your genetic makeup? This debate has raged for years among biological scientists, and now it appears that each situation must be evaluated on its own.

Each sport is different in its physical demands. For example, coaches frequently say that "you recruit speed." Can *anyone* be a 100-meter-sprint gold medalist? There appears to be a set of genetic factors related to the type of neuromuscular system you must have in order to be successful at this very specific sport skill of going from point A to point B faster than any other human. Your neuromuscular system must have some very specific characteristics or you will not be able to run exceptionally fast. For example, the exceptional sprinter has a high percentage (greater than 70 percent) of Type II, or fast twitch, muscle fibers capable of rapid muscle action upon stimulation from very fast-type motor units (i.e., the motor neuron and associated muscle fibers) and an ideal body-mass-to-power ratio for maximum velocity over a 100-meter distance. Even if you have the basic genetics, other factors must be in place to promote a world-class performance. So building the optimal physiological strategy or profile for an athlete in some sports begins with genetics that support the primary needs of the sport. Without some of these characteristics an athlete's ability to compete at the highest level is limited. Being a 100-meter Olympic champion is not possible without an optimal set of genetic endowments for size, muscle fiber type, and nervous system characteristics.

The importance of genetics also can be seen on the other end of the continuum, where we find the marathon race, which is the ultimate running endurance event in the Olympics. Again, no one stands on the starting line for the Olympic marathon without possessing a distinct set of genetic and physiological capabilities. Today an Olympic marathon runner must be capable of running 26.4 miles in close to 2 hours and 10 minutes. This requires an optimal body size and muscle fiber type with a high percentage (greater than 75 percent) of Type I, or slow twitch, muscle fibers to support the endurance demands of the race. Although psychological factors, practice and competition opportunities, training environment (including altitude), supplemental conditioning programs, nutritional considerations, and a host of other factors are vital for pulling it all together, fundamental base genetics are needed for an elite performance at the extreme ends of the performance continuum.

Since many sports do not require such extreme abilities of speed or endurance, various combinations of physical and psychological characteristics can result in success. Nature is a factor in all of them, but nurture can play a bigger role. For example, would Tiger Woods be as great a golfer as he is if he had not started the game until he was in college? From all accounts he was immersed in golf from the cradle, showing off his amazing putting skills on *The Merv Griffin Show* at the young age of four. Environment or genetics? Nurture or nature? Our vote in this case goes to "nurture." However, the impact of genetics cannot be discounted due to the obvious interaction of the physical and psychological development necessary for an elite performance.

Mass practice (a motor learning term for the number of practices or trials performed in practicing a skill) of motor patterns from a young age appears to be an important factor in optimizing genetic talent in many high-skill sports. We see this in sports such as baseball and tennis, in which young athletes start to develop high-skill levels at an early age; this appears to be an important component of their success. Without exercise and skill training, the performance advantage goes to the child who has a biologically accelerated rate of growth and development.[1] However, psychological burnout from too much sport training and performance can become a real problem for young athletes. Today it is too often the large sums of money at the end of the rainbow that drive parents and their children to extreme measures in the pursuit of sport success. Creating an elite athlete becomes more difficult than first imagined. In the end it is the joy of sport, the development process, and the positive environment that surrounds sport participation that will benefit even the most motivated athlete. Conditioning—and more specifically, strength training can be a positive factor in an athlete's development, but without a healthy approach to the whole issue of athlete development the joy of sport can be lost.

Regardless of the source of influences on maturation, when developing conditioning programs for children you must understand that the influences are many and that they affect an outcome. Some of the influences are related to "nurture," meaning they can be readily changed (e.g., through practice of a motor skill or positive reinforcements for developing coping skills), while other developmental aspects are related to nature; and therefore environmental factors, including weight training, have only a minimal impact on them. For example, exercise and nutrition can help bone growth, but skeleton size is determined by genetics.

Skill and the Price of Success

When I was a junior high wrestling coach, I found out how much skill impacted the success of an athlete. My seventh-graders were just being introduced to the sport, learning the most basic moves and rules. As a young coach I had not realized that other schools in the conference had wrestling programs that started in kindergarten, so by the time those students wrestled my kids they had seven years of experience under their belts. This became obvious after we walked off the mat losing a match 55-0. Yet surprisingly, although the kids were disappointed by the loss, most of them had positive attitudes about it, saying, "Wow! Those guys are really good!" We continued on, and wrestling was fun and a part of their scholastic careers.

Skill development is important to success in many sports. But years later some of those same opposing wrestlers, including one NCAA Division I national champion, said, "I was tired of the sport by the time I left high school." So there are two sides to success to consider. The role of sport in each child's life can be different and is not necessarily based on absolute competitive success. Each parent and coach has to understand that not all children yearn for the same goals in a sport and that individual differences in goal setting need to be acknowledged.

DEVELOPING PHYSICALLY

Physical differences as well as performance capabilities at different ages are due to varying genetic potentials and growth rates. Adults need to realize that children are not just "little adults." Understanding some of the basic principles of growth and development allows you to develop realistic expectations for children. It also prevents children from becoming frustrated by unrealistic demands. Ultimately, sensitivity to these growth and development issues will also help you develop solid starting points for training programs, proper goals, and appropriate exercise progressions. The exercise program must match the child's physical and emotional ability to tolerate its stresses.

How Genetics Plays a Role

Growth and development of a child involve many factors, not simply a single element such as height. To an extent we are all limited by our genetic potential; many people, on seeing a great athlete, acknowledge that "it is important to have picked your parents wisely." Although there is truth in this statement, we have already discussed that many factors other than genetics go into the making of a great athlete. There are physically gifted athletes who never succeeded in sports as expected. Psychological factors are also important.

Knowledge about our genetic makeup is increasing markedly every year. With the genetic code now in place due to the Human Genome Project, information about the effects of the many families of genes on everything from diseases to human performance will become more comprehensible and commonplace in our lives. But at present, beyond the hype of 21st-century science, we can use some of the basic concepts to design resistance-training programs that optimize what each child brings to the weight room.

Although genetic potential (called genotype) is the basis for a given trait, its expression (called phenotypic expression) can be positively affected by many factors, including exercise. Resistance exercise might not affect the length of the bones in your body, but it could have a positive effect on their density and so help prevent a fracture. It might even fight the aging process by combating the potential for osteoporosis, especially in women. So while a resistance-training program will not give one the height of a Shaquille O'Neal, it can help prevent sport injuries by building stronger bones.

Maturation

Every child makes progress toward adulthood on an individual time line, and therefore we must remember that each one has both a chronological age and a physiological age. This is readily apparent when you see a group of young athletes in junior high school. Their differences are due to varying rates of growth and pubertal development. In addition, dramatic differences can exist between boys and girls in their maturation process. Training presents a decided advantage in physical performance for both boys and girls during the growth years from ages 10 to 17;[2] a child's skeletal system changes as a result of sport- and strength-conditioning programs.

Maturation has been defined as the developmental progress toward adulthood. In a clinical evaluation of maturity, a physician assesses several areas, including

- physical size,
- bone maturity,
- neuromuscular maturity,
- reproductive maturity, and
- emotional maturity (discussed in the following section).

As we've said previously, each individual has a chronological age and a physiological age; physiological age is the more important and determines the functional capabilities and performance for that person. Maturation occurs over a wide age span among children. In girls the range is from ages 8 to 14 years and in boys, from ages 9 to 15 years. Typically girls begin puberty about two years before boys. Nevertheless, the fact that we cannot assume an identical time course in all children for the maturation process underscores the need for individualized training. Such variation in maturation emphasizes the need to focus on self-improvement with conditioning programs and sport performance. In addition, factors such as exercise-tolerance differences and responsibility must be considered when evaluating a child's development. Clearly, understanding the maturation process and its impact on a child's abilities is a critical part of designing a resistance-training program for the young athlete.

Physical Size

Physical stature is an obvious sign of growth; we use measures such as height and weight to assess physical growth from birth to adulthood. Obviously, all children do not grow at the same rate. From the moment of birth, growth occurs in what is called a pulsatile or "burst-like" nature; for example, within 24 hours a baby can increase in height 1 centimeter. Graphing changes in body height shows that they occur at varying rates at different ages. Dramatic changes in height, as well as other growth variables, can be seen at various ages. Figure 2.1, which depicts the height growth-rate curves of two boys who are identical in age, shows the pronounced differences in growth patterns that are possible. It also shows that the significant size differences that can occur at certain ages may be ultimately reduced when the boys reach adulthood.

Conversely, you can see in figure 2.2 that patterns of height growth can be similar yet yield considerable differences in the ultimate height achieved. You can observe examples of such responses every day. In figure 2.1, one boy is smaller than another at ages 11, 12, and 13, but due to similar genetic potentials their height difference in high school is minimal. Conversely, figure 2.2 shows that one boy, perhaps the tallest child in the class, might maintain that relationship to his classmates into adulthood. The key is the genetic potential for a particular physical trait. As we have pointed out, subtle differences can occur when other factors (such as exercise and nutrition) influence the expression of a trait, but the absolute magnitude of those variables is fixed by a person's genetic endowment.

From studies of twins we have learned that some traits are more tightly genetically controlled than others. Yet even in twins a trait may vary by 5 to 30 percent. The most remarkable evidence from twin studies comes in obesity research. Genes may dictate your basic body type, but your lifestyle may dictate the actual amount of fat you carry. A recent study showed that when one identical twin exercised and watched what he ate, he had much lower body fat and was thinner than his twin, who ate more and did not participate in any rigorous conditioning program. For the first time we see evidence that body fat and body mass can be modified by behavioral differences in food intake and exercise patterns. Conversely, two identical twins living apart had identical heart problems detected at the same time, showing that traits such as inherent pathology are remarkably linked genetically. Thus, while height is a rigid gene type, making a change in adult height very difficult to achieve, body fat is more easily

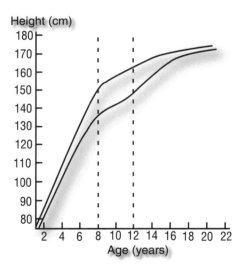

Figure 2.1 Height growth-rate curves of two boys identical in age. Early differences sometimes disappear at older ages.

changed. Exercise programs provide an external influence that can make a difference in a child's physical development. On the other hand, the impact of various competitive sports (e.g., wrestling, gymnastics, baseball) and their associated practice demands on mechanisms related to body size, growth, and development remains to be determined.[3] However, appropriate resistance-training programs can positively contribute to the growth potential and limit the negative effects (increased injury, physical stress) of sport in young children.

There are many aspects of physical growth. One child may be taller, but another may weigh more and have better muscular

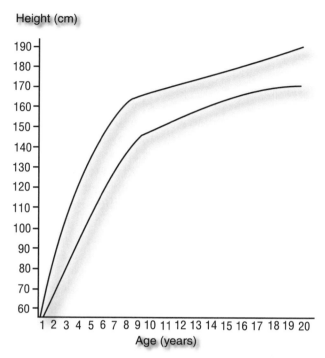

Figure 2.2 Growth rates of two different boys.

development. Each physical trait is dictated by its own genetic pattern for development. Although certain physical traits appear to favor specific sports—height in basketball, body mass in football—no single physical variable can guarantee athletic success. Many times children are pushed into a particular sport because of a single physical attribute. A tall child might find athletic success in swimming, rowing, or track and field, yet a parent may push him to play basketball due to his height alone. This can be a mistake. Such an approach negates common sense and fails on several different levels to optimize the child's success by making assumptions that he enjoys the sport, finds pleasure in practicing it, has other attributes (e.g., neuromuscular skills) needed, and desires to commit part of his life to this activity. Thus this one trait may not truly represent the child's physical and mental aptitudes for a particular sport.

Bone Development

As we have discussed, bone is one tissue that can be affected by modifying factors, such as nutrition, menarche, exercise, and disease. In the past, many health professionals feared bone injury in a child who lifted weights, but such fears are now far outweighed by the documented physical benefits of resistance training. Bone maturity involves the progression toward a fully ossified skeleton, or solid bone structure. This process includes the sealing of growth plates, which determine long-bone growth in a child, and bone mineralization, which is the deposition of minerals in the bone that determines bone density. Mineralization is evaluated clinically by bone scans. The process of mineralization varies, so children of the same age may have skeletons of different physiological ages. Children who do not have normal bone densities for their age are more prone to skeletal injury. This is particularly true in athletics, because some sports, such as football, soccer, and gymnastics, demand tolerance of high forces. Bone health is of great importance, especially for girls; osteoporosis has been called a "pediatric disease" because its development (or more precisely, the lack of sufficient bone mineralization during childhood) may result in osteoporosis later in life. Young girls in particular should participate in resistance exercise and other physical activities to improve the rate of bone deposition.[4]

One provocative concept of interest to scientists studying osteoporosis in women is the use of training to increase the peak bone mass in young girls; the hope is that they will enter adulthood with a much higher bone density, thereby reducing the potential for osteoporosis. Preliminary findings offer some hope, because children do increase bone mineral density with exercise training.[5] So despite the obvious need for further study, resistance training can only support optimal bone growth.[6-9] One report concluded that "during the very early stages of puberty, bone may be particularly responsive to weight-bearing, high-impact exercise, attainable in a range of youth sports and activities or in brief sessions of jumping activity," suggesting that resistance training may enhance bone development in younger children during this optimal time.[7] The greatest bone mineral content peaks occur in girls from about ages 11.5 to 13.5 years and in boys from 13 to 15 years, so resistance training may well be important during these times. Although the greatest proportion of bone mineral content increases in girls has been attributed to growth, the lumbar spine mineral content gain achieved by plyometric-like (a training method that uses exercises with a eccentric lengthening of the muscle followed by a rapid shortening of the muscle such as in jumps and bounding movments or medicine ball throws) jump training has been maintained for a year after training stopped.[5] Still missing from the literature is the study of more advanced lifting exercises (squats, pulls), which may better stimulate bone development.[10, 11] Nevertheless, hedging one's bet on future research in this case may be worth the risks. Why? Because if the peak bone mass developed in youth is carried into the adult years, it would offer a distinct biological advantage, perhaps decreasing the need for constant training in adulthood in order to maintain or increase the low bone density that occurs with aging and is caused by lack of exercise in childhood.[12] In addition, it now appears that other environmental factors such as nutrition (e.g., calcium and milk intake) can influence bone development as well.[8, 13] Thus a healthy lifestyle involving proper exercise and good nutrition can influence optimal bone growth and maximize a child's genetic potential.

Interestingly, scientific studies indicate that resistance training can influence bone growth in both boys and girls.[8] Research has shown that young Olympic weightlifters have greater bone densities than individuals who do not lift.[11, 14] The fear that resistance exercise is detrimental to bone growth appears inappropriate. In fact, resistance exercise can be the most potent exercise stimulus for bone growth and development.

Using the variable of height, you can approximate a child's growth rate by determining at a given age the percent of adult height the child has obtained. Such predictive values have some accuracy but, as we have discussed, might well be influenced by the environment, nutrition, and activity profile. Such predictive charts are valuable only during certain ages. From 3 to 8 years for girls and from 3 to 10 years for boys, the prediction is rather high. When children are older, predictions are accurate only for boys and girls who reach their peak growth rates at approximately 12 and 14 years, respectively. Table 2.1 shows such a height prediction chart.

Table 2.1 **50th Percentiles for Height and Weight in Boys and Girls Ages 11-18***

	Boys		Girls	
Age	Height (in)	Weight (lb)	Height (in)	Weight (lb)
11	57	78	57	85
12	59	88	59	95
13	61	100	62	105
14	65	113	63	110
15	67	123	65	115
16	68	133	65	118
17	69	140	65	120
18	70	147	65	122

*Data are current from the Centers for Disease Control (CDC).

Neuromuscular Maturity

Figure 2.3 shows that the development of muscle and nerve cells is ongoing throughout the adolescent years. Anaerobic capacities are less developed in children compared to endurance capabilities associated with aerobic metabolism.[15] In part this is due to the slower maturation of the neuromuscular system, including muscle fiber and neural tissue, which continues into early adulthood.

This progressive maturation also affects both power and anaerobic function, in part due to an approximately 15 to 20 percent increase in the percentage of body weight that is made up of muscle over the growth phases shown in figure 2.3. Peak muscle mass in women occurs between ages 18 and 25 and in men between ages 17 and 25, depending on maturation rates. In healthy adolescent boys the sexual stages (Tanner stages), which indicate physiological, not chronological age, are most correlated to arm muscle area, arm circumference, and skinfold thickness.[16] Thus muscular development is very much linked to reproductive maturity (see next section) and also appears to affect how well children, especially boys, respond to training the muscle component of their bodies.

Training the nervous system is specific to the development of motor pathways. However, there are no data to suggest that training before puberty positively affects

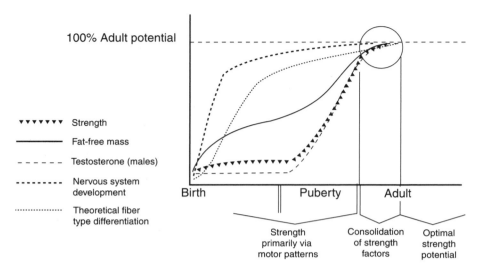

Figure 2.3 Many developmental factors converge in adulthood to complete maturation of a child.

neurological function, especially in the more complex motor tasks. Training specificity (e.g., matching the type of training with demands of the sport) appears to be maintained even in younger (11-year-old) athletes, indicating a need to develop specific sport-conditioning programs.[16] In children, general training is needed to set the basis for future development, and this is where the greatest gains in sport performance occur. After a generalized base has been developed with a well-rounded program, sport-specific training can be added as the child grows older to enhance specific skills and prevent injury. Strength-training programs need to have components of specificity (training the muscles the way they will be used in a sport, for example, explosive jump training for basketball) in order to benefit sport performance.

Reproductive Maturity

Maturity also includes development of a child's reproductive capacity, which dramatically affects growth and overall development. Changes in hormonal secretions are responsible for many of the physical changes in both boys and girls during pubescence. In males, for example, increased secretion of testosterone is related to increases in body weight, muscle size, and strength. As a boy grows older, he will become bigger and stronger without any training at all, due to the influence of hormonal changes alone (see chapter 1). In addition, testosterone in young boys is responsible for the changes that result in the maturation process with increasing chronological age.[17] Figure 2.4 shows a theoretical relationship between increased testosterone concentration and strength in males. As pointed out in chapter 1, in girls and women other hormones (estrogen, growth hormone) play similar roles to compensate for the significantly lower amounts of testosterone in their bodies. Testosterone concentrations are 10 to 30 times greater in men than in women, which accounts for the differences in muscle size and strength between the genders. It is especially important in the developmental aspects of the upper-body musculature in girls from prenatal to postnatal potential

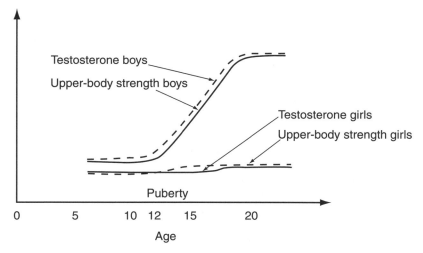

Figure 2.4 Theoretical basis between testosterone and upper body strength.

for muscle fiber numbers during gestation and absolute size in adulthood. In other words, differences in testosterone during prenatal development impact the number of muscle cells. Thus, the number of muscle cells are lower in girls when compared to boys. In addition, during adolescence differences between boys and girls are due in part to the androgenic differences such as body hair, voice depth, and shoulder width between the genders. Boys ultimately have much stronger upper-body musculature, which is explained by the much greater number and size of muscle fibers when compared to girls. This advantage is maintained in adult men compared to women; the average man has a decided advantage in absolute strength and size over the average woman.[18, 19]

Menarche in Girls

In young girls, *menarche* is a significant biological marker of increasing reproductive maturity. The onset of the first menstrual flow is the culmination of many hormonal changes that take place in the growing female. In American girls, menarche is typically observed at about 12 to 13 years of age. Over the past 10 years, physicians and scientists have questioned the extent to which intense physical activity affects the age of menarche. To date, studies have been inconclusive. Researchers have observed that certain female athletes and those who start to train during their prepubescent years exhibit later menarche than average. Yearly physicals and medical follow-ups are prudent when menarche is delayed because late onset can affect other growth functions such as bone health or indicate some other medical problem. Active young athletes need to have medical examinations that are specific to their needs and that involve the counsel and perspective of a physician trained in sports medicine. Still, research has not definitively demonstrated harmful

(continued)

(continued)

effects from delayed menarche or *sport amenorrhea* (the temporary absence of menstruation). Inadequate and improper nutritional intakes in girls and women are also linked to amenorrhea; this correlation is the subject of prolific research. The impact of sport and intense physiological stress on adolescents is an ongoing topic of interest and concern.[20]

Increasing Hormonal Signals

As the body changes and adapts, certain tissues and glands become more responsive to the exercise stimuli. In addition the body starts to learn how to repair itself from the stress of exercise, which in fact does damage structures such as muscle and connective tissue. For years scientists went back and forth on these issues, but it is the stimulation of the repair process due to physical activity that allows the body to come back stronger, with bigger muscles, stronger bones, and more dense ligaments and tendons, which in turn help resist the forces and stress of sports and everyday activities.

Chapter 1 pointed out that the endocrine system is important to the repair process because its anabolic hormones send signals to build muscle (testosterone and growth hormone) and fight inflammation (cortisol). But to produce such physiological signals that tell the body to increase the size and density of muscle and bone takes time, and thus training adaptations can take months to achieve. The nervous system, as we have said, is very responsive to training and assists the muscles of a young child in producing force without much help from larger muscles. The body learns to repair itself and send anabolic signals to other tissues and glands to make changes in muscles, bones, tendons, and ligaments, which all contribute to greater strength and power and injury prevention. So it's clear that the exercise responses of hormone signals in the body are important to a child's adaptive capability. With resistance training these signals become stronger and their effects more obvious, as demonstrated by the changes that can occur during puberty.

Resting serum testosterone in young boys (11.6 to 12.6 years) who have had a year of resistance training has been shown to be increased over a control group of boys who did not weight train, and the changes correlate with changes in speed, strength, and isometric endurance.[21] In addition, in elite young athletes, testosterone has been found to be important for the development of strength.[22] However, an exercise-induced response in young boys to a resistance-training workout has not always been observed, therefore limiting the anabolic impact of hormonal signals to muscle.[23] It may take two years of training for a young boy to produce an increase in testosterone after a workout. If boys in their adolescent years (14-17 years) had been training for at least two years or more, they were capable of increasing their blood testosterone concentrations following a resistance-training workout.[24] If they did not have at least two years of weight-training experience, no changes occurred. These data were the first that linked this effect or lack thereof to the amount of prior training time. Training time and the resulting hormonal responses to a workout can play a vital role in the growth and maturity of physical development, especially as training time progresses. Thus training time "banked" for a child is associated with different adaptation stimuli, which leads to a different training outcome and supports the concept that consistent training is necessary not only to maintain an advantage over untrained peers who are also growing but also to create a more effective physiological response to workouts. How such mechanisms respond to training time in young girls as it relates to other hormones such as growth hormone remains unclear at this time.

DEVELOPING PSYCHOLOGICALLY

Psychological growth is important because it interacts with a variety of training-process factors. The child who is in training needs to have the proper interest, attention span, and attitude. As she grows, she exhibits differences in group interaction, self-esteem, and mood states. In fact, some 7- or 8-year-old children may be easier to teach and motivate than some 12- or 13-year-olds. The psychological development of a child influences the type of activities that she can perform safely and effectively and dictates how much immediate supervision will be needed for various lifts and training methods. The type of program you can implement will depend on the child's interest, dedication, attitude, and motivation. Proper teaching progressions, supervision of progress, and positive motivation of the child are important aspects of an exercise-training program. Each of these components interacts with the child's psychological mind-set either positively or negatively.

Carefully examine your approach to training, teaching progressions, and methods used to monitor the child's exercise tolerance. Implement the program with common sense and the best interests of the child in mind. The key is to not do too much too soon.

A training program should optimize the workout protocols and take into account both the child's physical and psychological maturity so that young athletes can adjust to the changes in their bodies, enjoy training, and make progress.

Motivation, Program Philosophy, and Self-Esteem

Every program, whether conducted at home, at school, in a private health club, or in a public recreation facility, must provide an environment conducive to training for children. This requires a program philosophy that includes motivational considerations and realistic expectations for children and is based on a sound understanding of their psychological and physiological needs and capabilities. In today's world of "infomercial hype" many children, affected by overt messages targeted for adults, are getting misinformation about physical fitness and body development. This is especially true for adolescent boys and girls who are growing up too quickly in a media-rich world and who already feel a desperate need to cope with social pressures. For these young people, factual information is especially critical for self-esteem.

The media are powerful forces in relaying information on fitness—from screaming fitness gurus to equipment ads, both promising a model's body in weeks. The underlying message is that fitness will fix your problems with relationships and make you more attractive. Resistance training can positively affect self-esteem, body image, and confidence.[25,26] But inappropriate expectations from such training or an ineffective program will result in the child feeling betrayed when he doesn't see the desired changes in his body or in a sport or physical performance. This can negatively affect the gains that can be achieved through consistent long-term participation in properly designed weight-training programs.

Resistance training can have positive effects, but boys and girls key in on different outcomes. Self-esteem is associated with body satisfaction. Boys are more likely to focus on changing muscles, whereas girls are more interested in body image.[27] Care must be taken with girls not to send messages that promote or lead to eating disorders. The so-called Barbie figure is not only physiologically impossible, but the pursuit of this mythology can lead to serious health problems. Take a proactive approach and provide education to better frame the positive outcomes of resistance training that both boys and girls can achieve (e.g., improved muscle function, bone density, performance, and health). Don't leave it up to the child to determine what the benefits of resistance training are; her perceptions may be incorrect due to limited exposure and inappropriate signals coming from the environment (e.g., TV, older children, media).

Promoting physical fitness can

- increase physical performance capabilities;
- reduce body mass, promoting a more favorable body shape and structure;
- provide more positive social feedback and recognition from peer groups; and
- improve self-image.

The array of training promises, from "six-pack" abdominal muscles to getting rid of fat, are messages that resonate with everyone, but it takes proper interpretation of these messages to place them in reality. It is up to adults to clarify and bring the more factual messages to the child without destroying the dreams and hopes of a better body or the glory of higher levels of athletic performance that resistance training conjure up in young minds. Facts are important to combat the mythologies created by the world around us.

Adults should do the following to help children see through the hype:

1. Identify the fact and fiction about achieving certain goals.
2. Be honest with children about what is possible.
3. Tell them that goals such as weight loss will take hard work in areas other than a resistance-training program.
4. Support their dreams and hopes for the future, but put them into a realistic set of goals.
5. Create an action plan.
6. Prioritize and let them know that you cannot go after everything at once.

Motivation is an individual phenomenon that should always be viewed from a child's perspective; what motivates one child may not motivate another. The first step is to get the child genuinely interested in physical fitness. This has been a problem, especially in young girls. A recent study showed that the top barriers to physical activity for the girls were: "I am self-conscious about my looks when I exercise," and "I am not motivated to be active."[28] In healthy children, factors related to positive exercise compliance include social support, perceptions of competency and self-esteem, enjoyment of the activity, and availability of a variety of activities.[29]

We live in a world where children from the United States to Australia are seeing an epidemic of obesity fueled by inactivity. A recent study by P. Gordon-Larsen (2001)[30] showed that in girls, physical activity, inactivity, and perception of ideal body size were the most important factors contributing to obesity. Adolescents shown to be overweight had significantly lower levels of physical activity and a perception of larger ideal body size than non-overweight adolescents. Knowledge and attitudinal factors (with the exception of perceived ideal body size) had far less association with obesity than activity-related behavioral factors. For girls, intervention strategies need to focus on physical activity and body image attitudes. However, children who are forced to participate in fitness programs usually do not enjoy the activities and resent participating. Their unwillingness makes adherence to the program almost impossible, because the fundamental aspects that motivate children are *fun* and sociability. Children who are inappropriately motivated in fitness programs may later turn away from physical activity. Inappropriate motivation is typified by the classic example of a coach assigning exercise as a punishment for unwanted behaviors, such as missing a catch or a free throw.

Appropriate motivation hinges on appropriate exercise demands. Don't overshoot the child's physical capabilities or make the experience physically painful. For example, asking a child to perform too many sets during the early training sessions of a program can result in severe muscle soreness. Use proper progression to gradually prepare each child both physically and mentally for resistance training. Each day thousands of young athletes are exposed to sport activities for which they are not prepared physically and mentally. This lack of preparation corresponds to low fitness levels in young people. Thus, it is important that we positively promote fitness activities, including resistance training, in order to promote better health habits and safer participation in sports.

Differences Between Boys and Girls

Differences between males and females are obvious in the way they grow and mature. In general, girls mature much sooner than boys. The growth spurt in girls may start as early as age 10 and peak at age 12 or 13, with the onset of menstruation following shortly thereafter. A boy's primary growth spurt occurs between the ages of 12 and 15. Production of testosterone appears to govern many of the changes in the physical development of muscle and bone of young boys during puberty. Generally boys go through a later growth spurt than girls, catch up to the girls, and eventually pass them.

An 11-year-old girl can be significantly taller and stronger than an 11-year-old boy, and you must teach children that such differences are normal. Resistance-training benefits should focus on the individual's growth, development, and accomplishments.

Adults should discourage children from comparing themselves to others. Although this is easy to say, children will want to make such comparisons. It is up to you to explain why individual progress is much more important—and then reward it! The greatest thing an adult can do for a child is to express joy and appreciation for the child's improvement and accomplishment. Promote the idea that the child competes only against himself, and alter the program to meet each child's goals and needs. Focusing on progress is the most important factor in long-term adherence to an active lifestyle.

Exercise Tolerance

The importance of the child's ability to tolerate exercise stress cannot be over-emphasized. In order for the concepts of individualized exercise prescription, proper supervision, and program monitoring to work, you must communicate with the child: Encourage discussion, provide feedback, and listen to concerns and fears. The program's design and development should reflect those concerns. Use common sense and provide exercise variations, active recovery periods, and rest from training. Do not operate on the belief that more is better.

Start the child with a program that she can easily tolerate, and increase the difficulty as she becomes accustomed to training and matures. Maturation may bring dramatic changes in the ability to tolerate resistance training, sports, or any exercise program, but don't overestimate that ability. It is better to start out at a conservative level than to overshoot the child's exercise tolerance and reduce her enjoyment. You can design a program that reflects the developmental nature of the child yet does not compromise her enthusiasm or physical and mental tolerance of the program. By using the proper guidelines for program development, you can implement a resistance-exercise program that fits each stage of development. Remember that the child should not be forced to participate. It is up to you to provide a positive environment that promotes the child's success.

SUMMING UP AND LOOKING AHEAD

Growth and development are multidimensional; prediction of athletic success based on one variable at one point in time is difficult at best and typically does not represent the best interests of the child. Participation in different sports promotes proper physical training, sparks a child's interests, and provides him with a realistic view of sport. It is up to parents, teachers, and coaches to promote the fun associated with a game and the training needed to participate, and not view sport participation as a future profession. In a time when burnout in children is common, the correct attitude concerning the role of sports and training in a child's life will help make participation in sports a positive experience. Furthermore, promotion of better physical exercise training, including weight training, can enhance a child's health and fitness and help him develop habits that will influence health and well-being over a lifetime. In the next chapter we examine various administrative and weight-training program development concerns.

Determining Individual Needs

When beginning a resistance-training program, children, like anyone else, should be examined by a physician and given clearance to participate. Ideally, this should include a careful analysis of each child for pre-existing medical problems (past injuries or medical conditions) and a musculoskeletal exam that ensures that the joints and body structures are sound and can take the physical demands of training. From the results of this exam, one can design a specific program to accommodate special needs. For example, if a child has Osgood-Schlatter disease (degeneration of the bone at the point where the patellar tendon attaches to the tibia), exercises involving extreme bending of the knee may be contraindicated. Or if a child has had a prior shoulder injury, the program should strengthen the shoulder joint with the goal of preventing further injury. After medical clearance or identification of any medical or prior-injury concerns, the child should begin a balanced resistance-training program that exercises all the major muscle groups around all the major joints.

Programs for children participating in a certain sport or activity may be similar, but individualization is key to success. Children vary in physical and mental maturity, training goals, genetic potentials, and desire to participate in a resistance-training program. Thus, individualized programs must be placed in the context of each child's expectations and potential.

THE NEEDS ANALYSIS

Before designing a resistance-training program, you should perform a needs analysis to determine specific goals for each child. The easiest way to conduct a needs analysis is to answer a series of questions concerning the desired goals of the resistance-training program. Some common goals follow:

- Increased strength of specific muscle groups
- Increased power of specific muscle groups
- Increased local muscular endurance of specific muscle groups
- Increased motor performance (ability to jump, run, or throw)
- Increased total-body mass (age dependent)

- Increased muscle hypertrophy (age dependent)
- Decreased body fat
- Increased self-confidence
- Improved sport performance

A well-planned program can allow the athlete to meet all these goals. However, expectations for changes in these characteristics must be kept within reasonable limits based on the child's age and biological potential for change (see chapter 2). In addition, one must carefully prioritize all the components of fitness. Progress toward some of these goals is easy to assess. For example, if the trainees are performing exercises for specific muscle groups, those muscles should increase in strength. Progress toward other goals, such as increased muscle hypertrophy, especially in prepubescent youths, is more difficult to observe.

Strengthening by Muscle Group

A program designed to increase general fitness and strength typically includes exercises for all the major muscle groups of the body, including the muscles around each joint, or in other words in the front and back of the body (e.g., biceps and triceps or front of the arm and back of the arm) and the upper and lower body. To ensure proper symmetry of development, each body part should be addressed (i.e., neck, shoulders, upper back, lower back, abdominal muscles, and the front and back of the upper and lower extremities.

When developing a sport-specific program, the trainer needs to find exercises in the weight room that mimic the major movements used in the sport. If a program goal is to increase sprinting ability, the major muscle groups that should be strengthened are the thighs and the lower leg, or more specifically the front of the thigh (quadriceps), back of the thigh (hamstrings), calf (gastrocnemius), and buttocks (gluteal muscles). You can train each muscle in isolation (for example, using knee extensions to exercise the quadriceps); however, multi-joint exercises for the thighs, such as the squat, should also be included.

Obsession With Big Biceps in Boys

Younger boys can get obsessed with their biceps as they grow into adolescence, and some resistance-training programs include an overabundance of biceps curls. Such training can create a dramatic imbalance not only of the arm but the entire body as well. A balanced program is needed for optimal training.

Determining Muscular Action by Sport

The three major types of muscle actions are isometric, dynamic concentric, and dynamic eccentric. During an isometric action the muscle contracts but no movement takes place, as when a lifter attempts to perform a leg press with a resistance that he cannot lift. A dynamic concentric action takes place when the muscle contracts and shortens and movement occurs; for example, during a knee extension, the front of the thigh contracts and the knee joint extends. A dynamic eccentric action takes place when the muscle is active and lengthens. For example, lowering a weight from an extended knee position is a dynamic eccentric action of the quadriceps. During knee extensions, the quadriceps performs a dynamic concentric action to lift the weight and a dynamic eccentric action to lower the weight. Other examples requiring eccentric actions of the quadriceps are descending a flight of stairs or slowing down. Dynamic concentric and eccentric actions occur in most daily and sporting activities, so a weight-training program should include both of these muscle actions. Should a lifter perform isometric contractions to be successful in the activity he's training for? For a sport like wrestling, which requires isometric muscle actions, yes; for one like swimming, no. Figure 3.1 depicts the three major types of muscle actions.

Since dynamic concentric and eccentric actions are needed for virtually all recreational activities and sports, be sure the equipment your lifters use can exercise both phases of movement. Some pieces of equipment provide no resistance as the movement returns to the starting position; the lifter must pull the resistance back into the starting position. This produces not an eccentric action but a concentric action of muscles on the other side of the joint that is moving. If your lifters are training for sports in which direction must be changed quickly and often, include some specific eccentric exercises for the muscles involved in those movements. To accomplish this, exercises can be performed in the typical manner of lifting a resistance with a concentric action and lowering it with an eccentric action. Eccentric-only training involves only the lowering of a weight with loads greater than can be lifted concentrically. Care must be taken when performing eccentric-loaded exercises due to the heavy resistances (105 to 120 percent of maximum 1RM concentric strength) that can be handled in what are popularly called "negatives." Care must be taken and advanced supervision is needed when performing negatives due to the increased possibility of injury. Heavy eccentric-only training should not be performed by prepubescent children or inexperienced resistance trainers. (See chapter 13 for specific program recommendations.)

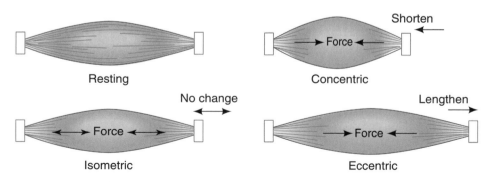

Figure 3.1 Three major types of muscle actions.

Research has shown that using both concentric and eccentric motions in a repetition is superior to using only one type of movement in achieving strength gains. Children can gain eccentric benefits in training by lowering normal concentric loads in a controlled manner. Although using a controlled speed when lowering a resistance yields optimal results, exceptionally slow speeds will result in the need to use very light weights (as low as 25 percent of 1RM), which are not effective in developing strength.

Choosing the Correct Energy Source

Consider the time needed to perform the sport or activity and its intensity. Because a sport such as marathon running requires a long time to complete (two to three hours), the muscular demands are submaximal in order to perform over such a long duration. Conversely, shot putting takes a very short time to complete (one or two seconds) and is performed with maximal muscular actions. Of course, many sport skills and performances fall between these two extremes, such as the 400-meter run, which takes one to two minutes to complete and requires near-maximal muscular actions. The duration and intensity of muscular actions used in the activity determine whether its energy source is more aerobic or anaerobic (see table 3.1). Long-duration events performed with submaximal actions are aerobic, which means the body uses oxygen to produce energy by breaking down carbohydrates and fats. Events of very short duration performed with maximal or near-maximal muscular contractions are anaerobic, which means the body uses energy already stored in the muscle in the form of high-energy molecules. Activities of moderate duration that require near-maximal actions are also anaerobic. However, their major energy source is not the stored energy molecules in muscle but the breakdown of stored carbohydrates (glycogen) without the use of oxygen, which produces lactic acid. Lactic acid is associated with fatigue; it gives the athlete's muscles a tired, heavy feeling after completing an event like a 400-meter sprint. Although one energy source may predominate in a particular activity, all three sources contribute some energy in any activity.

Table 3.1 **Guidelines for Primary Energy Sources for an Activity**

Energy source	Muscular contractions	Duration of activity
Anaerobic	Maximal	Very short (seconds)
Lactic acid	Near maximal	Short to moderate (15 seconds to 4 minutes)
Aerobic	Submaximal	Long (4 minutes to hours)

Note: Although one energy source may predominate, any activity uses all three energy sources to some extent.

COMMON INJURIES
AND SPECIAL CONSIDERATIONS

When designing a resistance-training program, consider the sites of common injuries in a particular sport or activity along with the sites of an individual's previous injuries, if any, then incorporate exercises to strengthen these areas. Common sites of injury in many activities are the knees, elbows, shoulders, neck, and ankles.

Today, overuse injuries can be a prominent problem with young athletes. Too much activity without planned periods of rest, improperly sized equipment, improper sport skill techniques, and a lack of proper communication with parents and coaches can lead to overuse injuries.[1] Training programs should address these causes of overuse injuries and balance flexibility, strength, and endurance training to counteract the stress imposed on the body during activity. Parents, coaches, and team physicians share the responsibility of ensuring properly periodized training that prevents the child from doing too much too soon or combining too many activities. Often young athletes are set up for injury by the accumulation of inappropriate stresses and strains on their bodies. Care should be taken to reduce "hyper-parenting" and overscheduling activities. Allow children to communicate feelings of fatigue that may merit a decrease in the number of physical activities. Every activity should fit into a total program, with the absolute amount of activity carefully monitored for successful coping and positive physical and psychological adaptations.

Due to their immature skeletal and muscular systems, children are more prone than adults to certain types of injury (e.g., growth cartilage injury). In addition, certain muscle groups, particularly in the upper body, are chronically weak in many children, and exercises to strengthen them should be included in weight-training programs. Carefully consider the health and functional ability of the joints involved in the sport or activity so that injury does not occur in prepubescent or pubescent children.

Growth Cartilage

Growth cartilage, a type of connective tissue, is located at three major sites: the growth plate, or epiphyseal plate, of the long bones; the site of tendon insertion onto bone, or apophyseal insertion; and cartilage on the joint surfaces, or articular cartilage (see figure 3.2). The long bones of the body grow in length from the epiphyseal plates located at their ends. Severe damage to these plates before they ossify (which happens late

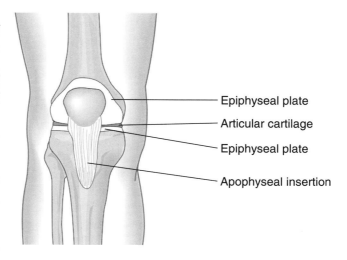

Figure 3.2 Locations of growth cartilage.

in puberty) can result in no further growth in bone length. Growth cartilage at the apophyseal insertions ensures a solid connection between the tendon and bone. Damage to these areas may cause pain with movement and increase the chance of the tendon separating from the bone. Articular cartilage acts as a shock absorber between the bones of a joint; damage to it may lead to rough surfaces on the bones of a joint and pain with movement. Growth cartilage has been documented as an injury site of particular concern in young athletes performing resistance training.[2]

Damage to all three sites of growth cartilage may occur due to either a single, or acute, injury or repeated microtraumas, which result in an overuse injury. Damage to the epiphyseal plate is the most common acute injury; in prepubescent athletes, this includes fractures caused by resistance training. The majority of injuries occur during unsupervised performance of overhead lifts (such as overhead press or push press) with near-maximal resistances. Children should take two precautions to minimize the chance of epiphyseal plate fracture: They should not perform overhead lifts with near-maximal or maximal resistances (in fact, it may be wise for them to use lighter-than-normal weights), and they should use proper form during any exercise, especially overhead lifts.

Articular cartilage can also be damaged by repeated microtraumas. This is one of the factors responsible for osteochondritis dissecans, or separation of a portion of the articular cartilage from the joint surface. This can occur at the elbows of Little League pitchers and at the ankles of young distance runners. Damage to the growth cartilage at the apophyseal insertions may be in part responsible for the pain associated with Osgood-Schlatter disease. Investigators have proposed that early heavy physical exercise by children can cause epiphyseal plate damage resulting in bone deformation.

An example of how repeated microtraumas can cause overuse injuries is the shoulder pain associated with throwing in preteens, often called "Little League shoulder." Pain can result from damage to the epiphyseal plate of the upper arm bone, the humerus, caused by repeated throwing. However, it is also likely that the rotator cuff muscles of the shoulder are weak or out of balance (that is, one of the muscles is substantially stronger than the muscle that causes the opposite movement); this sets the stage for shoulder pain and injury. Resistance training can increase rotator cuff strength; exercises that strengthen these muscles are presented later in this book. You should incorporate these exercises into resistance-training programs designed for a throwing sport or any activity in which the shoulder is extensively involved (such as swimming). In general, most athletes can benefit from these exercises.

Damage to growth cartilage is not a necessary outcome of resistance training. Microtraumas can be caused by all activities; an overuse injury in a child performing resistance training may be due not to the training but to other activities or the cumulative effect of the child's activities. However, you must consider the potential for damage when you design a program for children and take appropriate precautions. Resistance training does help prevent overuse injuries such as Little League shoulder, tennis elbow, runner's knee, and swimmer's shoulder. Proper exercise-training techniques help eliminate all types of injury related to resistance training, including overuse problems.

Lower-Back Problems

The lower-back musculature and vertebral column are not well developed in pre-pubescence; therefore children may be at greater risk of lower-back pain and injury than adults. During growth spurts many children develop lumbar lordosis, an anterior (forward) bending of the spine often accompanied by a forward tilting of the top of the pelvis (see figure 3.3). Factors contributing to lordosis include tight hamstrings and growth of the front (anterior) portion of the vertebrae to a greater extent than growth of the back (posterior) portion.

Lower-back problems in children and adults can be a result of an acute injury; in resistance training they are primarily caused by improper lifting technique, which can result in strains and sprains of the muscles and ligaments of the lower back. In many cases, attempting to lift maximal or near-maximal resistance contributes to improper technique, especially in exercises that stress the lower back, such as dead lifts and squats. When performing such exercises, children must keep their backs straight and as upright as possible and use their legs to lift the weight. This minimizes the torque on the lower back and keeps the weight over the child's feet, protecting the lower back from injury. Leg-press machines can also cause back problems, because the seat may flatten the normal curve of the spine. If lower-back pain persists, the child should see a physician.

You can help prevent lower-back problems by having your lifters perform strengthening exercises for the lower back and abdominal musculature and flexibility exercises for the lower-back area and hamstrings. Use exercises such as back extensions and sit-ups to strengthen the lower back and abdominal regions, respectively. Resistance

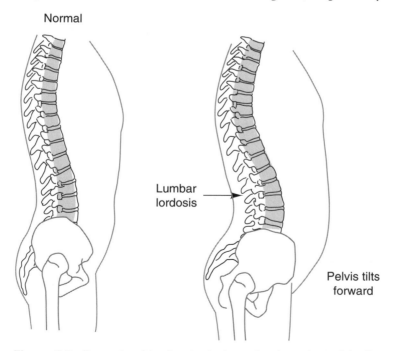

Figure 3.3 Example of lumbar lordosis; notice how the pelvis tilts forward.

should be light to moderate in exercises for the lower back, allowing at least eight repetitions to be performed.

Upper-Body and Abdominal Strength and Endurance

The American Alliance of Health, Physical Education, Recreation and Dance measures abdominal muscular strength and endurance by the number of sit-ups a person can perform in one minute. The mean number of sit-ups in one minute for girls (27-31) shows little improvement from ages 10 to 17. The President's Council on Physical Fitness and Sports (PCPFS) test shows no increase in the number of sit-ups beginning at age 14 and a decrease after age 16 for both boys and girls. Weak abdominal muscles can limit an athlete's proficiency in many sports; therefore, a resistance-training program for children must include exercises for those muscles.

Upper-body strength is often assessed by the number of pull-ups boys can perform and by the amount of time girls can maintain a flexed-arm hang. Sixty percent of girls ages 6 to 17 years cannot perform one pull-up. The PCPFS has concluded that upper-arm and shoulder-girdle strength and endurance for both boys and girls are significantly weak.[3] Lack of upper-body strength limits many sport-specific tasks, even at the recreational level, so resistance training for prepubescent and pubescent children should include exercises for the upper body.

PREPARING A TRAINING SCHEDULE

In order for a program to bring about continual increases in strength and local muscular endurance and prevent boredom, training sessions must be varied. An unchanging or constant loading type (e.g., using the same program like 3 sets of 10RM, or 1 set of 12RM, or 3 sets of 5RM without variation except for resistance over a training period) eventually results in plateaus, or long periods when no progress is made. All programs should be varied in the ways discussed next.

Periodization

Periodization is a popular way of varying the training volume and intensity of an adult's workout. There are two types of periodized training programs: linear periodization, in which the intensities are increased and the volume of exercise is decreased sequentially over a long-term training cycle (4 to 12 months), and nonlinear, or undulating, periodization, in which the load and volume of each workout vary over a 7- to 10-day training cycle.

Linear Periodization

In a linear periodized, or classic strength/power training format, major changes are made every two to four weeks, many times only to the multi-joint exercises (bench press, squats, leg press); however, they can be made to all exercises. An example of a linear periodization model is presented in table 3.2 for an adult strength/power athlete, such as a shot putter or weightlifter. This model is characterized by a high initial training volume and a low training intensity. As training progresses, volume

Table 3.2 **Traditional Periodization for an Adult Strength/Power Athlete**

Training phase	Sets	Reps	Intensity
Base	3-5	8-15	Low
Strength	3-5	2-6	High
Power	3-5	1-3	High
Peaking	1-3	1-3	Very high
Active rest	Physical activity (not necessarily resistance training)		

decreases and intensity increases in order to maximize strength, power, or both. Each training phase emphasizes a particular physiological adaptation. For example, hypertrophy is stimulated during the initial high-volume phase, while strength is developed during the later high-intensity phases. Studies have shown that classic strength/power periodized training is superior to nonperiodized models for increasing maximal strength (1 repetition maximum ability, or 1RM), cycling power, motor performance, and jumping ability.[4] However, a short-term study has shown similar performance improvements in multiple-set nonperiodized models. Training programs need time to produce results, and longer training periods (more than three months) are necessary to compare the benefits of periodization and nonperiodization. Studies demonstrate that both periodized and nonperiodized training are effective in the short term, whereas variation is necessary for successful long-term resistance training.

The goals of initial training phases are to prepare the individual for the later, heavier exercise and to increase muscle size (or in the case of younger athletes, improve the quality of the muscle proteins). The major goals of the strength and power phases are to increase maximal strength and power. The peaking phase is designed to maximize strength and power for a short-term, high-intensity activity. Linear periodization increases maximal strength and power to a greater extent than nonperiodized resistance training.

Nonlinear Periodization

Nonlinear periodization varies intensity and volume within each 7- to 10-day period by rotating a variety of training protocols over the course of the program. Nonlinear methods also attempt to train the various components of the neuromuscular system within the same cycle. During a single workout, only one characteristic is trained in a given day: strength, power, or local muscular endurance. For example, the core exercises in an adult training program use heavy (4- to 6RM), moderate (8- to 10RM), and light (12- to 15RM) resistances, which are randomly rotated over a short period. For example, on Monday, Wednesday, and Friday the resistances used would be 8- to 10RM, 4- to 6RM, and 12- to 15RM, respectively. Children could use heavy 6- to 8RM loads, moderate 9- to 11RM loads, and light 12- to 15RM loads in rotation or randomly on a given day, depending on their feelings or trainability. For example, a trainer might choose light loads on an in-season training day after a hard practice. This model compares favorably with the classic strength/power periodized and nonperiodized single- and multiple-set models. It has advantages in helping to meet schedule demands and provides enough flexibility to adjust to the fatigue level of the young athlete on a given day.

The use of periodization with children has received little study. However, research has demonstrated that use of the traditional periodization model with a high school football team leads to greater gains in 1RM strength and vertical jumping ability than nonperiodized resistance training. A recent study in teenage boys has shown that a nonlinear periodized model is effective in producing strength improvements and positive changes in body composition, such as enhanced muscle mass and bone mineral density.[5]

The traditional adult strength/power periodization model requires exercises to be performed with near-maximal and maximal resistances (1- to 3RM); therefore, it may not be applicable to prepubescent athletes. However by modifying the RM resistances used, trainers can adapt the traditional model to meet the guidelines of a program for young athletes (see table 3.3). The nonlinear or undulating periodization model shows the most flexibility in dealing with the busy schedules, multi-competition schedules, and long-season sports such as tennis, wrestling, and basketball. It has become popular over the past several years.

Table 3.3 Periodization Model for a Prepubescent Child

Training phase	Sets	Repetitions (RM range)
Base	3	10-15
Strength	3	6-10
Power	2-3	6-8
Peaking	1-2	6-8
Active rest	Physical activity (not necessarily resistance training)	

A lighter warm-up set can be used prior to heavier resistances (6- to 8RM).

Resistance, Repetitions, and Sets

Changing the resistance used for a particular exercise is the easiest and most common way to vary a program. The use of RMs (or better yet, an RM zone) ensures progression as the trainee becomes stronger. If a child can perform eight but not nine repetitions on the bench press with 50 pounds, then 50 pounds is an 8RM resistance for that child. As he becomes stronger, 60 pounds may become his 8RM resistance for the bench press. If you design the program so that the child uses 8RMs for three weeks, as he becomes stronger you increase the resistance so that he is still training at the desired 8RM. When using an RM training zone, the amount of resistance should produce a repetition number within that zone. For example, a training zone of 6 to 8RM may be achieved with 50 pounds, but once the child can do more than eight repetitions, the resistance has to be increased to keep it within the zone. The trainee does not have to go to absolute failure (when only a partial repetition can be performed); this can create stress on the joints and cause breath holding as he squeezes out the last repetition. Most children know when they cannot perform another repetition, so an all-out push to absolute failure is not needed. Determining the weight for an RM training zone is quite easy: If the child cannot perform the desired number of repetitions, you should make the weight lighter; if he can perform more than the desired repetitions, make the weight heavier. However, changes in resistance may be difficult to accomplish and monitor in some body-weight exercises such as push-ups and self- or partner-resisted exercises.

You can also change resistances from one training session to the next on a weekly basis to provide heavy, moderate, and light exercise sessions. Some athletes and coaches believe this is important to ensure continual gains in strength, power, and local muscular endurance. For example, a heavy training day may involve a 10RM load. On moderate and light training days the lifter may use 90 and 80 percent of that 10RM load, respectively. Therefore, if a child's 10RM for the leg press is 100 pounds, a heavy training day will include sets of 10 at 100 pounds. A moderate training day will include sets of 10 at 90 pounds (.90 × 100 pounds) and a light training day sets of 10 at 80 pounds (.80 × 100 pounds). A normal sequence for this type of load variation for three training sessions per week using nonlinear periodization might be Monday, light; Wednesday, heavy; and Friday, moderate. Three training sessions per week are considered sufficient to cause maximal gains in strength/power. This arrangement provides for recovery before and after the heavy training day, which allows the trainees to perform up to their potential on the heavy training days. Heavy, moderate, and light training days also minimize the possibility of fatigue buildup during training, which could prevent further gains in strength, power, or local muscular endurance.

You may also vary RM loads every two to four weeks using the linear periodization method so that training emphasizes either strength/power or local muscular endurance. Using this concept you can design resistance-training programs similar to the traditional periodization model for an adult strength/power athlete and still remain within the guidelines of resistances for prepubescent children. Sets can vary from one to three per exercise so that a considerable amount of variation in volume is possible. The same loading scheme can be used for nonlinear periodization, but each RM training zone uses a single day rather than a two- to four-week period.

There are other ways to vary resistance and sets and still remain within the guidelines for prepubescent athletes. A training session designed to predominantly increase local muscular endurance may consist of 3 sets of 15 repetitions at a 15RM resistance for each exercise. One designed primarily to increase strength/power may consist of 3 sets of 10 repetitions of each exercise at a 10RM resistance. And if the goal is to maintain increases in strength/power and local muscular endurance (for example, in an in-season maintenance program), the session may consist of only 1 set of 12 repetitions of each exercise at a 12RM resistance.

Rest Periods

The length of the rest periods between exercises and sets should vary based on the goal for the session and on the major goals for a particular phase of the training cycle. For example, in a session designed predominantly to increase strength/power, use rest periods of two to three minutes or longer. Generally, the heavier the resistance used, the more rest is needed between sets and exercises. However, in a training session designed to maintain gains in strength/power and local muscular endurance, using 12- to 15RM resistances, rest periods may be one minute or less. Short rest periods lead to a buildup of lactic acid in the muscles and blood, resulting in fatigue, which can lead to weakness in the limbs. Short rest periods usually necessitate using lighter resistances, while longer rest periods allow the lifter to use heavier resistances. Care should be taken; if a child begins a program that includes short rest periods before she is physically ready for this type of stress, she may become light-headed and nauseated. In addition, short-rest programs can lead to psychological stress and feelings of anxiety, anger, and fear before a workout.[6] Children need to progress gradually and carefully toward rest periods of one minute or less in order to develop the needed tolerance and acid-base buffering capacity (i.e., the ability to neutralize lactic acid). It usually takes 8 to 12 weeks to achieve tolerance to such short-rest sessions. Take care to explain the fatigue process to the children so that they understand what is happening and are ready to cope with it psychologically. Again, if a child does not want to participate in such a protocol, it is a mistake to force or pressure them to do so.

Exercise Variation

Empirical evidence suggests that variation in exercises for the same muscle group causes greater increases in strength/power than no variation. This does not mean that every training session should include different exercises or that all exercises must be changed at the same time. However, you may want to introduce some new exercises every two to three weeks or vary some exercises every other training session. For example, initially include the bench press for the arms and chest, then change to the incline press or a bench press with dumbbells after two to three weeks. Or, have children perform the bench press on Monday and Friday and the incline press on Wednesday. However, remember to maintain some major-muscle-group exercises throughout the training program in order to see adaptations in the primary movements being trained. A guiding principle is that every time you change an angle of an exercise, such as a narrow grip as opposed to a wide-grip bench press, you have changed the exercise. Some possible training variations follow:

- Increased resistance for a particular RM
- Variation in the RM used (6- to 20RM)
- Variation in the number of sets (one to three)

- Heavy, moderate, and light training days during a week
- Use of a periodized training model
- Variation in exercises for the same muscle groups

TOTAL CONDITIONING PROGRAMS

The key to a successful program is adherence to basic program principles. The training should also be comprehensive in nature, using a total conditioning program that includes resistance-, cardiovascular-, and flexibility-training components and a sport-skills program. Keep the following points in mind when planning weight-training programs for young athletes:

- Total conditioning of all fitness components (strength, flexibility, cardiovascular endurance, sports skills)
- Resistance training for development of muscular strength and local muscular endurance with supplemental training where needed for agility, coordination, balance, and speed for sport-related skills

- Evaluate each athlete's body composition and be sure that a solid nutritional program is supporting the energy needs for activity and tissue recovery
- Balanced choice of exercises for upper- and lower-body development
- Balanced choice of exercises for muscles around each joint
- Use of body-part (single-joint) as well as structural exercises (multi-joint)

Prioritizing various conditioning components over a training cycle is important in a total conditioning program.

© Human Kinetics

By using a total conditioning program, children greatly improve their overall athletic abilities.

Too many coaches make the mistake of trying to train all of the fitness components maximally at the same time. Doing too much too soon can lead to injury or even muscle and joint overuse syndromes. Different conditioning programs can in fact work against each other (e.g., too much running can reduce the power development needed for vertical jump performance); therefore, you must prioritize each child's training goals. By prioritizing the goals over each training cycle based on the child's needs analysis, you develop a total athlete.

Medicine-ball training can be very effective in helping children gain muscular power, especially in the upper body. It provides a type of plyometric training and is an effective supplement to many sports, such as basketball (practicing chest and overhead passes with a medicine ball), volleyball, and baseball and softball (overhead throws and rotational throws). Programs for children can integrate the use of medicine balls and plyometric drills twice a week. While plyometric training might be thought of as an advanced technique, it can provide an important component of sport specificity for the young athlete.

Every resistance-training program should begin with an active warm-up of light cardiovascular exercise for 5 to 10 minutes, flexibility exercises, and a very light set of the resistance exercise itself. The workout should be individualized and exercise each of the major muscle groups of the upper and lower body and each side of a joint or front and back of the body (for example, balance arm curls with triceps extensions or bench press with seated rows). You can add additional sport-specific exercises and those that target individual needs after the child has learned basic lifting techniques. Each workout should be followed by a cool-down that emphasizes flexibility exercises for the entire body.

You don't need to make a major distinction between boys and girls when planning resistance-training programs, because general fitness requires training of all major muscle groups and successful performance of a particular sport skill depends on the strength and power of particular muscle groups, not the participant's gender. However, a program specific for girls may emphasize the upper body and shoulder girdle, because many girls lack strength and power in these areas. Differences in maturation and development of boys and girls, which are discussed in chapter 2, are also important considerations in designing a program.

In a total conditioning program resistance training produces benefits in the development of the neuromuscular system, cardiovascular training benefits the cardiovascular system, and flexibility improves the range of athletic motion. Table 3.4 illustrates the adaptations related to these different types of conditioning.

Consider the Child's Feelings

Recovery is not only physical but also mental. How the young athlete feels about his training is important! Proper progression, goals, and a basic understanding of training can help him explore this newfound physical expression and potential. Don't force him to do anything he is unsure about. Never underestimate the importance of a child's feelings, and take time to explain even the most obvious concept. Be sure each child knows the following:

Table 3.4 **Adaptations Observed With Other Types of Conditioning Programs**

Training modality	Primary adaptation in the body
Aerobic long-duration training	Cardiovascular fitness, endurance, improvements in oxygen delivery and aerobic capacity
Flexibility training	Improvements in the ranges of motion in both rested and dynamic movements
Interval training	Improvements in high-intensity exercise tolerance and repeat-burst activities (all-out short-duration efforts such as sprints in the game of soccer) and aerobic capacity
Speed training	Improvements in velocity of movements
Plyometric training	Improvements in explosive power

- The purpose of the exercise program
- The expected stress and fatigue from the exercises performed. (It is normal to experience some fatigue, but no pain, excessive discomfort, or excessive fatigue should be present during or following an exercise session.)
- That it is OK for the child to tell you how he feels about an exercise session or the training program and, more important, that he can expect you to make appropriate modifications
- That he should feel adequately recovered before starting successive workouts

Remember, you are working with the child to develop a program he is comfortable with and feels excited about, and it is up to him whether he wants to participate in it.

Assure Proper Progression

The saying "no pain, no gain" sends the wrong message to many young athletes. Research shows that a painful resistance-training workout does not necessarily yield optimal gains in strength. Thus, it is important to think about the signals we—and the rest of the world—communicate to young people. Take time to explain the basic principles of resistance training, correct misconceptions, and state realistic expectations.

These steps can help you establish proper progression:

1. Show the child how to perform each exercise using little or no resistance. Do not rush this period of orientation and physical interaction.
2. For the first workout, start the child with only one set of relatively light resistance (12- to 15RM).

3. Plan for a three- to four-week learning period. Start out with simpler body-part exercises, then very slowly add specific multi-joint structural exercises based on individual needs.

4. Gradually increase the number of sets and the resistance used so that after four to five weeks the child reaches the starting point for a program.

5. Carefully monitor the child's recovery so that you don't overshoot physical or mental abilities to recover; cut back if needed.

As the child gains muscular strength and endurance, the amount of resistance and the number of repetitions performed can increase. Do not allow the child to become obsessed with maximal performance in each exercise session; this causes undue stress and discourages participation. Look for improvement, but be positive and allow for normal ups and downs in training. Don't ever let young athletes become self-critical because of their performance in an exercise-training session; the workout is merely a goal or guide, and you must be realistic about and sensitive to variations in performance as training progresses.

Because children mature at different rates, they must learn to value the improvements they make and not compare themselves to others. You should play a vital role in developing their self-esteem and helping them to focus on their own training gains. Provide rewards and support for improvement. Furthermore, help children understand that although improvement might slow down in one area, gains can be made in other areas; constant improvement in all areas isn't possible.

Schedule Realistically

Resistance training should not be the only activity for children; they should participate in a total conditioning program. You must develop a realistic schedule that doesn't overstress the child. Some examples follow:

• **Schedule 1:** The athlete trains three days per week, performing both aerobic and resistance exercises on the same day. Flexibility training is part of the warm-up and cool-down. Aerobic and resistance training can be performed in the same session or at different times (e.g., aerobic in the morning and resistance in the afternoon). If the athlete wishes to split the two training sessions in order to spend more time on a particular activity, allow several hours between workouts. This schedule allows four days for sports and other activities.

• **Schedule 2:** This schedule splits up the aerobic and resistance-training sessions, and the flexibility program is part of the warm-up and cool-down. This type of schedule allows the athlete to spend more time on a particular training activity but is demanding and typically is not needed until the athlete has gained considerable training experience. Still, it accommodates those who do not have large blocks of time available on three training days.

Limitless scheduling variations are possible. The previous two schedules may work well for a high school athlete or someone very dedicated to staying physically fit, but for children involved in numerous activities they may be too restrictive. Use your imagination when designing schedules for children. For example, a young child can resistance train on Monday and Wednesday and perform aerobic training on Tuesday and Thursday. Although sessions are less frequent and gains would be made more slowly with this schedule, it's a viable alternative. Remember, training must be fun, not frightening, if children are to perform it willingly and establish good fitness habits.

Again, children must have adequate time to recover from exercise stress or positive physical changes will not occur. Training is more than physical; you need to be sensitive to its mental aspects as well. Starting with a low frequency of training in the beginning or alternating heavy, moderate, and light days of training allows the child to progress into the training program more easily.

It is typically recommended that adults train three times per week so that the exercise stress will bring about physiological changes. The optimal exercise frequency for children is unknown, but three days per week appears to be an appropriate starting point. Schedule constraints may alter the frequency, but training fewer than three days per week may not be optimal. The body must have enough exposure to exercise stress to stimulate change. Too much stress can cause distress or overtraining; too little can make a program ineffective. This is why you must observe how the child handles the physical and emotional stress of training and make immediate changes if he does not tolerate a session physically or emotionally.

PHYSICAL TESTING

One way to determine children's readiness for a strength-training regimen is through physical testing. This can be done in many ways, but the most popular tests determine the maximum number of repetitions they can complete, local muscular endurance, and motor performance.

Repetition Maximum

In children, establishing the maximal weight possible for one repetition of an exercise (1RM) is not necessary to evaluate strength gains; a weight that allows six or seven repetitions is sufficient. You should closely control RM testing because the length of the rest periods and the number of sets performed will affect the results. An estimation of the RM will help you determine warm-up resistances to be used in RM testing. If the child has weight-training experience, you can get an estimation of the RM for a particular exercise from her training log. If she has been tested for an RM previously, you can estimate it from those results. The following is a procedure to determine a 6RM:

1. The child warms up with 5 to 10 repetitions using 50 percent of the estimated 6RM.

2. After one minute of rest and some stretching, she performs six repetitions at 70 percent of the estimated 6RM.

3. She repeats step 2 at 90 percent of the estimated 6RM.

4. After about two minutes of rest, depending on the effort needed to perform the 90 percent set, the child performs six repetitions with 100 or 105 percent of the estimated 6RM.

5. If she successfully completes six repetitions in step 4, add 2.5 to 5 percent of the resistance used in step 4, then have her attempt six repetitions after two minutes of rest. If she does not complete six repetitions in step 4, subtract 2.5 to 5 percent of the resistance used in step 4 and have her attempt six repetitions after two minutes of rest.

6. If the first part of step 5 is successful (the child lifts 2.5 to 5 percent more resistance than used in step 4), retest her starting with the higher resistance after at least 24 hours of rest. If the second part of step 5 is successful (she lifts 2.5 to 5 percent less than the resistance used in step 4), this amount of resistance is her 6RM. If the second part of step 5 is not successful, retest her after at least 24 hours of rest, starting with less resistance.

As an example, let's say a child's estimated 6RM for the leg press is 100 pounds. She performs 5 to 10 repetitions with 50 pounds as a warm-up (100 pounds × .50 = 50 pounds; step 1). After one minute of rest and stretching, she then performs six repetitions with 70 pounds (100 pounds × .70 = 70 pounds; step 2). After two minutes of rest she performs six repetitions with 90 pounds (100 pounds × .90 = 90 pounds; step 3). Let's say this child performs the six repetitions at 90 pounds very easily, so you decide to use 105 percent of the estimated 6RM resistance. After two minutes of rest the child performs six repetitions with 105 pounds (100 pounds × 1.05 = 105 pounds; step 4). Performance of the set at 105 pounds appears to be very difficult, so you decide to have her try another set at 108 pounds (105 pounds × 0.025 = 2.6 pounds; 105 pounds + 2.6 pounds = 107.6 pounds; step 5). It is impossible to get a resistance of 107.6 pounds on the leg press being used, so you have the child use 108 pounds. After two minutes of rest she completes only four repetitions, so this child's 6RM resistance for the leg press is 105 pounds. (It is often impossible to get the exact weight needed for RM testing on the bar or machine the child is using, so you will have to use a resistance that's as close as possible to what's needed.)

On some machines it is possible to make changes in resistance of as little as 5 pounds by sliding a 5-pound weight on and off the stack with a built-in mechanism or hanging small weights (usually 2.5 or 5 pounds) off an additional weight-stack pin. When using the latter method, make sure the additional weights do not interfere with the movement of the weight stack.

Correct RM testing does require a relatively long time (10 to 15 minutes per child per exercise). However, you can reduce the total amount of time by staggering the testing so that when one child is resting another is performing a set or by having more than one testing station going on at the same time.

RM testing must be performed at least 24 hours after the previous training session so that fatigue does not affect the results. Whether machines or free weights are used, body, hand, and foot position must be the same for all testing. If the child's feet are blocked for one test, they should be blocked for all. The seat and any other adjustments on a machine must be in the same position for all tests. If the child grows significantly between tests, she must attempt to achieve the same relative body position (e.g., same angle at the elbows, shoulders, and knees) after adjustments for height, such as seat position, are made. Correct exercise technique must be used for all testing and spotters must be present to prevent injury. You must use correct and repeatable procedures for all testing to ensure both reliable results and the safety of the lifters.

Recent evidence indicates that testing a 1RM can be done safely in children. Maximal 1RM strength testing is safe in 6- to 12-year-olds if conducted using supervision and proper technique.[7] However, 1RM testing is often related to research; determination of the safer 6RM provides a good idea of how much loading to use for heavy training in children. Remember, by using RM target zones and recording session results in a log, it's possible to see progress in strength of all muscles, which can greatly reduce the need for RM testing.

Local Muscular Endurance

If increased local muscular endurance is a training goal, you may want to evaluate it before starting training. You can perform a simple test by having the child do as many repetitions as possible at a specified percentage of his body weight or his 6RM resistance. RM testing and local muscular endurance testing should be spaced at least 24 to 48 hours apart so that fatigue does not affect the results. You can use 60 to 80 percent of the 6RM to test relative local muscular endurance. Terminate the tests when technique deteriorates to a point that endangers the child's safety. As with RM testing, use spotters and require proper technique for all repetitions.

Motor Performance

A goal of some resistance-training programs, especially those designed for a sport, is to improve motor performance. Common motor-performance tests are short sprints (30-50 yards) and vertical jumping. It is beyond the scope of this text to describe proper procedure for motor-performance tests. (For a detailed overview of testing, see Harman and Pandorf, 2000, and Harman et al., 2000.)

SUMMING UP AND LOOKING AHEAD

No one type of training can effect all of the changes needed to promote cardiovascular endurance, muscular strength, health, and improved sport performance. A varied training schedule also exposes the young athlete to various types of exercise, such as lifting, running, and skiing.

Although a child's chosen sport may require only one type of conditioning, encourage him to participate in a total conditioning program and not become a specialist at a young age. Total conditioning will lead to a better overall physical development and enhance health and fitness. In chapter 4, we discuss how to create an individualized program and in chapter 6 we examine the various factors involved in teaching exercise techniques, which is an important part of implementing a program.

4

Creating Individualized Programs

Children need a considerable amount of education about fitness, training, and sports before they start a program of exercise training. They must understand why they perform the exercises and must wish to participate. Thus, adults must make programs attractive to children and allow them to see the benefits, including the bottom line of fun and socialization. The goal is for children to participate in exercise training because they want to be involved, not merely to please an adult. Through goal setting, understanding personal responsibility, and evaluating progress, your child is more likely to continue a strength-training program and become a healthier, happier athlete.

SETTING REALISTIC EXPECTATIONS AND GOALS

Realistic expectations of what resistance training can accomplish are based on understanding how the body responds at various ages to different training programs. A goal of developing larger muscles in a 10-year-old boy is not consistent with the adaptations that occur in young children. Setting proper expectations and goals requires a basic understanding of what is realistic and possible. Statements such as "You should be about 25 pounds heavier if you want to play" or "Anyone can be a world champion" are irresponsible and misleading to children. The results range from losing the trust of the child, to lowering his self-esteem, to possibly contributing to anabolic substance abuse. Although a discussion of anabolic drugs and alternatives to their use is beyond the scope of this book, parents, coaches, and teachers should educate themselves about these potentially hazardous substances.[1, 2] For more information, visit the National Strength and Conditioning Association's Web site at www.nsca-lift.org.

Children must learn to measure themselves against their own progress, not against others. Because children mature at different rates and have genetic predispositions for physical characteristics, self-improvement is one of the most important concepts that you can promote. Encourage this viewpoint and you will contribute to each child's self-esteem. Each individual has a genetic potential for growth and performance. The purpose of training is to enhance the genetic potential for fitness, health, and performance. Parents, teachers, and coaches are important influences on how young children think about training and performance, so they need to send out the right signals. Let young athletes know that the rewards of sport participation come from self-improvement, not only from winning. For example, a football coach might tell a young athlete that he must gain 30 pounds to play on the team. This is not a realistic training goal, and the methods required to achieve it are not ethically acceptable. Coaches and athletes need to be patient and realize that making true physical gains takes time; there is no quick fix. Only through commitment to a developmental conditioning program that includes exercise, good nutrition, and skill practice can the athlete safely make gains and improve sport performance.

Let's look at some examples of starting goals for two children. Dan is a 13-year-old boy who plays soccer and wants to use resistance exercise to help him prepare for the sport; Anna, a 15-year-old girl who plays tennis, wants to start a resistance-training program to help her with her sport and possibly make the varsity team.

Dan has multiple goals related to general fitness and soccer. His goals for resistance training would be (1) to gain overall body strength by training each of the major muscle groups around each joint; (2) to develop local muscular endurance in order to be able to perform optimally throughout an entire soccer game; and (3) to strengthen the knee joint, because knee injuries in soccer are the highest in youth sports.

Anna's goals for general fitness and tennis might include (1) gaining overall body strength by training each of the major muscle groups around each joint; (2) developing total body power to enhance performance in each of the tennis strokes; and (3) including rotator cuff exercises, as well as and shoulder and arm exercises, to prevent injury.

At the beginning of any training program, strength and endurance gains are made quickly, typically because the individual starts at a low level of fitness. Then as training continues, the magnitude of the gains slows down until the trainee reaches a plateau. In reality small day-to-day changes are taking place, but they are so slight that our methods of measuring progress (e.g., amount of resistance) cannot pick them up. For example, in the first three months of training, the weight a child lifts for 10 repetitions may increase by 50 pounds in a leg press. Then, over the next 3 months, the improvement may be only 10 pounds. The child cannot expect constant, large increases during training because physiological changes slow down after the initial adaptations.

Children's potentials for strength at a given age can be noticeably different depending on their maturation status. For example, during a growth spurt a young boy's muscle size and strength will increase without any training at all. Keep in mind that strength changes occur during all periods of maturation, but only long-term training will increase strength beyond normal growth-related changes.

Changing Training Goals With Age

Training methods and goals evolve as a child grows older because of changing interests in different sports and other factors. Even if he maintains a long-term interest in a particular sport, his exercise prescription will change to address increased physical maturity and the more rigorous demands of advanced sport competition. Each child's motivations are unique, and parents, teachers, and coaches must understand the changing world of children as they grow, develop, and mature both physically and emotionally. Adults have only to look at the culture, movies, video games, magazines, television, and schools to see the world that affects children's views on many things, including resistance training.

Presenting the Program Philosophy

For formal programs in schools or health clubs, the environment must reflect the program philosophy: Web sites, signs, wall charts, and handouts need to send the right signals to the child. This is especially important when both adults and children train in the same facility. You can present the program philosophy in the following ways:

- Post age-related instructions for children next to the adult guidelines on wall charts, Web sites, and computer-based programs (see figure 4.1).
- In the weight room, gym, or on the Web site, choose posters and pictures that depict boys and girls rather than adults, thereby promoting proper expectations from resistance training.

Use charts, contests, and awards to promote the principles and proper context for training; these can include

- training-consistency charts and awards,
- exercise-technique contests and awards,
- total conditioning fitness awards that focus on progress in other components of physical fitness, such as endurance runs and flexibility,

Training Day Schedule

Adult
Heavy day: 100% of 3- to 5RM
Moderate day: 90% of 3- to 5RM
Light day: 85% of 3- to 5RM

Child (15 and under)
Heavy day: 100% of 8- to 10RM
Moderate day: 90% of 8- to 10RM
Light day: 85% of 8- to 10RM

Figure 4.1 Sample wall chart for adults and children.

- fitness-preparation awards prior to a sport season,
- maintenance-program awards during a sport season, and
- best-buddy-support awards for training partners.

BEING RESPONSIBLE

Participating in any strength-training regimen requires a lot of responsibility on the part of parents, coaches, and the athletes themselves. Before beginning any training each person involved needs to recognize, understand, and accept responsibility for the factors that are necessary for safety and growth.

- **Responsibilities of adults.** Parents are often concerned about a child's growth for purposes of sport and athletic competition. They usually desire to see a child grow larger in order to allow for superior sport performance and may become quite obsessed with trying to predict his future height and weight. Although a physician should monitor growth rates to make sure that no underlying pathology exists, parents should not give children impossible objectives to meet, because their genetic basis cannot be altered. It is up to parents to enhance the positive factors that can improve a child's health and active lifestyle. Parents should also remember that success in athletics involves more than size; each sport has particular requirements for success at every level. In fact in some sports that have weight classes, such as wrestling and judo, body size is not important; in others, such as road cycling and gymnastics, a large body mass is a disadvantage.

Further, adults should not select a child's activities based only on the potential for future professional success. A child can enjoy playing basketball despite the fact that she may never be a WNBA player. It's up to adults to link sport participation to fun and fitness rather than to professional or financial success. Of course, that's easy to say but hard to do in today's world of big money, where young athletes start so early to gain the skills needed for elite competition in sports such as golf, tennis, and baseball. Resistance training should not be looked at only as a tool for sport performance—it is also a lifetime fitness activity as well. Sports should be fun, and adults must provide children with adequate preparation so that they can participate safely.

Adults are also responsible for optimizing the child's sport experience. Resistance training along with proper coaching can prepare the child for the demands of a sport, whether it is recreational or competitive. So many times we want our children to be successful but do not provide them with the proper tools to do so, such as appropriate teaching or training methods. Adults must not only allow children to have fun, grow, and develop; they must provide them with the tools to reach their potential.

- **Responsibilities of children.** Children too have important responsibilities as participants in a resistance-training program. They should ask questions whenever they are unsure about what they are doing or why. By learning each of the exercise techniques and understanding the spotting and safety aspects, children take an active role in their training. They should feel free to communicate their feelings and thoughts about a workout, know how to distinguish between fatigue and pain that may be due to an injury, and understand how to listen to their bodies to determine

---

Working With Young Elite Athletes

When working with young athletes who are especially talented, trainers must guard against burnout, which is a big problem for children. Physical conditioning should be a stress reliever, not an added stress to an athlete at any age. To achieve this, monitor the athlete's ability to recover from workouts and use a periodized training program to provide needed variation and fun. Excess work for the sake of working harder than the other guy is not a formula that will meet with much success.

In reality children must get more out of the sport experience than participation in their growth as individuals. Chasing the dream of money and fame in the hope of being the next Tiger Woods or Annika Sorenstam will likely reduce the sport experience and the training for it to something negative. Successful athletes love not only the sport but the culture of preparation and training that surrounds it. The dream must arise from the children themselves, and the human spirit needs to gain something in the process. This is what can be lost in the world of big-time money sports. In the world of big business in sports today, the cost is high for thousands of aspiring young athletes trying to hit it big and forsaking other parts of their life. Good physical conditioning programs can help a talented young athlete succeed, but without the needed genetics, no amount of conditioning will create an elite athlete. So care must be taken to see the human side of each child and develop not only a total conditioning plan but a "total life plan" for the young athlete.

---

how they should recover from an exercise session. Documenting their workouts in a log with the help of a trained adult teaches them how to track their workout sets, resistances, rest periods, and each aspect of the workout protocol. Also, they must be responsible for knowing how to dress properly for a workout and take care of themselves. Ultimately, children must accept the responsibility to grow and develop in their understanding of resistance training, learning about each aspect and the concepts related to it, just as they would with a sport. Finally, they must have the freedom to decide that a workout or a program is not for them.

EVALUATING THE PROGRAM

You should evaluate the training program to determine whether it meets the goals for which it was designed; if not, it needs to be altered or redesigned. Strength gains and changes in motor performance are common evaluation factors. An athlete should train for at least eight weeks before a program is evaluated in order to allow time for training adaptations to occur. Young athletes also need enough time to gain initial tolerance to resistance-exercise stress before they face the additional physical strain of testing. Resistance-training injury often is related to doing too much too fast, inappropriate exercise techniques, and accidents, so evaluations should be added in a progressive manner, especially when starting out with a new program.

Examining a training log is the easiest and quickest way to evaluate strength gains since it documents the improvements children have made in repetition maximum resistances. You can do this in a cursory manner or calculate percent gains for individuals or a group. Remember that during the first three to four weeks of training large gains in strength (up to 20 percent) will occur. After 8 to 14 weeks of training, previously untrained children have demonstrated gains in strength of up to 43 percent. Thus, increases of approximately 30 to 40 percent in 8 to 14 weeks indicate a successful program in terms of strength gains. However, improvement of this magnitude may not occur if the children have had previous resistance-training experience.

Testing for strength gains involves determining repetition maximum (RM) resistances, which we will discuss later in the chapter. The RM is a resistance that allows the performance of no more than a specific number of repetitions. It is not necessary to test for RMs for all exercises in the program; this is very time consuming, and in many instances training-log data can answer questions concerning strength gains. Normally trainers determine RMs for two or three multi-joint exercises, such as the leg press, squat, bench press, or incline press. These provide a general view of the upper- and lower-body strength capabilities. Determining a 1RM for every exercise requires far too much testing; RM zones can improve program implementation, aid in strength-gain evaluations, and keep the training resistance optimal (see chapter 3).

Keeping a record of the number of sets, repetitions, and resistances for each exercise per session in a training log is useful in several ways: It demonstrates the progress of each lifter in terms of resistance used and repetitions performed and provides other information that can be motivational for children. The log also helps the trainer evaluate the success of the program and determine when the resistance should be increased for a particular exercise. Last, it is a reminder of the order of exercises to be performed, the resistance to be used, and the number of repetitions to be performed during a training session.

Recording body weight prior to each training session is useful, especially if an individual is attempting to lose or gain weight. Training logs also may have a place for comments about each session, such as whether it seemed easy or difficult. Additionally, they should have a place for notes on necessary equipment modifications (see figure 4.2).

A child can keep a training log in a notebook (see figure 4.3), a three-ring binder, or a handheld computer. For example, the notation "bench press 3 × 10RM at 70, 60, 55 (1 min)" means the lifter performed three sets of the bench press with resistances for the first, second, and third sets being 70, 60, and 55 pounds, respectively, and he rested one minute between the sets. Use this type of notation to record each exercise of a training session. Make notes on the workout and record the starting poundage for each exercise in preparation for the next workout.

Many young children want to see how strong they are by trying to lift as much as possible for one repetition (1RM). To satisfy the competitiveness of some children, you can hold lifting-technique contests. Typically, contests that stress correct lifting technique rather than the total resistance lifted use lifts that involve multi-joint movements and a higher degree of skill, such as the squat, bench press, power clean, or power snatch. Figure 4.4 contains technique evaluation forms for these lifts. You can develop your own forms for other lifts following these examples. It suggests the amount of resistance you should use for technique evaluation, but you should adjust this to the strength levels of the children in a particular group and for specific exercises. Correct technique for all of these lifts is described in detail in later chapters.

Name _____ Age _____

Week _____   Week _____   Week _____

Day _____   Day _____   Day _____

Weight _____   Weight _____   Weight _____

Exercise	Set 1		Set 2		Set 3		Set 1		Set 2		Set 3		Set 1		Set 2		Set 3	
	Weight	Reps	Weight	Reps	Weight	Reps	Weight	Reps	Weight	Reps	Weight	Reps	Weight	Reps	Weight	Reps	Weight	Reps

Comments: _____

_____

_____

_____

Exercise   Modifications

_____   _____

_____   _____

_____   _____

_____   _____

Figure 4.2   Sample training log.

Training Log

	Jan 16
●	Body weight - 101 lb.
	Leg press 3 x 12RM - 100,95,90
	Bench press 2 x 12RM - 65,60,55
	Leg curls 3 x 10RM - 25
	Arm curls 3 x 10RM - 15
●	Military press 3 x 8RM - 50,45,40
	Leg extensions 3 x 10RM - 35
	Incline sit-ups 3 x 2 - Board at 2nd
	highest position
	Comments:
●	1 - 2 min. rest between all exercises.
	Felt good. Almost time to increase
	leg press resistance to 105.

Figure 4.3 Notebook training log.

Figure 4.4 Technique Evaluation Forms

The amount of resistance used in technique competition should be only enough to require the lifter to demonstrate balance, control, and coordinated movement during the lift. The resistance used depends on the strength level of the child.

Front or Back Squat Technique

Resistance Used Back squat, 60 to 70 percent of body weight; front squat, 50 to 60 percent of body weight

Starting Position

Feet are shoulder-width apart and pointing forward or slightly out; back is straight; bar is on spines of scapulae and hands are slightly wider than shoulder-width for back squat; elbows are rotated up and bar is on upper chest and front of shoulder for front squat; bar is centered and horizontal; head is in a neutral position.

Points Available 0-4

Points Earned

Lowering (Eccentric) Phase

Feet stay flat; descent is performed in a controlled manner; back stays straight; no excessive forward lean; bar stays horizontal; descent is to where thighs are parallel to the floor; head stays in line with rest of back.

(continued)

Figure 4.4 *(continued)*

Points Available   0-9
Points Earned

Lifting (Concentric) Phase

Feet stay flat; back stays straight; legs (not back) lift weight; no excessive forward lean; bar stays horizontal; head stays in line with rest of back.

Points Available   0-9
Points Earned

Finishing Position

Knee and hip extension is complete; position is same as starting position.

Points Available   0-3
Points Earned

Total Points Available: 0-25

Total Points Earned

Bench-Press Technique

Resistance Used   40 to 50 percent of body weight

Starting Position

Elbows are straight; feet are flat on the floor; buttocks and shoulders touch bench; back is not excessively arched; bar is over upper chest; bar is horizontal.

Points Available   0-6
Points Earned

Lowering (Eccentric) Phase

Descent of bar is controlled; elbows are out to side; bar touches chest at approximately nipple level; there is no bounce on chest touch; bar is horizontal; feet stay flat on floor; back is not excessively arched; head stays still and in contact with the bench.

Points Available   0-7
Points Earned

Lifting (Concentric) Phase

Back is not excessively arched; elbows are out to sides; bar is horizontal; both arms straighten at same speed; motion is smooth and continuous; head stays still and in contact with the bench; buttocks remain in contact with the bench; feet stay flat on floor.

Points Available   0-9
Points Earned

Finishing Position

Same as starting position.

Points Available	0-3
Points Earned	
	Total Points Available: 0-25
Total Points Earned	

Power Clean Technique

Resistance Used	40 to 50 percent of body weight
	Starting Position
	Bar is over balls of feet; feet are hip-width or slightly wider apart; shoulders are over or slightly in front of bar; grip is slightly wider than shoulder-width; head is in neutral position, back is straight.
Points Available	0-5
Points Earned	
	Lifting (Concentric) Phase
	Back stays at the same angle to floor as in the starting position until it is at knee height; shoulders stay over bar; bar stays close to body; bar does not bounce off thighs during second pull; second pull is explosive; elbows stay above bar; shoulders shrug; lifter rises on toes; elbows do not bend until shoulder shrug and rise on toes is complete; bar is horizontal.
Points Available	0-9
Points Earned	
	Catching the Bar
	Elbows rotate under bar quickly; back is straight; knees are bent as bar is caught; bar is horizontal.
Points Available	0-9
Points Earned	
	Finishing Position
	Back is upright; knees are straight; bar is horizontal; elbows are high in front of bar so that it rests on front of shoulders.
Points Available	0-2
Points Earned	
	Returning Bar to Floor
	Elbows rotate down; bar is returned to floor, not dropped.
Points Available	0-2
Points Earned	
	Total Points Available: 0-27
Total Points Earned	

Snatch

Resistance Used	30 to 40 percent of body weight
	Starting Position

(continued)

Figure 4.4 *(continued)*

Bar is over balls of feet; feet are hip-width or slightly wider apart; shoulders are over or slightly in front of bar; back is straight; head is in neutral position; grip is at correct width.

Points Available 0-5
Points Earned

Lifting (Concentric) Phase

Back stays at same angle to floor as in the starting position until bar is at knee height; shoulders stay over bar; bar stays close to body; bar does not bounce off thighs during second pull; elbows stay above bar; shoulders shrug; lifter rises on toes; elbows do not bend until shoulders are shrugged and rise on toes is complete; bar is horizontal.

Points Available 0-9
Points Earned

Catching the Bar

Elbows rotate under bar quickly; elbows extend quickly; bar is not pressed out; bar is above ears in overhead position; knees are bent as bar is caught; back is straight; bar is horizontal.

Points Available 0-7
Points Earned

Finishing Position

Knees straighten completely; bar is above ears; elbows are straight; back is straight.

Points Available 0-3
Points Earned

Returning Bar to Floor

Bar is returned to floor, not dropped.

Points Available 0-1
Points Earned

Total Points Available: 0-25

Total Points Earned

SUMMING UP AND LOOKING AHEAD

Development and administration of a resistance-training program comprise an ongoing process of many factors, from daily correction of exercise technique and adjustment of resistances to program evaluation and the adjustments needed to meet the changing goals of the program. In the next chapter we will discuss factors you should consider when designing a resistance-training program for children.

5

Safe Training Environments

The primary goal of any conditioning program is to create a safe environment for the child to work in. This includes the physical setting, the people involved, and the equipment used. The adults who implement the program are responsible for its safety and must assure parents, guardians, and caretakers that such protective measures are in place. In this chapter we examine some of the components vital to a safe training environment; attention to each is important. Creating a safe training environment ultimately takes effort: Do your homework and check things out so that proper safeguards are in place prior to the implementation of any program. (Exercise photos courtesy of Life Fitness Academy, except where noted.)

SELECTING A TRAINING FACILITY

When evaluating where to train, pay attention to the number and type of people who typically train during the times your child would be there in order to get a feel for the environment. Weight rooms have their own training environments, ranging from upscale health clubs to serious gyms for bodybuilders and weightlifters to places for young adults to socialize.

Be aware of the messages being sent in the training environment you choose for a child. Recently many gyms that cater only to children have popped up all over the United States; seek them out as well as the classic choice of a well-equipped YMCA/YWCA with a family environment. Many commercial venues cater to a specific market and may not have appropriate equipment and personnel available to help train certain age groups of children. You must carefully determine whether the environment is right for a young athlete. One of the worst approaches is to send a young athlete into an environment without a careful analysis of the equipment, who trains there, and the professional qualifications of the personnel.

Some fitness facilities can limit effective training of the young athlete by not having certain types of equipment. Some may not reflect any real understanding of what younger athletes need, especially prepubescent children. Many schools provide training facilities, but due to overcrowding, lack of supervision, or sole use by older athletes, they may not be appropriate for the younger child. Very few adequate training facilities exist below the high school level in most public school programs. Nevertheless, make sure the facility has what is needed for optimal training. Not all facilities are equal, even if the corporation name is the same. The addition of a parent, coach, or personal trainer accompanying each child can make for a crowded weight room in smaller facilities. In addition, when planning a home gym area make sure that the flooring, ceiling height, temperature control, ventilation, and safety elements are all appropriate. There are numerous tales of accidents involving young children who train in a poorly lit basement with no supervision. Expect the same safety standards from a home gym as you would from a health club. With children, supervision and guidance in the implementation of a workout program are vital to success.

Selecting a Supervisor

Supervision is crucial in a resistance-training program for children. Coaches, personal trainers, athletic trainers, and in some cases parents all can play a part in this role. Each must have the background necessary to be a knowledgeable supervisor. Incompetent supervision can be as detrimental as none at all. No matter what the adult's title is, they must demonstrate minimum competence in understanding of the equipment, exercise techniques, spotting, and safety aspects of each exercise as well as basic knowledge about exercise, fatigue, and injury.

Current first-aid and cardiopulmonary resuscitation (CPR) certifications are also a must. Equally important is a healthy perspective on what a workout and training program for children should be like. Certifications also provide clues to an adult's background and exposure, which is especially important when parents are evaluating a coach's credentials. Are they certified as strength and conditioning specialists by the National Strength and Conditioning Association (NSCA)? Have they attended United States Weightlifting Coaches clinics and certifications? Many times adults who express an interest in working with young athletes played a sport in high school but are not necessarily qualified to work with children. The availability of qualified adult supervision is limited at times, which has led to the use of inadequately credentialed or even incompetent adults in some situations.

The NSCA has developed a locator service to help people find personal trainers and identify those with strength and conditioning qualifications in various areas of the United States; contact them for the names of professionals in your area.

Choosing a Health Club

Chapter 1 points out that using high-tech equipment and simulating the environment of a health club have been shown to be effective for children in a school setting. But in a commercial setting you need to carefully evaluate a number of factors.

When you are considering enrolling a child at a spa or health club, evaluate the equipment and consider the factors listed in the box that follows. The NSCA can also give you advice or recommend a qualified professional in your area. Too many trainers get by with an outgoing personality and great looks, but there's little substance or competence underneath the so-called hard body. Remember, although a fitness professional should look the part, body development does not reflect competence in teaching and coaching in the field of strength and conditioning.

Factors to Consider When Purchasing a Club Membership for a Child

The following factors are important when selecting a club membership for your child.

1. Are the instructors certified by a nonprofit, professional organization concerned with knowledge and understanding of resistance training?
2. Are the instructors certified in first aid and CPR?
3. How many children are members of the club?
4. Are there special times or classes for children?
5. Do the instructors know how to train children?
6. Do parents have to be present for children to use the resistance-exercise facilities? How old must children be to use the facilities alone?
7. Is the resistance-exercise room well supervised?
8. Are testing programs used to help design the program?
9. Is the program individually designed?
10. Is aerobic training monitored by use of a physiological variable (e.g., heart rate)?
11. Does the club have a medical or scientific advisory board?
12. What is the medical emergency plan?
13. Is the equipment maintained and in good working condition?
14. Is there an obvious plan for cleaning and maintenance of the equipment to protect health and prevent injury or disease (more than a spray bottle to wipe off equipment with a used cloth from a hook)?
15. Does the equipment properly fit children or can it be modified to do so? Is there a variety of equipment options to accommodate children of different sizes?

ENSURING FACILITY SAFETY

The availability of equipment, space, and time for resistance training, along with the number of children training and their maturity levels, all have a great impact on the training program. In the initial design of the program, however, you should not consider these administrative concerns. First, design an optimal program, then make any needed changes due to administrative concerns. Try to remedy those problems that severely compromise the program design as soon as possible. For example, if an exercise in the optimal program cannot be performed because of lack of proper equipment, plan to obtain the equipment.

Equipment Modification and Availability

Equipment made for children is now becoming more available, with barbells as light as 5 pounds, mini benches, and 2- to 3-pound dumbbells that allow even the youngest children to get a feel for the concept of a workout. Even some machine lines have been downsized to properly fit young children's limb lengths and smaller statures. Surfing the Internet, you can even find equipment for 5-year-old-sized bodies. The key is to allow younger children the chance to learn about performing a workout and developing healthy exercise habits, which may be more important than strength gains for the very young child.

Equipment setups must be altered properly to fit children, or you could complicate the exercise and increase the potential for injury. However, modifying equipment to fit children also creates organizational problems. For example, each exercise station must have the pads and blocks necessary to modify the equipment to fit the child. Equipment such as dumbbells must be available so that the child can perform an alternate exercise when a machine does not fit or cannot provide the proper resistance. Each child must know how to set up the necessary modification for each exercise. Equipment modifications change as a child grows; thus you will need to check equipment for proper fit as frequently as every month. Prior to the training session, preparation of the resistance-training facility is needed to address any equipment modification concerns. If you use timed workouts, you must factor in the time needed for equipment modifications, especially when several children are training and modifications are being made for many exercises. One way to solve this problem is to note the necessary modifications on each child's workout card. Although adults can make the modifications for the children, this may be impractical with a large group of children.

To find out how long it takes to make a particular equipment modification, have the child perform a trial training session including the modifications. Then adjust the rest periods to allow the time needed for each piece of equipment. Younger children (8 to 10 years old) may require more time to make the modifications themselves, or an adult may have to make the modifications for them. This requires more adult supervision but it may be needed to ensure the safety of the children. Although one-minute rest periods may be desirable in a particular training session, organizational problems such as equipment fit may make this impossible. For example, exercise machines typically require more modifications than free weights due to fixed movement patterns and positions. You must resolve these organizational problems as best as possible without sacrificing the safety of the children or lessening the training session's effectiveness.

The availability of resistance-training equipment, especially in elementary, junior high, and high schools, is perhaps the greatest obstacle to many programs. Although some programs do not require a great deal of equipment (participants can use body-weight and partner-resisted exercises), many exercises do require some equipment.

If you plan to purchase equipment, evaluate it for safety, cost, construction, and proper fit for children. Plan your purchases so that all of the body's major muscle groups can be trained. Do not buy resistance-exercise machines that duplicate your capabilities or equipment for a specific sport or small muscle group until you have equipment to train all the major muscle groups. Obtaining equipment that you can use to train several different muscle groups should be a higher priority than that which can train only one group.

If the available equipment is minimal, find viable alternatives for the muscle groups for which you have no equipment. In these situations consider body-weight-resisted and partner-resisted exercises or elastic stretch bands. Dynamic drills (e.g., hill running and stair running) are also acceptable substitutions for some conditioning requirements.

Facility Availability

Many times a training facility has adequate equipment to train all the major muscle groups, but the facility is too crowded. The number of children who can be effectively trained at one time depends in part on their maturity (i.e., their ability to follow directions and their desire to train). These factors in turn may depend on the children's understanding of what they are doing and why. In many instances, a facility is overcrowded only at certain times of the day, such as noon or after school.

One solution to overcrowding is to develop a master schedule of training times for teams or individuals. Having accurate information about the facility's use also aids requests for it to be open for a greater number of hours, such as before or after school and during free periods, and provides strong support for requests for more equipment and space. The largest numbers of people typically train at noon, after school, and late in the afternoon, when athletic teams are training and children have free time. When attempting to schedule athletic teams, obtain from coaches the times they desire to use the facility and possible alternate times, such as in the morning before school. Inform all parties using the facility that staying with the established schedule will increase the amount of actual training that takes place because it will reduce overcrowding and the wait time for equipment. Consider the presence of adult supervisors when developing the schedule of the facility's open hours; for safety reasons, the number of people in the facility needs to be carefully monitored and controlled.

A second solution to overcrowding is to better organize the flow of lifters during their training sessions. To do this, you must know which pieces of equipment are used most often in various training programs and where the lines develop due to people waiting to use equipment. Requiring children to wait to use a piece of equipment is an open invitation to horseplay, distraction, and possible injury. Furthermore, excessive delays reduce the effectiveness of timed training programs. Several measures can help improve the flow pattern within the training facility:

- Use timed training sessions (specified times for each exercise and rest period), so that lifters must move quickly from one piece of equipment to the next. However, remember to account for the time needed to modify equipment so that it fits the children and to change the resistance.

- Use predetermined exercise sequences so that lines do not form by the group's favorite piece of equipment.

- Schedule individuals who follow a similar training program at the same time of the day. This also gives children an opportunity to have training partners.

• Schedule children who need similar equipment modifications at the same time of the day, if possible. Have the pads or blocks needed to make the modifications available at each exercise station.

• Carefully plan programs for groups that use different exercises or time sequences and that need to train at the same time of the day so that they do not interfere with each other's movement through the exercises.

For timed training sessions, you can use a whistle and stopwatch to control the rest-period length between sets and exercises and length of time allowed for each set. The big digital clocks that are now popular in weight rooms have a timing feature that allows countdowns for rest periods or time at each exercise station. You can also play a tape recording of the rest-and-exercise sequence on a facility-wide audio system. For example, play music during the training session and use a voice-over to indicate the rest periods and when to move to the next exercise. In addition, you can help control the flow pattern by indicating the exercise sequence on the floor with color-coded tape and having lifters carry workout sheets that explain the sequence. All of these measures free you to assist the children with exercise technique instead of acting as a traffic cop. These methods may be mandatory when you are training a large group, but they also help you stress the proper exercise sequence and rest periods for each program.

Space Availability

The amount of total floor space in the resistance-training facility should be adequate enough not only to house the equipment but also allow for walkways between pieces of equipment. Ideally at least 6 feet should separate each piece of equipment. This space is necessary for lifters to move about safely and change the resistances, and for the spotters to perform their exercise monitoring during a lift. When free weights are used, space is needed where the lifter can drop the weight if necessary; this is especially true for *ballistic-type* lifts (e.g., power cleans and snatches or exercises that are explosive in nature). Before you obtain any new equipment for a facility, be sure sufficient space to meet these needs is available.

Time Availability

The best-designed program is of no use to children if they do not have sufficient training time. Calculate the total amount of time needed for a training session, including rest periods and time to change the resistance and make equipment modifications. You can do this by having one or two children perform the workout, including any equipment modifications.

Be careful when making modifications to a training program in order to reduce the total training time. Don't simply drop the last exercise in a session; if an exercise needs to be dropped, it should be the one that is least essential, based on the needs analysis (see chapter 3) of the group or individual. If there are more than one exercise for a major muscle group, it may be possible to drop one of them. Don't decrease rest periods simply to save time. Increased blood lactate levels, a by-product of lactic acid, which are associated with increased exercise discomfort, result when rest periods are reduced. Pay close attention to whether a child can tolerate more demanding, high-lactate workouts. Rest periods should be reduced only when you want to increase the lifter's *high-intensity* local muscular endurance. This may be desirable for children participating in such sports as certain track events (400- and 800-meter sprints) or wrestling. But if the major goal of training is to increase strength/power, rest periods should not be less than two minutes. Carefully evaluate any changes you make in the training program to meet time constraints. Also evaluate how the changes affect the exercise training stimulus.

MAINTAINING EQUIPMENT

Resistance-training equipment is very durable; however, maintenance is necessary for safe operation and will increase the life of the equipment. Welds should be inspected for cracks and bolts checked for tightness at least weekly; a cracked weld or loose bolt can easily cause an injury. Be sure there is adequate air circulation so that excessive moisture does not cause machines to rust. Many facilities are air-conditioned, which keeps the humidity low. The simplest way to ensure adequate air ventilation in a facility that is not air-conditioned is to keep doors and windows open and use fans where possible. Install an air conditioner or dehumidifier if necessary. If rust does develop on a piece of equipment, use naval jelly to remove it immediately, then touch up the spot with a rust-resistant paint.

Cleaning and Disinfecting

Proper cleaning of surfaces and equipment is essential to a healthy training environment. Another way to keep germs away is to routinely clean and disinfect surfaces. In public facilities, wash your hands and be careful not to touch your mouth and nose areas without washing. The Centers for Disease Control in Atlanta, Georgia, offers the following hints for proper cleaning of surfaces (such as those in a weight room or gym facility) and distinguishes between cleaning and disinfecting.

Cleaning and disinfecting are not the same thing. In most cases, cleaning with soap and water is adequate to remove dirt and most of the germs. However, disinfectants, including solutions of household bleach, provide an extra margin of safety by destroying bacteria and other germs. You should disinfect areas where there are high concentrations of dangerous germs and a possibility that they will be spread to others. Even though surfaces may look clean, infectious germs may be lurking around. Given the right conditions, some germs can live on surfaces for hours or days. What is the best way to clean and disinfect surfaces?

• Follow the directions on the cleaning product labels. Be sure to read safety precautions as well.

• If you are cleaning up body fluids such as blood, vomit, or feces, wear rubber gloves, particularly if you have cuts or scratches on your hands or if it is possible that the fluid is infected with HIV, hepatitis B, or another blood-borne disease. It is also a good idea to clean and disinfect weight-room surfaces because someone may have come there sick.

• To begin, clean the surface thoroughly with soap and water or another cleaner.

• After cleaning, if you need to use a disinfectant, apply it to the area and let it stand for a few minutes or longer, depending on the manufacturers' recommendations. This keeps the germs in contact with the disinfectant for a longer period.

• Wipe the surface with paper towels that can be thrown away or cloth towels that can be washed afterward.

• Store cleaners and disinfectants out of the reach of children.

• Wash your hands after cleaning or disinfecting surfaces.

Lubricating

You should understand how each piece of equipment works and what its care and maintenance requirements are. Resistance-training equipment has many moving parts, which need to be lubricated to prevent wear; a spray-on silicone lubricant is best. Most machines now have belts made of rubber or a similar material instead of chains to connect handles and foot plates to the weight stack. However, if chains are present clean and lubricate them once a week to ensure smooth operation. Clean and lubricate the weight-stack rods weekly when they are in heavy use so that the plates slide freely and smoothly. Rub the weight-stack rods with fine steel wool to remove dirt. In addition, you should inspect the bushings in the weight-stack plates for wear and replace them if needed to ensure smooth operation and prevent damage to the rods.

• **Cables and pulleys.** Many pieces of equipment have a cable-and-pulley, rubber-belt-and-pulley, or chain-and-pulley arrangement, which can become worn. The cables, chains, belts, and pulleys should be inspected daily for proper alignment and smooth operation. Lubricate the bearings of the pulley regularly if needed; check it for side-to-side wobble and tighten it if needed. A pulley and cable, belt, or chain unit that is not operating smoothly will wear out very quickly. For safety reasons, replace worn components immediately.

• **Weight plates.** Free-weight plates and the plates in a weight stack on a machine do crack and break occasionally, most commonly when a lifter drops the resistance after completing a repetition. Discourage lifters from dropping free weights or "banging" the plates of a weight stack. It's possible to weld cracked or broken weight plates, but it is difficult due to the high graphite content in many of them. In most instances welding does not last; therefore it is best to replace the broken plate. For exercises in which the plates commonly hit the ground (dead lifts, high pulls), you can buy plates with rubber bumpers (called bumper plates) to minimize the effect of hitting the floor or lifting platform, but they are more expensive.

• **Olympic bars.** Olympic bars are barbells that are 7 feet 2 inches long that are used for Olympic and power lifting. They have sleeves on each end that allow the weights to rotate and the bar to revolve during a lift, which prevents skin from being ripped off the hands of the lifter or the wrist being injured (see figure 5.1). Olympic bars are very durable; however, a few problems can develop. The bar may become bent over time if the supports holding it are very close together and the bar is loaded heavily. This can easily happen if the bar is left loaded overnight or between training sessions, so unload it when it is not in use. The revolving sleeves become loose

Figure 5.1 Sleeves on each end of the Olympic revolving bar allow weights to rotate and the bar to revolve during a lift, preventing injury to the lifter.

at times; normally you can remedy this by tightening the Allen screw at the end of the sleeve. The revolving parts of the sleeves should also be lightly lubricated on a regular basis. After lubrication, wipe the sleeves clean; if lubricant remains on the outside of the bar, the plates will easily slide off. This is one reason that the use of collars on all free-weight bars should be mandatory. Olympic bars come in a wide price range, and typically it is the less expensive bars that develop problems, so make sure they are of quality construction and have good tensile strength.

Maintaining Upholstery

The benches and seats of resistance-training equipment are covered with vinyl or Naugahyde. Disinfectants used to remove moisture, sweat, and dirt from these coverings will cause them to crack over time; therefore, regular cleaning with a strong disinfectant should be followed by a mild soap rinse, and a vinyl restorative product should be applied regularly. To help prevent the buildup of dirt, make clean clothing mandatory in the facility and require lifters to wear shirts. In addition, lifters should use towels and a disinfectant to wipe sweat off the equipment after they have finished with it. If the covering becomes excessively cracked or ripped, it can be replaced; most companies sell replacement pads for their equipment. It is also possible to have a local upholsterer re-cover the pad with a high-grade vinyl or Naugahyde.

Protecting the Floor

If possible, install a dark, rubberized flooring throughout the facility. Place rubber mats where weight plates will most likely be placed on the floor or dropped, especially in the area where such lifts as dead lifts and cleans are performed. Typically, facilities place lifting platforms in the areas where power cleans and variations of the Olympic lifts are performed. An official Olympic lifting platform is a square that measures 13 feet and 1.25 inches per side. Constructed of wood, it is designed to protect the floor if the barbell is dropped. You can obtain construction plans for a weightlifting platform from U.S.A. Weightlifting, One Olympic Plaza, Colorado Springs, Colorado 80909.

Weight Room Tool Kit

Many simple equipment repairs require tools, so you should keep the most frequently needed tools in the facility. A training-facility tool kit should include the following:

- Complete set of Allen wrenches
- Complete set of screwdrivers (Phillips head and slotted)
- Files for smoothing rough spots on equipment
- Staple gun
- Complete socket set
- Paint touch-up supplies
- Bolt cutters
- Measuring tape
- Light silicone lubricant spray
- Naval jelly
- Strong disinfectant, rubber gloves, mild soap, vinyl restorative, sponge, and bucket to clean upholstery

For a more detailed inventory, refer to a comprehensive guide to facilities care and risk management by Greenwood and Greenwood (2000).

SUMMING UP AND LOOKING AHEAD

Creating a safe training environment is a function of qualified supervision, proper programs, proper equipment and spotting, and an understanding of the needs of each child. Of note is the fact that in some of the most sophisticated sporting cultures around the world the best coaches work with the youngest athletes. In our Western sport culture this concept has never really been embraced. Adults who are in charge of resistance training must understand the basic features described in this chapter and be able to deal with the changing needs of the children they work with. Within the context of the sporting continuum, resistance training as a conditioning modality is one of the safest activities. However, mistakes and tragedies have happened and in most cases they are due to incompetence and lack of proper supervision. In the next chapter you will start to read about the fundamental techniques so important to the actual performance of exercises. Such knowledge is the cornerstone of a safe resistance-training program.

6

Teaching Technique

The two most important characteristics needed to teach any activity, including resistance-training exercise techniques, are patience with trainees and knowledge of the material being taught. Proper exercise and spotting techniques are two of the most important aspects of a safe, effective program.

BASICS OF PROPER EXERCISE TECHNIQUE

Proper exercise technique involves many interrelated factors, all of which are important. They include:

- Understanding the exercise movement
- Spotting techniques
- Use of collars with free weights
- Proper grips
- Properly adjusting machines to fit a lifter
- Knowing how and when to make changes in the resistance used
- Correct breathing techniques
- Giving lifters feedback concerning their technique
- Choosing exercises that promote symmetrical muscular development

It is impossible for people to teach what they do not know. Therefore, you must completely understand the proper technique of an exercise, especially multi-joint exercises such as the squat, before attempting to teach it to others. Chapters 7 through 12 cover many commonly performed exercises. Study and practice the lifts you intend to include and teach in a training program. When you are learning a new exercise, starting with a very light resistance allows you to concentrate on proper technique. Critique your exercise technique by watching yourself in a mirror or have an experienced lifter, such as a personal trainer or strength coach, critique it for you.

One aspect of correct technique is performing the exercise with the fullest range of motion possible. Full range of motion normally means lifting and lowering the resistance as far as possible during each repetition. Another aspect of correct technique is using only those muscles that are supposed to be involved in the exercise. Frequently, lifters use another muscle group to start the weight moving when beginning a repetition, such as using the back to start an upper-body exercise such as arm curls. Using muscles other than those that the exercise is supposed to target compromises the training effect on the intended muscles.

Attempting to use too much weight too quickly for a certain number of repetitions can result in improper exercise technique. Although one training goal is to increase strength (which results in the ability to use more weight for a certain number of repetitions), take care that any increase in resistance does not result in improper exercise technique. Improper technique can also be the result of a weak muscle group in a multi-joint exercise, in which case exercises to strengthen those muscles should be added to the training program. For example, weak lower-back musculature results in too much forward lean or rounding of the lower back when performing a squat.

With children another aspect of improper exercise technique is equipment fit. Most resistance-training machines are made to fit the average-sized adult; many children's arms, legs, and torsos are too short to allow proper exercise technique when using these machines. If a machine does not fit a child, he should not use it. Improper exercise technique, no matter what the cause, can result in injury; therefore it must be corrected immediately.

Spotting

Spotting is the practice of having one or more individuals present to assist the lifter if needed. Spotters not only assist with completion of a repetition if needed, they also correct improper technique; their presence is vital in a safe resistance-training program. Spotters should use the following checklist at all times:

1. Know proper exercise technique.
2. Know proper spotting technique.
3. Be sure you are strong enough to assist the lifter with the resistance he is using.
4. Know how many repetitions the lifter intends to do.
5. Be attentive to the lifter at all times.
6. Stop the exercise if incorrect technique is used.
7. If incorrect exercise technique is used, correct it.
8. Know the plan of action if a serious injury occurs.

Since the major goal of spotting is to prevent injury, lifters should always have one or more spotters. No child or young adult should perform resistance training without proper supervision, including spotters. Trainers and children should know correct exercise and spotting techniques for all exercises in a program. If children are responsible enough, they should spot each other. If they cannot spot each other, as may be the case in some situations (special education classes, classes of children with handicaps, or when training partners are of unequal strength), enlist the help of other adults or reduce the number of children training at one time.

One- and Two-Person Spotting

More spotting is generally needed with free-weight exercises than with machine exercises. Most exercises are spotted by either one or two people. One spotter can be utilized for many barbell exercises when the weight is not extremely heavy. For example, the free-weight bench press can usually be spotted by one person, who stands behind the lifter's head. Some free-weight benches, such as incline benches, have a platform the spotter can stand on to make his task easier and safer. Barbell exercises that use heavy weights, such as back squats, are commonly spotted by two individuals who stand facing each other at opposite ends of the barbell. Additionally,

some barbell exercises, such as squats and overhead lifts, can be performed in a power rack with the pins of the power rack set at the lowest point in the exercise's range of motion. That way, if the lifter loses control of the barbell it will be caught by the pins of the power rack (figure 6.1).

Generally, when using dumbbells two spotters are necessary, with each one responsible for spotting one dumbbell. This is normally accomplished by the spotters standing facing each other on opposite sides of the lifter. Some free-weight exercises are not spotted, such as the barbell dead lift, because the lifter can either drop the barbell or lower it to the floor if he can't complete a repetition. Dynamic lifts, such as power cleans, are also generally not spotted because they must be done at

Figure 6.1 A power rack can aid in safety when lifting.

a relatively high velocity; by the time spotters could react to the lifter losing control of the weight the lift might already be over or the barbell already returned to the floor. However, even though it may not be necessary to spot these types of exercises, spotters still should monitor and correct the lifter's exercise technique and perform the other duties listed in the spotter's checklist. Spotters are an important safety aspect of all weight-training programs and are necessary at all training sessions.

The Spotting and Technique Connection

Correct exercise and spotting technique are highly interrelated. A safe and effective resistance-training program requires that both be practiced at all times.

When you teach a new exercise, be sure to demonstrate proper exercise and spotting techniques and discuss their major points. Then allow each child to try the exercise using a very light resistance so that fatigue or excessive weight does not result in incorrect exercise technique. For free-weight exercises a light resistance could be a barbell or dumbbell with no weight plates, or even a broomstick. For a machine exercise a light resistance might mean removing all weight from the machine or taking the pin out of the weight stack. After a child attempts to perform the exercise, point out any technique flaws, then continue to practice with light resistances. Do not increase the resistance until the child has mastered correct technique. In addition, all children should be expected to learn and demonstrate proper spotting techniques for each exercise.

Usually more time is needed to teach proper exercise and spotting techniques for free-weight exercises than for machine exercises. This is in large part due to the need for the lifter to balance the resistance in all directions (left, right, forward, backward, up, down) when using free weights. Machines, however, generally allow movement in only one plane and therefore require little if any balancing of the resistance. (Some new machines do allow movement in two planes.) Additionally, free-weight exercises generally require more spotting than machine exercises because free weights can be dropped. Even if a lifter loses control of a machine exercise, the handles, foot plates, or weight will follow the path directed by the machine.

Teaching proper exercise technique for multi-joint exercises, in which the lifter must learn to coordinate several muscle groups and joints, usually requires more time than teaching single-joint exercises. This is especially true for free-weight multi-joint exercises, such as squats, where the lifter must also balance the weight in all planes of movement.

Attempting to teach techniques for too many exercises at the same time, especially multi-joint exercises, will slow learning. The number of new exercises children can learn at one time will vary from child to child. A good starting point is seven to eight exercises, of which three or four may be multi-joint exercises.

Collars

Collars keep weight plates from sliding off of barbells, dumbbells, and some weight-plate-loaded machines. If a weight plate slides off it may hit the lifter, a spotter, or a bystander, resulting in injury. The danger of a weight plate hitting someone if it comes off a bar is perhaps most likely during overhead lifts. If the weight plates on a free weight, especially on a barbell, slide toward the end of the bar or come off completely, the resulting twisting motion of the bar could cause injury. Collars should be used all times and it is the duty of the spotters to make sure that they are.

Loading

One aspect of correct exercise technique that is frequently overlooked is how to load weight plates onto a barbell or machine. Loading is a very simple task, but it needs to be done correctly and safely. Obviously one aspect of this task is to grasp the plate firmly with both hands to avoid dropping it. Lifting a weight plate off the floor or a weight tree (particularly if it's a child lifting a heavy weight) should be done by using the legs, not by bending over at the lower back. Correct lifting technique applies to loading equipment as well as performing weight-training exercises.

Grips

Many exercises, with both free weights and machines, involve grasping a bar or handle. The three major types of grips are the overhand, underhand, and mixed. Most exercises use an overhand, or pronated, grip (see figure 6.2). In an overhand grip the back of the hand and knuckles are facing forward when grasping a bar handle that is horizontal to the floor. (If grasping a handle that is vertical to the floor, the back of the hand and knuckles will face outward.) In an underhand, or supinated, grip the back of the hand and knuckles face backward if grasping a handle that is horizontal to the floor. With a mixed, or alternate, grip one hand uses an overhand and the other an underhand grip. A mixed grip is the least common and is used for exercises such as a dead lift, where grip strength may limit how much weight can be lifted.

Another aspect of grips is the direction in which the palms of the hands face. On some machines and with dumbbells it is possible to have the palms face each other. For example, when performing a machine seated row or overhead press, handles allow the palms to face each other. This position is considered safer for the shoulder joint because there is less chance of a shoulder impingement syndrome (results from mechanical impingement of the rotator cuff tendon beneath the anteroinferior

Figure 6.2 *(a)* Overhand grip, *(b)* underhand grip, *(c)* mixed grip.

portion of the acromion, especially when the shoulder is placed in the forward-flexed and internally rotated position).

Center of Rotation

Machines have a center of rotation, which is normally located at the middle of a cam or a pulley. For example, the center of rotation for a knee extension machine is located at the center of the machine's cam (see figure 6.3). Some manufacturers mark the machine's center of rotation with a colorful dot. In single-joint exercises the moving joint's center is aligned with the machine's center of rotation, which allows for smooth performance of the exercise. For example, if during the knee extension exercise the knee's center of rotation is not aligned with the machine's, the shin pad will slide up and down during each repetition. If a machine's pad slides up and down an extremity or the handles stretch or compress the lifter's arms during repetitions, the two centers of rotation are improperly aligned. By adjusting the seat or back pad of the machine you can correct the alignment.

This general rule of aligning the joint's and machine's centers of rotation does have exceptions, the majority of which occur during multi-joint exercises. For example, during the T-bar row the machine's center of rotation is located near the feet of the lifter, but the elbows and shoulders are the joints that move during the exercise.

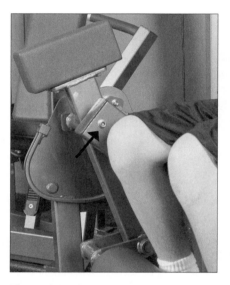

Figure 6.3 Arrow locates the machine's center of rotation.

Progression

Increasing the resistance too quickly when a child is attempting to learn proper technique slows the learning process and can result in injury. An increase in resistance that results in poor technique is too great. This is true for both beginning and experienced lifters.

It is also important to progress slowly when increasing the number of sets performed. If the training program calls for an increase from one to three sets of an exercise, have the child perform one set for several weeks, then two sets for several weeks, then finally progress to three sets. Progressing too quickly can result in muscular soreness and even injury.

Breathing

When breathing correctly, the lifter inhales just before and during the lowering phase and exhales during the lifting phase of each repetition. Trainers discourage breath holding or performing a Valsalva maneuver during weight training because it results in higher blood pressures. However, some breath holding will occur during the last repetition of a set due to fatigue or when lifting heavy weights (6 to 8 repetition maximums). Excessive breath holding or doing so for an entire repetition or set should not be allowed. The resulting increase in blood pressure makes it more difficult for the heart to pump and eventually reduces blood flow to the brain. If this happens, the lifter may become light-headed or even faint during or after an exercise, which can result in loss of control of the resistance and possible injury. Because lifting maximal or near-maximal resistances is not the goal of weight-training programs for children, there is no need for excessive breath holding; proper breathing should be taught and encouraged at all times.

Feedback

All lifters, especially children, should receive constant feedback about their exercise and spotting techniques in language they can understand. Feedback is as important after weeks or even months of training as it is at the start of a program. Without feedback about technique, it is easy for a child to gradually develop a flaw in lifting technique as a program progresses. Children also need constant feedback about their duties and competency as spotters.

SYMMETRICAL MUSCULAR DEVELOPMENT

Symmetrical muscular development depends on the use of single-arm and single-leg, or unilateral, exercises. If only double-arm or double-leg, or bilateral, exercises are performed, the stronger limb can compensate for the weaker one, particularly in machine exercises. For example, the machine will move during a two-legged leg press even if one leg produces all the needed force. Although it is natural for one arm or leg to be stronger, the difference in strength between limbs ideally should be less than 10 percent. Proper exercise programming and use of unilateral exercises can reduce any drastic differences. Large strength differences between right and left limbs may increase the possibility of injury as it is the goal to keep differences between the right and left limbs as small as possible thereby promoting symmetrical physical development. Although bilateral exercises are important, unilateral exercises should also be included in any program.

Examples of unilateral exercises are single-leg knee extensions, single-leg knee curls, and most exercises that use dumbbells. A leg press or bench press where the lifter uses both legs or arms at the same time is a bilateral exercise, as are barbell exercises. Doing bilateral barbell exercises makes it easy to tell if one limb is stronger than the other. For example, during a bench press if the barbell slants toward the left or right, that arm is weaker than the opposite arm.

Muscle balance around a joint is also important for injury prevention and total strength development. Although strength differences between muscle groups on opposite sides of a joint do exist, a weight-training program should not exaggerate them. Thus if a lifter performs a quadriceps exercise, such as knee extensions, he should follow it with a hamstring exercise, such as knee curls.

Emergency Plan

Safety considerations and proper supervision are important for all conditioning programs for children and adolescents. Injuries rarely occur when a resistance-training program is properly supervised; those that do occur are most commonly muscle strains. Most serious injuries occur in unsupervised settings. The following are possible causes of injury during resistance training:

- The lifter attempts to lift too much weight for a certain number of repetitions.
- The lifter uses improper lifting technique.
- The lifter improperly places his feet or hands on a machine so that they slide off the pedals or handles.
- The lifter places his hands on the machine's cable, belt, pulley system, or weight stack.
- The lifter drops free weights or the weight stack of a machine after completing a repetition.
- The spotters are inattentive and do not perform all their duties.
- There is improper behavior in the weight room.
- A bench or piece of equipment moves or breaks during the exercise.
- Worn-out equipment, such as cables or belts, breaks during lifting.
- The lifter does not use collars with free weights.
- The lifter drops weight plates while loading or unloading a bar or machine.

Even though injuries are rare, all resistance-training facilities should have an emergency plan to deal with a serious injury. The plan should be posted in the weight room and all supervisors should be familiar with it. As mentioned previously, it is highly recommended that supervisors be certified in CPR and basic first aid. An emergency plan should include the following:

The phone number of the nearest ambulance service and/or hospital

The location of the nearest hospital or emergency room

The training facility's address and directions for how to locate the weight room (for paramedical personnel)

An alphabetical card catalog of contact information for the children, including parents' or guardians' home and business phone numbers and addresses

If there is no phone in the weight room, supervisors should know the location of the nearest one or have a cell phone with them. Taking the time to develop an emergency plan is well worth the effort even if the plan is never utilized.

MACHINES VERSUS FREE WEIGHTS

We've established that most machines allow movement only in a predetermined plane or movement path so that balancing the resistance in all directions is not necessary. However, free-weight exercises require balancing the weight in all directions, which makes learning exercise technique for them more difficult than for machine exercises. Balancing the resistance requires the use of muscles other than the prime movers. For example, the prime movers in the military press are the deltoid, located on the outside of the shoulder, and the triceps, located on the back of the upper arm. However, the muscles of the upper and lower back, smaller muscles around the shoulder area, and even the abdominal muscles are all used in balancing the resistance. The involvement of these secondary, stabilizing muscle groups needed for balancing the weight is greater with free weights than with machines. Advocates of free weights point out that sporting events and daily life activities require balancing any resistance moved, so having to balance the weight during resistance training is an important aspect of preparing for those activities. Conversely, machine advocates believe that the lack of a need to balance the resistance allows greater isolation of the prime movers and so provides a greater training stimulus to those muscles. In addition, machine advocates believe that proper exercise technique is easier to achieve because movement is allowed only in one plane and direction. The truth is that both machines and free weights are beneficial at different points in a weight-training program. Also, some exercises, such as knee extensions and knee curls, cannot be safely performed with free weights.

Both machines and free weights offer training advantages. Machines that allow movement in only one plane and direction, thus isolating a muscle group, are useful when the training goal is to increase strength/power or local muscular endurance. Additionally, this ability to isolate a muscle group is ideal for some rehabilitation programs after an injury or when the goal is to increase strength/power or local muscular endurance of a muscle group or joint that is prone to injury or that is the weak link in the performance of a certain sport. Free-weight exercises are a good choice if the training goal is to strengthen total-body movements and improve coordination between various muscle groups.

Additionally, although the research is not conclusive, it appears that for adults free-weight exercises, such as squats, result in greater increases in vertical jumping ability than do machine leg press exercises. This is probably due to the greater mechanical similarity of squat exercises to the jumping motion. However, both squat and leg press exercises can cause an increase in vertical jumping ability.

Types of Machines

There are several types of weight-training machines. Today variable-resistance machines are the most common. These machines have a kidney-bean-shaped cam that varies the resistance throughout the exercise's range of motion. When the belt or cable leaves the cam a short distance from the cam's center, or point of rotation, the resistance seems light, and when it leaves the cam further from the center, the resistance seems heavy.

If a machine does not have a cam and uses only round pulleys for the belt or cable, the resistance does not vary. Other machines emphasize the lowering, or eccentric, portion of each repetition. These machines are utilized in what is commonly known as negative training, in which a heavier weight than can be lifted during the positive (concentric), or lifting, phase of a repetition is used for the lowering portion of each repetition. Eccentric strength is important for many athletic events and daily life activities; simply walking down steps involves eccentric actions of the quadriceps. However, the use of heavier weights than are possible during the lifting phase of a repetition to bring about optimal strength, muscle size, and fitness gains is controversial, especially for young children. Although negative training may have a place for advanced adult lifters, it is not generally recommended for children or beginning lifters.

Children and Machine Fit

When training prepubescent or pubescent children, the most important equipment consideration is that it fits them. With free weights, body-weight exercises, or exercises in which a partner supplies the resistance, fit is not the critical concern it is when using machines. Although some manufacturers do make machines designed to fit children, most resistance-training machines are made to fit adults and will not properly fit many children despite allowing many adjustments. Most prepubescent children's limbs are too short for many machines, which makes correct technique and full range of motion of the exercise virtually impossible. Most critical, a body part could slip off of its point of contact with a machine, such as a foot pad or an arm pad, resulting in injury to the child.

With some machines you can make simple alterations that allow a child to safely use the machine; for example, you can use additional back or seat pads on a knee extension machine. However, simply adjusting the seat often is not enough to make a machine fit the child; you may also need to adjust for proper positioning of the arms and legs on the contact points of the machine. In addition, changing the seat position might make it impossible for the child's feet to reach the floor. In many exercises the feet need to touch the floor to aid in balance, so you may also need to place blocks under the child's feet.

Altering a piece of equipment to fit one child does not guarantee that the equipment will fit another child. Check each child for proper fit before the equipment is used. Insure that padding and blocks do not slide during exercise performance, which could result in injury. Sometimes you can avoid this by attaching rubber matting to the top or bottom of the pads or blocks. Remember that safety is the major issue. If you cannot safely adapt a piece of equipment to properly fit a child, he should not use it.

Single-Joint Versus Multi-Joint Exercises

Both single- and multi-joint exercises can be performed with either machines or free weights. A single-joint exercise, such as knee or triceps extensions, allow movement at only one joint and require the action of only one muscle group as a prime mover. The goal of single-joint exercises is to isolate and train the prime mover. A multi-joint exercise, such as the bench press, allows movement at several joints and requires the action of several muscle groups. Both single- and multi-joint exercises have a place in a well-designed resistance-training program. For example, if isolation and training of a particular muscle group is the goal, then a single-joint exercise may be chosen. However, if the goal is to develop coordination of several muscle groups in unison, then a multi-joint exercise would be preferable. Training all of the major muscle groups of the body requires more single-joint than multi-joint exercises; if that's the goal and time is limited, using multi-joint exercises will result in a shorter training session.

Performance of some multi-joint exercises can be limited by a weak muscle group. For example, squat exercises are often limited by the lower-back musculature. Therefore if a training goal is to increase back squat ability, increasing the strength of the lower-back musculature, by using a single-joint exercise such as back extensions, should also be a goal. Any well-designed program usually includes both single- and multi-joint exercises.

PARTNER EXERCISES

If a particular piece of equipment is not available or does not fit a child, partner exercises, in which another person supplies the resistance, can be performed. These exercises are valuable during an in-season maintenance program because they can easily be performed on a playing field or in a gym. Partner exercises are also useful for small children who do not fit resistance machines. In addition, the resistance can be adjusted to match the strength curve of the trainee as he fatigues during a set. The major disadvantage is that determining the effort the trainee exerts is difficult; thus, keeping motivation high and ensuring adherence to such programs may be a challenge. This is why partner exercises are typically used in a beginning program or in situations where equipment is limited.

Proper technique during partner exercises requires cooperation between the partner and the trainee. Both must act in a mature manner, and in many exercises they must communicate so that the resistance provided is of the correct magnitude and applied in a constant manner. The partner must allow the movement to occur smoothly but also supply sufficient resistance so that it is difficult for the trainee. The partner's role is to help train the lifter, not impress her by showing how much stronger she is. A training partner must be a good personality match as well, to enhance the training environment.

In order to introduce the concept of partner exercises, descriptions of several exercises follow.

PARTNER-RESISTED BACK SQUAT

START POSITION

The lifter stands with the back straight, eyes looking forward, feet flat on the floor approximately shoulder-width apart (a). Toes should point directly forward or slightly to the outside. The partner positions herself on the lifter's back. The lifter grasps the partner's thighs.

MOVEMENT AND END POSITION

In a controlled manner, the lifter bends his knees and hips until the thighs are parallel to the floor (b). The lifter then returns to the standing start position. Throughout the exercise the lifter maintains an upright torso position as much as possible. Throughout the exercise the lifter keeps his head and neck upright.

SPOTTING AND SAFETY

No spotting is normally needed. If the lifter cannot complete a repetition he can simply release the partner. The lifter should inform the partner when he is going to release her.

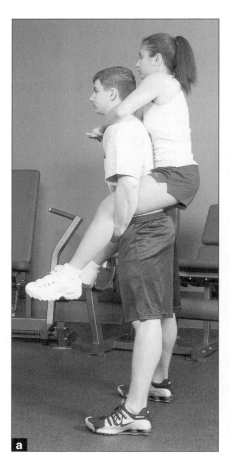

STANDING PARTNER-RESISTED ARM CURL

START POSITION

The lifter stands erect with feet approximately shoulder-width apart. The lifter's knees are slightly bent. The lifter grasps a towel in the middle with an underhand grip (a). The lifter's upper arms and elbows are at her sides. The partner kneels and grasps the ends of the towel. The partner's hands are below and slightly behind the lifter's hands.

MOVEMENT AND END POSITION

The lifter bends at the elbows until the hands touch or almost touch the chest (concentric, or lifting, phase). As the lifter's elbows bend, the partner supplies resistance by pulling on the towel (b). The exercise motion is then performed in reverse (eccentric, or lowering, phase) with the trainee resisting and the partner supplying force. The lifter's upper arms and elbows remain stationary and against the sides of the body throughout the exercise. One repetition should take approximately 10 to 12 seconds (5-6 seconds each for the concentric and eccentric phases).

SPOTTING AND SAFETY

No spotting is normally needed. The partner should give feedback concerning proper exercise position. Make sure the towel is strong enough to withstand the forces it must tolerate during the exercise.

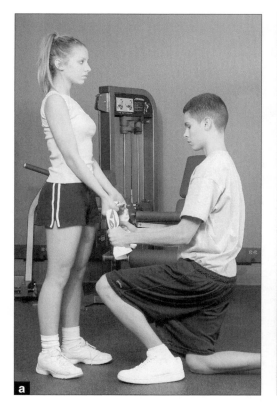

STANDING PARTNER-RESISTED TRICEPS EXTENSION

START POSITION

The lifter stands erect with feet approximately shoulder-width apart (a). The lifter's knees are slightly bent and the head upright. The lifter's upper arms are perpendicular to the floor with the elbows bent at 90 degrees. The lifter grasps a towel in the middle using the overhand grip. The partner grasps the towel at both ends. The partner's hands are below the lifter's hands.

MOVEMENT AND END POSITION

The lifter straightens the elbows. As the lifter's elbows straighten (concentric, or lifting, phase), the partner supplies resistance by pulling on the towel (b). The motion is then reversed (eccentric, or lowering, phase) with the lifter resisting movement and the partner supplying force. Throughout the exercise movement the lifter's upper arms remain parallel to the floor. One repetition should take approximately 10 to 12 seconds (5-6 seconds each for the concentric and eccentric phases).

SPOTTING AND SAFETY

No spotting is normally needed. The partner should give feedback concerning proper exercise position and technique. Make sure the towel used is strong enough to withstand the forces it must tolerate during the exercise.

RUBBER CORD EXERCISES

Rubber cord exercises offer another alternative with minimal expense. This type of training is performed using a thick rubber cord that resembles surgical tubing. Some sporting goods stores sell rubber cords with handles at the ends. The cords are available in varying thicknesses; the thicker the tubing the greater the resistance it provides. Rubber cords have several advantages and disadvantages as summarized below:

Advantages

- The equipment needed is minimal.
- The equipment is relatively inexpensive.
- The exercises are safe, so no spotting is normally needed.
- Both single- and multi-joint exercises can be performed.

Disadvantages

- No visible movement of a weight takes place, which can lead to motivational problems with some children.
- It can be difficult to judge the trainee's effort.
- The more the cord is stretched the greater the resistance, so completing a repetition in some exercises can be difficult.
- Lower-body exercises are more difficult to perform than upper-body exercises.

When performing a rubber cord exercise, the resistance is greatest as the movement nears completion as the stretched rubber becomes harder and harder to move, which is the opposite of what occurs in most sport movements, daily life activities, and other forms of resistance exercise. Thus, rubber band exercises best match the exercises with ascending strength curves where continued increases in the force production are possible over the range of motion (e.g., squat, bench press). Therefore when using this type of resistance care needs to be taken when performing movements that do not allow for continued increase in force production over the complete range of motion (e.g., arm curls, leg curls) as their strength curves do not match rubber band resistance. So if movement in an exercise becomes dramatically difficult at the middle to the end phases of the repetition, use a smaller rubber band, which will allow for the ability to move smoothly through the entire range of motion of the exercise.

During all rubber cord exercises the cord must be securely attached to an immovable object or the trainee must stand on it to hold it stationary. The resistance can be adjusted by using cords of different thickness and by prestretching the cord in the start position. To introduce the concept of rubber cord exercises, several of them are described here.

RUBBER CORD ARM CURL

START POSITION

The lifter stands on top of the midpoint of the cord. The lifter's back is straight, the head is upright, and the feet are approximately hip-width apart. The lifter grasps the handles with both hands or one for each handle or bar depending on the equipment used. The lifter's upper arms and elbows are against the sides of the body. An equal length of cord should extend from beneath each foot.

MOVEMENT AND END POSITION

Moving only at the elbows, the lifter performs an arm-curl movement until the elbows are completely bent. The lifter then returns to the start position. The elbows, back, head, and legs remain stationary throughout the exercise movement.

SPOTTING AND SAFETY

No spotting is normally needed. The lifter must not step off the rubber cord unless the arms are in the start position and there is no tension in the cord.

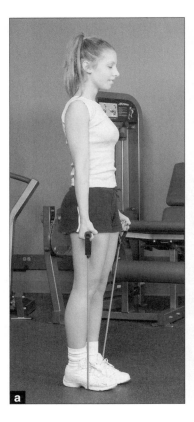

RUBBER CORD OVERHEAD PRESS

START POSITION

The lifter stands on top of the midpoint of the cord. The lifter's back is straight, the head is upright, and the feet are approximately hip-width apart. The lifter grasps the handles with both hands. The lifter's elbows are bent and the hands are at shoulder height.

MOVEMENT AND END POSITION

The lifter performs an overhead-press movement by straightening the elbows and moving at the shoulders. The lifter completely straightens the elbows, then returns to the start position. The back, head, and legs remain stationary throughout the exercise movement.

SPOTTING AND SAFETY

No spotting is normally needed. The lifter must not step off the rubber cord unless the arms are in the start position and there is no tension in the cord.

APPROPRIATE RESISTANCE PROGRESSION

No matter what type of equipment or exercise is performed, proper progression in the amount of resistance used is important. On some machines the resistance increases in increments that are too large to allow a smooth progression as a child becomes stronger. Some older machines have weight stacks that increase in increments of 10 to 20 pounds. Let's say a child can bench press 30 pounds; if the machine's weight stack increases in increments of 10 pounds, the next possible resistance is 40 pounds, which is a 33 percent increase—far too large for a safe and smooth progression. This problem can be remedied on some machines by purchasing specially designed weights, usually 2.5 and 5 pounds, that can be easily added to and removed from the weight stack. On many newer machines increments of 5 pounds are possible, which allows a smoother progression but can still be problematic when relatively light resistances are being utilized.

With plate-loaded machines and free weights the changes in resistance are limited by the smallest weight plates available. Normally 2.5-pound weight plates are available, but some as light as 1.25 pounds can be obtained. Thus a smooth progression in resistance is easier to obtain, especially when light resistances are being lifted.

On some machines the starting resistance is too great for a child to perform even one repetition. This may also be the case with free weights if only typical Olympic lifting bars, which weigh 45 pounds, are available. This situation can be remedied for free weights by obtaining bars of a lighter weight. If, however, a machine's starting weight or the available bars are too heavy for the child, an alternative exercise, such as body-weight or partner-resisted exercises, for the same muscle group(s) needs to be performed until the child is strong enough to utilize the available starting weight.

Despite the differences between the various types of resistance-training machines and equipment, virtually all equipment and types of training cause gains in fitness, such as increases in strength/power, muscle size, and motor performance. Decisions concerning equipment use should be based on the safety of the child. The following are other questions to consider when making decisions about equipment:

1. If the equipment does not fit children, can it be safely altered to do so?
2. If equipment is being purchased, what is its cost per exercise station?
3. How much will it cost to purchase sufficient equipment to train all major muscle groups of the body?
4. If equipment is being purchased, how long is its warranty?
5. What does the warranty cover?
6. Is the equipment made from heavy-gauge steel?
7. Is it sturdily constructed? (Are the welds solid?)
8. How easy is it to adjust the resistance?
9. How easy is it to adjust for proper fit (seat height and pad location)?
10. Does the resistance increase in increments suitable for children?

You may find that one manufacturer's equipment is best suited to all your needs, or perhaps one manufacturer's bench press and another manufacturer's knee extension machine are more appropriate. All of the equipment used need not be made by the same manufacturer or company.

Strength-Training Accessories

The three most commonly used strength-training accessories are weight-training belts, gloves, and shoes. Although they are not absolutely necessary for a safe and effective program, all three do offer some benefits.

Weight-Training Belts

A weight-training belt has a wide back and is designed to help support the lower back. Although they come in many sizes, belts small enough to fit little children are not commonly available. A belt is not necessary for resistance training; it is merely an aid to counteract a lack of strong abdominal and lower-back musculature.

Weight-training belts do help support the lower spine but not from the back as is commonly thought. Instead, the belt gives the abdominal muscles something to push against, creating a buildup of pressure in the abdomen that pushes against the lower spine from the front. The buildup of pressure in the abdomen also makes it more difficult for the lower back to bend forward in another way. Think of placing a football inside your abdomen and then pumping it up. The football would take up space and restrict the movement of your rib cage, making it more difficult for you to bend forward at the lower back. The buildup of pressure inside the abdomen acts in a manner similar to the football.

Wearing a tightly cinched belt during activity increases blood pressure. This makes the pumping of blood by the heart more difficult and may cause undue cardiovascular stress. Thus, wearing a belt during resistance exercises that don't involve the lower back is not recommended. Also, although a belt can be worn during lifts that involve the lower back, such as squats and dead lifts, it should not be used to alleviate technique problems due to weak lower-back and abdominal muscles. Instead, incorporate exercises into the program to strengthen those muscles. This helps eliminate chronic lower-back weakness, which can lead to improper exercise technique. Additionally, strong abdominal and lower-back muscles help prevent injury to the lower back during all physical activity and may aid physical performance in many sport and daily life activities.

Weight-Training Gloves

Gloves designed for resistance training cover only the palms, not the fingers. They protect the palms from such things as the knurling or ribbing on many barbells, dumbbells, and equipment handles, preventing the formation of blisters and calluses or the ripping of calluses on the hands. However, gloves are not essential to a safe or effective resistance-training program.

(continued)

(continued)

Weight-Training Shoes

Weight-training shoes provide good arch support, fit tightly, and have a nonslip surface on the sole. They offer little or no shock absorbance in the soles so that any force or power that the lifter develops by extending the leg or hip (for example, in such exercises as the squat or clean) is used not to compress the sole of the shoe but to lift the weight. Lifters should wear shoes with a nonslip sole and good arch support, but they do not have to be specifically designed for power or Olympic weightlifting. Many cross-training shoes offer the characteristics necessary for a good weight-training shoe.

SUMMING UP AND LOOKING AHEAD

Teaching proper resistance-training exercise technique requires not only knowing correct technique but also how to select equipment, properly fit children to equipment, and ensure smooth progression in the amount of resistance used. You must consider all these factors whether you're teaching technique for one exercise, implementing a program for total body strength, or developing a program to improve performance in a particular sport.

All of the information in this chapter needs to be kept in mind when learning and teaching correct exercise and spotting techniques for each exercise. The next several chapters describe and discuss proper technique for specific exercises.

7

Multi-Joint Upper-Body Exercises

Multi-joint upper-body exercises predominantly train the muscles of the upper arm, chest, shoulder, and upper back. The muscles of the forearm and torso also receive some training with many of these exercises. These muscle groups are obviously important for many sport, recreational, and daily life activities.

Using proper technique while performing these exercises is important for injury prevention as well as for training the targeted muscles. Improper exercise technique involves using the legs, lower back, or another muscle group to start the lifting motion, which not only compromises the training stimulus to the muscles but also can result in injury. Photos are provided for each starting and ending position.

UPPER BACK

Upper-back multi-joint exercises involve movement at the shoulder and the elbow joints. The elbow flexors, or biceps muscle group, located on the front of the upper arm, and other elbow flexors located in the forearm (brachioradialis) and the back of the shoulder area (posterior deltoid) often are also involved. However, these exercises are meant to target the musculature of the upper back, including the latissimus dorsi (lats), trapezius, and rhomboideus muscles, commonly referred to as the rhomboids.

Machines

The most common upper-back multi-joint exercise done on a machine is the lat pull-down. All machine upper-back multi-joint exercises train the lats, trapezius, rhomboids, and elbow flexors (biceps and brachialis). However, the seated cable row and seated machine row also train the back of the shoulder (posterior deltoid).

Common Technique Errors

Lat Pull-Down

- Leaning back to start the exercise movement
- Failing to move the shoulder blades toward the spine during the pulling motion

Seated Cable Row and Seated Machine Row

- Using the lower back or legs to start the lifting movement
- Failing to pull the shoulder blades together and hold them there during the exercise movement

Spotting and Safety

- No spotting is normally needed.

Lat Pull-Down

- Pulling the bar to the back of the shoulders places the shoulders in a potentially injurious position (possible shoulder impingement syndrome).

Seated Cable Row and Seated Machine Row

- Using the lower back to start the lifting movement can place strain on the those muscles.

Free Weights

Free-weight upper-back multi-joint exercises train the back of the shoulder (posterior deltoid), lats, upper back (trapezius and rhomboids), and the front of the upper arm (biceps, brachialis). The most common exercise is the bent-over row, which can be performed with either a barbell or a dumbbell.

Common Technique Errors

- Using the back or legs to start the lifting motion
- Failing to pull the shoulder blades together and hold them there during the exercise movement

Barbell Bent-Over Row

- Raising the torso so that it is not parallel to the floor

Dumbbell Bent-Over Row

- Rotating the back to start the lifting motion

Spotting and Safety

- No spotting is normally needed.

Miscellaneous Exercises

The pull-up uses body weight as resistance. For many people, doing a pull-up that uses their total-body weight as resistance is very difficult. Some machines do allow the use of less than total-body weight for resistance: The lifter stands or kneels on a platform, which pushes him upward so that he does not have to lift his full weight. The upward force of the platform is variable, so the resistance can range from little or none to the lifter's total-body weight.

CHEST AND TRICEPS

Multi-joint chest and triceps exercises can be performed with free weights and a variety of machines. All of these exercises involve some type of pressing movement, similar to that of a bench press.

Free Weights

A barbell or dumbbells and a flat bench or a resistive ball are used to perform these chest and triceps multi-joint exercises. All of these exercises train the chest (pectoralis major and minor), front of the shoulders (anterior deltoids) and triceps; however, the barbell bench press focuses on the chest and using a narrow grip emphasizes the triceps.

Common Technique Errors

All Free-Weight Chest and Triceps Multi-Joint Exercises

- Raising the hips and buttocks off the bench or arching the back excessively (bridging) during the lifting phase places undue stress on the lower back.

Barbell Bench Press and Narrow-Grip Barbell Bench Press

- Lowering the barbell and bouncing it off the chest to help start the lifting phase can injure the chest area.

Spotting and Safety

All Free-Weight Chest and Triceps Multi-Joint Exercises

- If the lifter feels shoulder pain during the exercise, especially at the chest-touch position, limit the range of motion so that the weight remains at least 4 inches above the chest. In the barbell bench press and narrow-grip barbell bench press this can be accomplished by placing a rolled-up towel or other soft object on the chest.
- If the lifter feels shoulder pain, especially at the chest-touch position, he should keep the upper arm close to the torso during the entire exercise movement.

Barbell Bench Press and Narrow-Grip Barbell Bench Press

- When a lifter uses light weights, one spotter can stand behind the lifter's head and assist if necessary.
- If heavy weights are used, two spotters should stand at the ends of the bar, facing each other.

Dumbbell Bench Press and Resistive-Ball Dumbbell Press

- Two spotters, one on each side of the lifter, are recommended.
- If the lifter feels shoulder pain he should use the palms-facing-each-other position for the grip.

Movement Variations

All Free-Weight Chest and Triceps Multi-Joint Exercises

- In all free-weight chest and triceps multi-joint exercises, the angle of the upper arm to the torso can be varied between 90 degrees to a position in which the upper arms are very close to the torso during the exercise movement.

Decline Bench Free Weights

These exercises are similar to the flat bench, free-weight chest and triceps multi-joint exercises except that they are performed on a decline bench, which places the feet and knees higher than the shoulders. Exercises performed using a decline bench train the chest (pectoralis major and minor), back of the upper arm (triceps), and front of the shoulder (anterior deltoids), but emphasize the lower-chest area.

Common Technique Errors

All Decline Bench Free-Weight Chest and Triceps Multi-Joint Exercises

- Lowering the weight toward the upper chest instead of the lower-chest area

Barbell Decline Press

- Bouncing the weight off the chest at the end of the lowering phase to help start the lifting phase can result in injury to the chest.

Dumbbell Decline Press

- Allowing the dumbbells to drift out to the side while lowering them makes the exercise much more difficult.

Spotting and Safety

Barbell Decline Press

- If the lifter is using light weights, one spotter can stand behind his head and assist if necessary.
- If heavy weights are used, then two spotters, one at each end of the bar facing each other, should be utilized.

Dumbbell Decline Press

- Two spotters, one on each side of the lifter and each spotting one dumbbell, are recommended.
- If the lifter feels shoulder pain he should use the palms-facing-each-other position for the grip.

Movement Variations

All Decline Bench Free-Weight Chest and Triceps Multi-Joint Exercises

- All decline bench free-weight chest and triceps multi-joint exercises can be varied by changing the angle of the upper arm to the torso from 90 degrees to a position in which the upper arms are very close to the torso during the entire exercise movement.

Incline Bench Free Weights

These exercises are similar to the flat bench, free-weight chest and triceps multi-joint exercises except they are performed on an incline bench, which places the shoulders higher than the feet and knees. Exercises performed using an incline bench train the chest (pectoralis major and minor), back of the upper arm (triceps), and front of the shoulder (anterior deltoid), but emphasize the upper-chest area.

Common Technique Errors

All Incline Bench Free-Weight Chest and Triceps Multi-Joint Exercises

- Lowering the weight toward the upper chest instead of the lower-chest area
- Raising the hips and buttocks off the bench during the exercise movement
- Raising the head off the bench during the exercise movement

Barbell Incline Press

- Bouncing the weight off the chest at the end of the lowering phase to help start the lifting phase can result in injury to the chest.

Dumbbell Incline Press

- Allowing the dumbbells to drift too far out to the side while lowering or lifting them makes the exercise much more difficult.

Spotting and Safety

Barbell Incline Press

- If light weights are used, one spotter can stand behind the lifter's head and assist if necessary.
- Many decline benches have a platform on which the spotter can stand.
- If heavy weights are used, two spotters, one at each end of the bar facing each other, should be utilized.

Dumbbell Incline Press

- Two spotters, one on each side of the lifter and each spotting one dumbbell, are recommended.

Movement Variations

All Incline Bench Free-Weight Chest and Triceps Multi-Joint Exercises

- All incline bench free-weight chest and triceps multi-joint exercises can be varied by changing the angle of the upper arm and the torso from 90 degrees to a position in which the upper arms are very close to the torso during the exercise movement.

SHOULDERS AND TRICEPS

All of these exercises involve an overhead pressing-type movement. They can be performed with free weights or machines. Free-weight exercises can be performed in either a standing or seated position with a barbell or dumbbells.

Shoulder exercises emphasize the shoulder area (deltoid) but also train the upper back (latissimus dorsi, trapezius, and rhomboids) and elbow extensors (triceps).

Common Technique Errors

All Free-Weight Shoulder and Triceps Multi-Joint Exercises

- Using the legs to start the lifting motion
- Failing to keep the elbows directly below the weight at all times
- Allowing the weight to move forward instead of lifting it straight up

Spotting and Safety

All Free-Weight Shoulder and Triceps Multi-Joint Exercises

- Two spotters, one on each side of the lifter, are recommended.

Barbell Overhead Press

- This exercise can be performed in a power rack with the pins set slightly lower than the height of the barbell in the start position.

SHOULDERS

Shoulder multi-joint exercises emphasize the shoulder area (deltoids), but also train the upper back (trapezius, rhomboids) and elbow flexors or biceps muscle groups.

Common Technique Errors

- Using the legs to start the lifting motion
- Not keeping your elbows above the barbell, dumbbells, or low-pull handle at all times

Spotting and Safety

- No spotting is generally needed.

MISCELLANEOUS UPPER-BODY EXERCISES

The push-up and bar dip exercises are common chest and triceps multi-joint exercises. These exercises focus on training the chest (pectoralis group), back of the upper arm (triceps), front of the shoulder (anterior deltoid), and upper-back musculature. Since they are performed with body weight as resistance, many people find them relatively difficult. However, they can be altered so that the resistance is less than full-body weight. For example, push-ups can be made easier by placing the hands on a bench or another sturdy object, and they can be made more difficult by elevating the feet in a similar manner. Some bar dip machines allow the resistance to be less than total body weight: The lifter stands on a foot plate or kneels on a knee pad, which pushes him upward and assists in the lift.

Common Technique Errors

Push-Up

- Raising the buttocks (sometimes called "camel-backing") to make the exercise easier

Bar Dip

- Moving the legs in an attempt to assist with the exercise movement

Spotting and Safety

Push-Up

- No spotting is normally needed.

Bar Dip

- Spotters can help the lifter get into the start position by placing their hands or arms under his armpits.
- Spotters can grasp the lifter's lower leg and assist with the exercise movement. (This technique should be used only with experienced lifters who can perform at least several bar dips.)

Multi-Joint Upper-Body Exercises

Machine upper back
Pulley-type lat pull-down (page 100)
Machine lat pull-down (page 101)
Seated cable row (page 102)
Seated machine row (page 103)

Upper back
Barbell bent-over row (page 104)
Dumbbell bent-over row (page 105)
Pull-up (page 106)

Chest and triceps
Barbell bench press (page 107)
Narrow-grip barbell bench press (page 108)
Dumbbell bench press (page 109)
Resistive-ball dumbbell press (page 110)
Machine bench press (page 111)
Barbell decline press (page 113)

Chest and triceps (continued)
Dumbbell decline press (page 114)
Machine decline press (page 115)
Barbell incline press (page 117)
Dumbbell incline press (page 118)
Machine incline press (page 119)

Shoulders and triceps
Barbell overhead press (page 121)
Dumbbell overhead press (page 122)
Machine overhead press (page 123)

Shoulders
Barbell upright row (page 124)
Dumbbell upright row (page 125)
Low pulley upright row (page 126)

Miscellaneous upper-body
Push-up (page 127)
Bar dip (page 128)

Multi-joint upper-body exercises are an important part of strengthening the upper-body musculature, and having a strong upper body aids with correct exercise technique in lower-body multi-joint exercises. This is largely because the upper-body musculature must support the heavy resistances used when performing lower-body multi-joint exercises.

PULLEY-TYPE LAT PULL-DOWN

START POSITION

The lifter begins in a seated position, with the thighs under the thigh pads provided. The height of the thigh pads should be adjusted if possible so that the lifter is held down when seated (a). The torso is upright, with the knees at a 90-degree angle (approximately) and the feet flat on the floor. The lifter grasps the handle with an overhand grip, palms facing forward. The hands are at least shoulder-width apart. The elbows are straight. The back is straight, with the neck and head in line with the back. The seat position should be set so that the handle can be pulled straight down to the front of the shoulders.

MOVEMENT AND END POSITION

The lifter pulls the handle down in a controlled manner until it touches the front of the shoulders (b). The pull is started by pulling the shoulder blades down and then pulling with the arms. The lifter briefly holds the handle in the shoulder-touch position. She returns the handle to the start position in a controlled manner. To return to the start position, she first straightens the elbows, then allows the shoulders to elevate. The torso and legs remain stationary at all times.

MOVEMENT VARIATIONS

Many different types of handles, such as ones that allow the palms to face each other, can be used for this exercise. Variation in grip width and hand position is possible with the use of different types of handles.

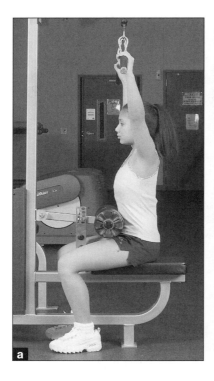 

MACHINE LAT PULL-DOWN

START POSITION

The lifter begins in a seated position, with the thighs under the thigh pads provided. Adjust the height of the thigh pads or seat height if possible so that the lifter is held down when seated (a). The torso is upright, with knees at a 90-degree angle (approximately) and the feet flat on the floor. The lifter grasps the handle with an overhand grip, palms facing forward. The hands are at least shoulder-width apart. The elbows are straight. The back is straight, with the neck and head in line with the back. The seat position should be set so that the handle can be pulled to the front of the shoulders.

MOVEMENT AND END POSITION

The lifter pulls the handle down in a controlled manner until it is at shoulder height (b). The pull is started by moving the shoulder blades down, then pulling with the arms. The lifter briefly holds the handle at shoulder height. He then returns the handle to the start position in a controlled manner. To return to the start position, he first straightens the elbows, then allows the shoulders to elevate. The torso and legs remain stationary at all times.

MOVEMENT VARIATIONS

The handles on some machines allow different hand positions, such as palms facing each other, and different grip widths.

SEATED CABLE ROW

START POSITION

The lifter sits on the seat with the torso forming an approximately 90-degree angle with the thighs. The feet are hip-width apart and rest flat on the foot plates. There is a slight bend in the knees. The torso is upright with the back slightly arched (a). The neck and head are in line with the back. The lifter grasps the handle with an overhand grip. The elbows are straight with the handles held at arm's length. The shoulder blades are relaxed and separated. Adjust the length of the cable or the seat position, if possible, so that resistance is felt in the start position.

MOVEMENT AND END POSITION

The lifter pulls the handle in a controlled manner until it touches the chest (b). The pull is started by pulling the shoulder blades together and then bending the elbows. When the handle touches the chest, the shoulder blades are still together and the elbows are slightly behind the back. Once the shoulder blades are together, they remain so for the entire pulling motion and do not separate until the end of the lowering motion. The lifter briefly holds the chest-touch position. He then returns the handle to the start position in a controlled manner by first straightening the elbows and then allowing the shoulder blades to separate.

MOVEMENT VARIATIONS

Several types of handles allow different hand positions as well as grip widths. The height and distance between the elbows and the body during the pull can be varied.

SEATED MACHINE ROW

START POSITION

The lifter sits on the seat provided, with the chest in contact with the chest pad. The feet are approximately hip-width apart and rest flat on the foot plates (a). The entire back is straight or slightly arched backward. The neck and head are in line with the back. The elbows are straight, with the handles held at arm's length. The shoulder blades are relaxed and separated. Adjust the seat height, if possible, so that the chest pad is in contact with the lifter's entire breastbone (sternum). Adjust the chest pad so that resistance is felt with the handles at arm's length.

MOVEMENT AND END POSITION

The lifter pulls the handles backward as far as possible, in a controlled manner. The pull is started by pulling the shoulder blades together and then bending the elbows. When the pull has been completed, the shoulder blades are still together and the elbows are slightly behind the back (b). The lifter briefly holds the handles in the farthest-back position. To return the handles to the start position in a controlled manner, he first straightens the elbows, then allows the shoulder blades to separate. Once the shoulder blades are together they remain so during the entire pulling motion and do not separate until the elbows are straight. The chest should remain stationary, in contact with the chest pad at all times.

MOVEMENT VARIATIONS

Some machines have handles that allow the palms to face each other or downward. The height and distance between the elbows and the body during the pull can be varied.

BARBELL BENT-OVER ROW

START POSITION

The lifter stands with feet slightly wider than hip-width and with a slight bend in the knees (a). She bends forward from the waist so that the torso is at approximately a 45-degree angle to the floor. The back is slightly arched. The neck and head are in line with the back. The lifter grasps a barbell with an overhand grip, palms facing backward and hands approximately shoulder-width or slightly wider apart. The elbows are straight, with the barbell held at arm's length. The shoulder blades are relaxed and separated.

MOVEMENT AND END POSITION

The lifter pulls the barbell upward in a controlled manner until it touches the mid-chest area (b). The pull is started by pulling the shoulder blades together and then bending the elbows. With the bar at the mid-chest position, the shoulder blades are still together and the elbows are slightly higher than the back. The lifter briefly holds the chest-touch position. To lower the barbell to the start position in a controlled manner, she first straightens the elbows, then allows the shoulder blades to separate. Once the shoulder blades are pulled together, they remain so for the entire pulling motion and do not separate until the end of the lowering motion. The back remains stationary throughout the exercise movement.

DUMBBELL BENT-OVER ROW

START POSITION

The lifter starts with feet slightly wider than hip-width apart and with a slight bend in the knees. He bends at the waist so that the torso is at approximately a 45-degree angle to the floor (a). The back arches slightly. The neck and head are in line with the back. The dumbbells hang straight down from the shoulder and the elbow is straight. The shoulder blades are separated so that the dumbbells hang down as far as possible.

MOVEMENT AND END POSITION

The lifter pulls the dumbbells upward in a controlled manner until the elbow is slightly higher than the back (b). The pull is started by pulling the shoulder blades together and then bending the elbow. The lifter briefly holds the elbow in the above-the-back position. To return to the start position in a controlled manner, he first straightens the elbow, then allows the shoulder blades to separate. Once the shoulder blades are pulled together, they remain so for the entire pulling motion and do not separate until the end of the lowering motion. The back remains stationary throughout the exercise movement.

MOVEMENT VARIATIONS

- The dumbbells can be held with the palm facing backward or facing each other.
- The distance between the elbow and the body during the exercise motion can be varied.

PULL-UP

Pull-ups train the lats (latissimus dorsi), upper back (trapezius, rhomboids), shoulder (deltoid), and front of the upper arm (elbow flexors, biceps, brachialis).

Common Technique Errors

- Raising the legs to help start the pulling motion
- Failing to get the chin above the bar
- Failing to completely extend the elbow at the end of each repetition

Spotting and Safety

- No spotting is generally needed.
- A spotter can assist when the lifter uses a normal pull-up bar by standing behind him and grasping him at the waist.

START POSITION

The lifter grasps the pull-up bar or machine handles with an overhand grip (palms facing forward). The hands are approximately shoulder-width apart. The elbows are completely straight. The entire body hangs straight down (a). If using a pull-up machine, the lifter stands or kneels on the platform provided. Adjust the force with which the platform pushes the lifter upward to the desired setting.

MOVEMENT AND END POSITION

The lifter pulls his body upward in a controlled manner until his chin is above the bar (b). He briefly holds the chin in the above-the-bar position. He lowers his body back to the start position in a controlled manner. The back and legs remain stationary at all times.

MOVEMENT VARIATIONS

The grip width can be varied. A grip that's wider than the shoulders emphasizes the lateral, or outside, portion of the lats and the superior (top) portion of the upper back. A grip that's narrower than the shoulders emphasizes the center portion of the upper back. Some pull-up machines allow a palms-facing-each-other grip.

BARBELL BENCH PRESS

START POSITION

The lifter lies on his back on a flat bench. He grasps a barbell with an overhand grip, palms facing upward. The hands should be wider than shoulder-width apart. The barbell is held at arm's length above the upper chest (a). The back of the head, upper back, and buttocks are in contact with the bench. The feet are wider than hip-width apart and flat on the floor. The knees are at an approximately 90-degree angle.

MOVEMENT AND END POSITION

The lifter lowers the barbell to the mid-chest area in a controlled manner. He allows the barbell to touch the mid-chest area, then extends the arms, returning the bar to the arm's-length position (b). The upper arms form a 65- to 90-degree angle to the torso in the chest-touch position. If viewed from the side, the end of the barbell travels in a smooth arc between the arm's-length position and the chest-touch position.

NARROW-GRIP BARBELL BENCH PRESS

START POSITION
Similar to barbell bench press except the hands are shoulder-width apart or narrower (a)

MOVEMENT AND END POSITION
Similar to barbell bench press except the upper arms are close to the torso at all times during the exercise movement (b)

DUMBBELL BENCH PRESS

START POSITION

Similar to barbell bench press except the lifter holds a dumbbell in each hand at arm's length above the upper chest (a). She holds the dumbbells at approximately shoulder-width or slightly narrower, with an overhand grip.

MOVEMENT AND END POSITION

Similar to barbell bench press except the lifter lowers the dumbbells in a controlled manner until they are at chest height (b)

MOVEMENT VARIATIONS

The lifter can hold the dumbbells with palms facing each other or palms facing forward. The lifter can lower and raise both dumbbells at the same time or by alternating them.

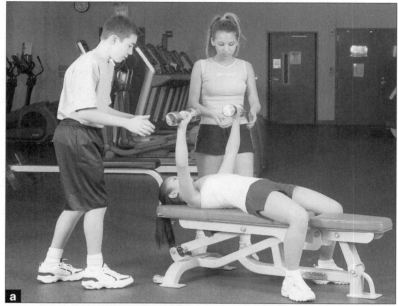

RESISTIVE-BALL DUMBBELL PRESS

a

b

START POSITION

Similar to the barbell bench press except the lifter holds a dumbbell in each hand at arm's length above the upper chest. The upper back is supported on a resistive ball (a). The knees are at an approximately 90-degree angle. The feet are flat on the floor.

MOVEMENT AND END POSITION

Similar to the barbell bench press except the lifter lowers the dumbbells in a controlled manner until they are at chest height (b)

MOVEMENT VARIATIONS

The lifter can hold the dumbbells with palms facing each other or palms facing forward. The lifter can lower and raise both dumbbells at the same time or by alternating them.

MACHINE BENCH PRESS

Most bench press machines allow the performance of an exercise that is very similar to the flat-bench, free-weight bench press, except that it is performed in a seated position. The muscles trained with this exercise include the chest (pectoralis group), back of the upper arm (triceps), and front of the shoulder (anterior deltoid).

Common Technique Errors
- Raising the hips and buttocks off the seat during the exercise movement
- Moving the head forward so that it is not in contact with the seat back at all times

Spotting and Safety
- No spotting is normally needed.
- If the lifter feels shoulder pain during the exercise, especially at the chest-touch position, limit the range of motion so that the weight remains at least 4 inches above the chest. (You can set the range of motion on some machines.)
- If the lifter feels shoulder pain, especially at the chest-touch position, he should keep the upper arms close to the torso during the entire exercise movement and use a palms-facing-each-other position if possible.

START POSITION

The lifter sits upright with the back and head flat against the seat back. The feet are flat on the floor or on the foot plates provided on some machines (a). The knees are at an approximately 90-degree angle. The lifter grasps the handles with an overhand grip. The grip is approximately shoulder-width or slightly wider. The elbows are directly behind the handles. The handles are held at arm's length. Adjust the seat height, if possible, so

(continued)

(continued)

that the handles are at mid-chest height in the end position. Some machines have foot pedals that help the lifter get the resistance to the arm's-length position.

MOVEMENT AND END POSITION

The lifter allows the handles to come backward in a controlled manner until they are even with the chest (b). She briefly holds the handles in the position where they are even with the chest. She then returns the handles to the arm's-length position by extending the arms. The elbows should remain behind the handles at all times.

MOVEMENT VARIATIONS

Some machines have handles that allow the palms to face downward or toward each other. The handles on some machines allow varying grip widths. The angle of the upper arm to the torso can be varied from 90 degrees to a position in which the upper arms are very close to the torso during the exercise movement.

BARBELL DECLINE PRESS

START POSITION

The lifter lies on his back on a decline bench. He places his shins underneath the shin pads, if provided (a). The back of the head, upper back, and buttocks are in contact with the bench. The lifter holds a barbell at arm's length above the lower-chest area. The hands are slightly wider than shoulder-width apart. The grip is overhand, with palms facing forward.

MOVEMENT AND END POSITION

The lifter lowers the barbell in a controlled manner to the lower-chest area (b). He touches the barbell to the lower chest, then presses it back to arm's length.

DUMBBELL DECLINE PRESS

START POSITION

Similar to barbell decline press except the lifter holds a dumbbell in each hand at arm's length above the lower chest (a). The dumbbells are held at approximately shoulder-width or slightly wider. An overhand grip is used to hold the dumbbells.

a

b

MOVEMENT AND END POSITION

Similar to the barbell decline press except the lifter lowers the dumbbells until they are at chest level (b). He holds the dumbbells at chest level briefly, then returns to the start position by extending the arms.

MOVEMENT VARIATIONS

- The dumbbells can be held in either a palms-facing-forward or palms-facing-each-other position.
- The starting palm position can be maintained throughout the exercise motion.
- If starting with the palms-facing-forward position, the dumbbells can be rotated during the lowering motion so that the palms face each other at the chest-height position, and rotated again during the lifting motion so that the palms face forward again at the arm's-length position.
- The lifter can lower and raise both dumbbells at the same time or alternate them.

MACHINE DECLINE PRESS

The exercise performed on the machine decline bench is similar to free-weight decline bench exercises except that it is done in a seated position. This exercise trains the chest (pectoralis group), back of the upper arm (triceps), and front of the shoulder (anterior deltoid), emphasizing the lower-chest area.

Common Technique Errors
- Failing to maintain contact of the head, shoulders, and buttocks with the bench at all times
- Raising the body off the seat during the lifting motion

Spotting and Safety
- No spotting is normally needed.
- If the lifter feels shoulder pain during the exercise, especially in the chest-touch position, she should limit the range of motion so that the handles do not come closer to the chest than 4 to 6 inches. (On some machines this can be accomplished by adjusting its range of motion.)
- If the lifter feels shoulder pain, especially at the chest-touch position, she should keep the upper arms close to the torso during the entire exercise movement and use a palms-facing-each-other hand position if possible.

(continued)

(continued)

START POSITION

The lifter sits on a decline press machine. The back of the head and upper back are in contact with the seat back. Using an overhand grip, the lifter grasps the machine's handles (a). A grip that's approximately shoulder-width or wider is used. The handles are held at arm's length. The feet are flat on the floor approximately hip-width apart or rest on the foot plates provided.

   Many machines have a foot plate that the lifter can push against to assist in getting the handles to an arm's-length position. Adjust the seat height so that when the handles are in the end position they are at the level of the lifter's lower chest.

MOVEMENT AND END POSITION

The lifter lowers the handles in a controlled manner until they are even with the lower chest (b). She then extends the arms to return the handles back to the start position. The elbows are directly behind the handles at all times. The back of the head, shoulders, and buttocks maintain contact with the seat at all times.

MOVEMENT VARIATIONS

Some machines have handles that allow the palms to face each other or face downward. The angle of the upper arms to the torso can vary from 90 degrees to a position in which the upper arms are very close to the torso at all times.

BARBELL INCLINE PRESS

START POSITION

The lifter sits on an incline bench. The back of the head, shoulders, and buttocks are in contact with the bench. The feet are flat on the floor and slightly wider than hip-width apart. The barbell is held at arm's length above the upper-chest and lower-neck area (a). The grip is overhand, with palms facing up and forward. The hands are slightly wider than shoulder-width apart.

MOVEMENT AND END POSITION

The lifter lowers the bar straight down to the top of the sternum in a controlled manner (b). He touches the the bar to the top of the sternum, then returns to the start position by straightening the arms.

MOVEMENT VARIATION

The grip can vary from shoulder-width to slightly wider than shoulder-width.

DUMBBELL INCLINE PRESS

START POSITION

Similar to the barbell incline press except the dumbbells are held with an overhand grip at arm's length above the upper-chest and lower-neck area (a). The dumbbells are held at shoulder-width or slightly wider apart.

MOVEMENT AND END POSITION

Similar to the barbell incline press except the lifter lowers the dumbbells in a controlled manner until they are at the level of the upper chest (b). The angle of the upper arms to the torso can vary from 90 degrees to a position in which the upper arms are very close to the torso at all times. The lifter briefly holds the dumbbells at the upper-chest level, then returns to the start position by straightening the arms.

MOVEMENT VARIATIONS

- The dumbbells can be held with palms facing forward or palms facing each other.

- The starting palm position can be maintained throughout the exercise motion.

- The lifter can rotate the dumbbells during the lowering motion so that the palms move from a facing-forward position to face each other at the chest-height position, and rotate them again during the lifting motion so that the palms once again face forward in the start position.

- The lifter can lower and raise both dumbbells at the same time or alternate them.

MACHINE INCLINE PRESS

The machine incline bench press is similar to the free-weight incline bench exercises except that the exercise is performed in a seated position. This exercise trains the chest (pectoralis group), back of the upper arm (triceps), and front of the shoulder (anterior deltoid), emphasizing the upper-chest area.

Common Technique Errors
- Failing to keep the head, shoulders, and buttocks in contact with the bench at all times
- Raising off the seat during the lifting motion

Spotting and Safety
- No spotting is normally needed.
- If the lifter feels shoulder pain during the exercise, especially in the chest-touch position, he should limit the range of motion so that the handles do not come closer to the chest than 4 to 6 inches. (On some machines this can be accomplished by adjusting its range of motion.)
- If the lifter feels shoulder pain, especially in the chest-touch position, he should keep the upper arm close to the torso at all times and use a palms-facing-each-other hand position if possible.

(continued)

(continued)

START POSITION

The lifter sits on the machine's seat. The back of the head, upper back, and buttocks are in contact with the seat back (a). The feet are flat on the floor and slightly wider than hip-width apart or rest on the foot plates provided. The lifter grasps the handles with an overhand grip. The handles are held at arm's length. Adjust the seat position, if possible, so that the handles are at upper-chest height when the lifter's arms are in the end position.

MOVEMENT AND END POSITION

The lifter lowers the handles in a controlled manner until they are even with the upper chest (b). He holds the handles at the upper-chest position briefly, then returns the handles to the start position by bending the arms. The elbows are directly behind the handles at all times.

MOVEMENT VARIATIONS

Some machines have handles that allow the palms to face each other or downward. The angle of the upper arms to the torso can vary from 90 degrees to a position in which the upper arms are very close to the torso at all times.

BARBELL OVERHEAD PRESS

START POSITION

The lifter stands erect with feet slightly wider than hip-width apart and staggered slightly front to back for balance. The head is upright and the gaze is straight ahead (a). The knees are bent slightly. The hands grasp the barbell slightly wider than shoulder-width apart. The grip is overhand, with the palms facing forward. The elbows are directly below the barbell. The barbell touches the upper sternum. The barbell can be taken from a power rack to get into the start position.

MOVEMENT AND END POSITION

The lifter extends her arms in a controlled manner, lifting the barbell to an overhead arm's-length position (b). She briefly holds the barbell at arm's length, then returns to the start position by bending the arms in a controlled manner. The elbows remain directly below the bar at all times. Bending the knees slightly when returning the bar to the top of the sternum at the end of the lowering phase helps to cushion the return of the barbell to the start position.

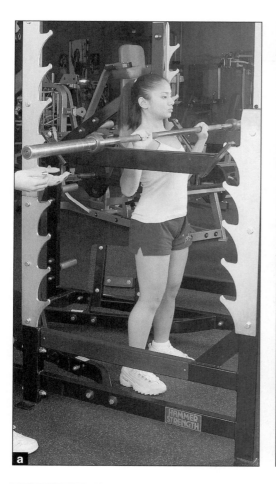

DUMBBELL OVERHEAD PRESS

START POSITION

Similar to the barbell overhead press except the lifter holds a dumbbell in each hand at shoulder height. The dumbbells are held with an overhand grip (a).

MOVEMENT AND END POSITION

Similar to the barbell overhead press except the lifter raises the dumbbells to an overhead arm's-length position by straightening the arms (b). She briefly holds the dumbbells at arm's length, then returns to the start position by bending the arms in a controlled manner.

MOVEMENT VARIATIONS

- If the exercise is performed while the lifter is seated on a bench or resistive ball, the knees should form an approximately 90-degree angle and the feet should be flat on the floor.
- In this exercise and all variations, both dumbbells may be lifted at the same time or by alternating them.
- In this exercise and all variations, the palms can face each other or forward.
- From the start position, the lifter can rotate the palms from the facing-each-other position to face forward in the end position. Then she rotates them again to face each other upon returning to the start position.

MACHINE OVERHEAD PRESS

The machine overhead press exercise is performed in a seated position, and its movement is very similar to free-weight shoulder and triceps multi-joint exercises. This exercise trains the front of the shoulder (anterior deltoid) and back of the upper arm (triceps).

Common Technique Errors

- Using the legs to start the lifting movement, which results in the buttocks rising from the seat
- Failing to keep the elbows directly below the handles at all times
- Bouncing the weights out of the lowest position after completion of a repetition to help start the lifting portion of the next repetition

Spotting and Safety

- No spotting is normally needed.
- If the lifter feels shoulder pain, he should use a palms-facing-each-other position if possible.
- If the lifter feels shoulder pain, he should limit the range of motion so that the handles do not come all the way to shoulder height; the handles should be stopped at a height that doesn't produce shoulder pain.
- Some machines have settings that limit the range of motion.

START POSITION

The lifter is seated, with his head and back against the seat back. He grasps the handles with an overhand grip (a). The grip is approximately shoulder-width or slightly wider. The elbows are directly below the handles. The feet are flat on the floor and slightly wider than hip-width apart. Tighten the seat belt (if provided). Adjust the seat height, if possible, so that the handles are at a height parallel to the top of the lifter's shoulders.

MOVEMENT AND END POSITION

The lifter raises the handles to an arm's-length overhead position by extending the arms in a controlled

manner (b). He briefly holds the handles at arm's length. He lowers the handles back to the start position in a controlled manner. The head and back remain in contact with the seat back at all times. The buttocks remain in contact with the seat at all times.

MOVEMENT VARIATIONS

Some machines have handles that allow the palms to face each other or forward.

BARBELL UPRIGHT ROW

START POSITION

The lifter stands erect with feet slightly wider than hip-width apart and slightly stag-gered front to back for balance. The knees are slightly bent. The lifter grasps a barbell with an overhand grip and palms facing backward (a). The hands are approximately 6 inches apart. The elbows are straight and the barbell lightly touches the thighs. The back is straight and the shoulders are back. The head is upright and the neck is in line with the back.

MOVEMENT AND END POSITION

The lifter pulls the barbell straight up along her body to shoulder height in a controlled manner (b). She briefly holds the barbell at shoulder height, then returns the barbell to the start position in a controlled manner. She keeps the elbows above the bar at all times. The back and legs remain stationary at all times.

DUMBBELL UPRIGHT ROW

START POSITION

Similar to the barbell upright row except the lifter grasps a dumbbell in each hand with an overhand grip and palms facing backward (a)

MOVEMENT AND END POSITION

Similar to the barbell upright row except the lifter raises the dumbbells to shoulder height in a controlled manner (b). She then lowers the dumbbells back to the start position in a controlled manner.

MOVEMENT VARIATION

The lifter can raise and lower both dumbbells at the same time or by alternating them.

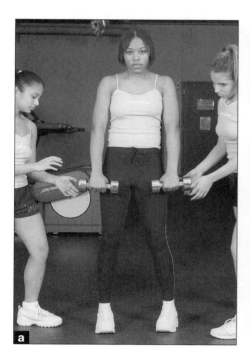

LOW PULLEY UPRIGHT ROW

START POSITION

Similar to the barbell upright row except the lifter stands close to a low pulley so that the handle can be pulled nearly straight up and lowered nearly straight down. He grasps a straight bar attached to the low pulley with an overhand grip and palms facing backward (a).

MOVEMENT AND END POSITION

Similar to the barbell upright row except the lifter pulls the handle to shoulder height in a controlled manner (b). He then lowers the handle back to the start position in a controlled manner.

PUSH-UP

START POSITION

The lifter supports his body weight on his hands and toes. The arms are straight and the hands are slightly wider than shoulder-width apart (a). The toes are approximately hip-width apart. The back is straight. The head is positioned so that the lifter looks at the floor slightly in front of his hands.

MOVEMENT AND END POSITION

The lifter lowers his body by bending the elbows. He touches the chest to the floor (b). He then returns to the start position by straightening the elbows. The back remains straight at all times.

MOVEMENT VARIATIONS

- Make the exercise more difficult by elevating the feet (for example, by placing them on a bench).
- Make the exercise easier by elevating the hands (for example, by placing them on a bench).

BAR DIP

START POSITION

The lifter supports her weight on straight arms. She grasps the bar dip handles with an overhand grip (a). The palms face each other. The torso and legs are straight. Some machines have a foot plate to stand on or knee pad to kneel on.

MOVEMENT AND END POSITION

The lifter bends the elbows, lowering the body until the upper arms are parallel to the floor (b). She straightens the elbows to return to the start position.

MOVEMENT VARIATION

If using a machine with a foot plate or a knee pad, adjust the amount of upward force to the desired setting.

8

Multi-Joint Lower-Body Exercises

Multi-joint lower-body strength and power are important to virtually all running and jumping sports activities, thus they usually are included in weight-training programs for athletes as well as for individuals interested in general fitness. These exercises, grouped into squats, machines, and lunges, target the muscle groups of the quadriceps, hamstrings, and buttocks. However, many of them also train the lower back and calf. Some, such as squats, also require sufficient upper-body strength to support the weight the lower body is lifting; thus total-body strength is important to the successful completion of these exercises. Photos are provided for each exercise's starting and ending positions.

SQUATS

There are several variations of squat exercises—the body-weight squat, free-weight squats, and the resistive-ball squat. Each is unique in the way it applies resistance to the body. However, all squat exercises train the entire leg and hip area, front of the thigh (quadriceps), back of the thigh (hamstrings), buttocks (gluteals), inside of the thigh (adductors), outside of the thigh (abductors), and lower-back area (back extensors).

Body-Weight Squat

The body-weight squat is the easiest because it uses only the relatively light resistance of the lifter's body weight. However, it is an excellent lead-in to other squat exercises.

Common Technique Errors

- Failing to keep the torso as upright as possible at all times during the exercise movement
- Rising onto the toes during the exercise movement

Spotting and Safety

- No spotting is normally needed.

Free-Weight Squats

Free-weight squats are very common lower-body exercises that require substantial lower-back and abdominal muscle strength for proper exercise technique. Often, these muscle groups are the weakest muscles involved in squats. Therefore, if a training goal is to increase squat ability, strengthening the lower-back and abdominal musculature is usually required. Increasing total upper-body strength also improves squat ability.

Common Technique Errors

All Free-Weight Squats

- Failing to keep the feet flat on the floor and the weight on the mid-foot and heel areas; in some instances this problem can be corrected by placing a sturdy 2- or 3-inch-high nonslip object beneath the heels.
- Tall people usually have difficulty squatting correctly, especially in the barbell back squat, because their long legs and back normally cause them to have more forward torso lean than shorter individuals.
- Strengthening the abdominal muscles and lower back will help with correct exercise technique.

Barbell Back Squat

- Placing the barbell too high on the upper back (above the spines of the scapulae) so that it rests on the lower neck rather than on the shoulders can result in neck strain.

Barbell Front Squat

- Failing to maintain a position in which the elbows are rotated up and forward so that the barbell does not rest on the front of the shoulders at all times

Spotting and Safety

Barbell Back and Barbell Front Squat

- The exercise should be performed in a power rack with the pins set slightly lower than the lowest barbell position achieved by the lifter.
- Two spotters, one at each end of the barbell, are recommended.
- Too much forward torso lean places undue stress on the lower back.

Barbell Front Squat

- Failing to maintain a position in which the elbows are rotated up and forward so that the barbell does not rest on the front of the shoulders can result in wrist, elbow, and shoulder strain.

Dumbbell Squat

- No spotting is normally needed. The dumbbell squat is easier to perform with the torso in an upright position, which results in reduced lower-back strain.

Resistive-Ball Squat

This exercise involves performing a squat-type movement with the lifter's back leaning against a resistive ball that's up against a wall. It can be performed with only body weight as resistance or with added resistance in the form of dumbbells.

Common Technique Errors

- Failing to keep the feet flat on the floor at all times

Spotting and Safety

- No spotting is normally needed.

MACHINE EXERCISES

Because these exercises require a machine to be performed and because of the way the resistance is applied, the amount of resistance that can be utilized is not limited by the lifter's lower-back and upper-body strength, as is often the case in free-weight squat exercises. The muscles trained include the entire leg and hip area, front of the thigh (quadriceps), back of the thigh (hamstrings), buttocks (gluteals), inside of the thigh (adductors), and outside of the thigh (abductors).

Common Technique Errors

- After completing one repetition, bouncing the weight out of the start position in an attempt to assist in beginning the next repetition
- Failing to keep the feet flat on the foot platform at all times

Spotting and Safety

No spotting is normally needed for any of the exercises in this group. However, allowing the knees to bend so much that the buttocks or lower back loses contact with the seat or back pad (due to inadequate hamstring flexibility) can result in lower-back strain. Make sure stops or range-of-motion limiters, if available, are set to keep the weight from pinning the lifter in the start position.

LUNGES

Lunges are a relatively common free-weight multi-joint lower-body exercise that predominantly trains the musculature of one leg at a time. In these exercises it is easier to maintain an upright torso position than in a free-weight squat exercise. The muscles trained include the entire leg and hip area, front of the thigh (quadriceps), back of the thigh (hamstrings), buttocks (gluteals), inside of the thigh (adductors), outside of the thigh (abductors), and lower-back area (back extensors).

Common Technique Errors

- The step forward is too short so that the knee of the stepping leg is in front of the toes when the knee is bent.
- The step forward is too long so that the knee of the stepping leg is behind the heel when the knee is bent.
- Failing to keep the feet hip-width apart after completion of the step forward, which makes it difficult to maintain balance during the exercise motion because of a narrow base of support
- Failing to keep the torso as upright as possible, which places undue stress on the lower back

Spotting and Safety

All Lunges

- A step forward that is not of the correct length places undue stress on the knee of the stepping leg.

Barbell Lunge

- Two spotters, one at each end of the bar, are recommended.

Dumbbell Lunge

- No spotting is normally needed. It is easier to keep the torso upright in the dumbbell lunge than in the barbell lunge, thus there is less potential for lower-back strain.

Movement Variations

- The lifter can step in a direction other than forward. The most common variation is to step to the side at a 45-degree angle.
- Initially the exercise can be performed using only body weight as resistance.
- The lifter can return to the start position after each repetition.
- Repetitions can be done with the same leg or by alternating legs.
- The lifter can push off the front leg with enough force to return to the start position in one motion rather than taking two short steps. This variation should be used only after the lifter masters the normal return to the start position (taking two short steps).

Multi-Joint Lower-Body Exercises

Squats
Body-weight squat (page 134)
Barbell back squat (page 135)
Dumbbell squat (page 136)
Barbell front squat (page 137)
Resistive-ball squat (page 138)

Machine
Leg press (page 139)
Hip sled (page 140)

Lunges
Barbell lunge (page 141)
Dumbbell lunge (page 142)

Multi-joint lower-body exercises are an important part of virtually all weight-training programs, whether for an athlete or for someone interested in general fitness. However, single-joint upper-body exercises, the subject of the next chapter, also have a place in weight training.

BODY-WEIGHT SQUAT

START POSITION

The lifter stands erect with his arms at his sides. The feet are flat on the floor and approximately hip-width apart. The toes point forward or slightly to the outside (a). The head is upright and the gaze is straight forward.

MOVEMENT AND END POSITION

The lifter bends at the knees and hips in a controlled manner, keeping the feet flat on the floor, until the thighs are parallel to the floor (b). He briefly holds the thigh-parallel-to-floor position, then returns to the start position in a controlled manner. The back and head stay as upright as possible at all times. The feet stay flat on the floor at all times. As the knees and hips bend, the lifter may bring his arms directly out in front of the shoulders to help with balance; then as he returns to the start position, the arms move back to the sides of the body.

MOVEMENT VARIATIONS

The lifter places his hands on his hips and keeps them there at all times. A broomstick or light bar may be placed on the lifter's shoulders as if doing a back squat or held on the front of the shoulders as if doing a front squat.

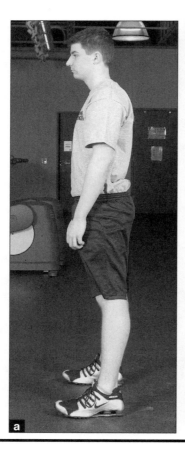

BARBELL BACK SQUAT

START POSITION

The lifter stands erect, with feet hip-width or slightly wider apart. The feet are flat on the floor and the weight is on the mid-foot and heel areas. The toes point forward or slightly to the outside. The head is upright and the gaze is forward. The barbell rests on the spines of the shoulder blades (a). The lifter grasps the barbell with an overhand grip and palms facing forward. The hands are shoulder-width apart or wider. The lifter removes the barbell from a power rack or squat rack to get into the start position.

MOVEMENT AND END POSITION

The lifter bends his knees and hips in a controlled manner until the tops of the thighs are parallel to the floor (b). The knees should move forward and stay in line with the toes as the knees bend. The lifter returns to the start position in a controlled manner. The torso will lean forward but should remain as upright as possible at all times. The feet remain flat on the floor and the weight on the mid-foot and heel area at all times. The head stays upright and the eyes look forward at all times. The shoulders stay back at all times.

MOVEMENT VARIATIONS

If knee discomfort or other physical problems contraindicate going to the thigh-parallel-to-the-floor position, partial repetitions can be performed. The foot position can vary from hip-width to wider than hip-width. A wider foot position emphasizes the inner-thigh muscles (hip adductors).

a

b

135

DUMBBELL SQUAT

START POSITION

Similar to the barbell back squat except the lifter holds a dumbbell in each hand with an overhand grip and palms facing the thighs. The arms hang straight down at the sides from the shoulders (a).

MOVEMENT AND END POSITION

Similar to the barbell back squat except the dumbbells remain at arm's length, hanging straight down from the shoulders at all times (b). The palms face the thighs at all times.

MOVEMENT VARIATIONS

Performing the exercise while holding the dumbbells at shoulder height can be used as a lead-up to a barbell squat. If knee discomfort or other physical problems contraindicate going to the thigh-parallel-to-the-floor position, partial repetitions can be performed. The foot position can vary from hip-width to wider than hip-width. A wider foot position emphasizes the inner-thigh muscles (hip adductors).

BARBELL FRONT SQUAT

START POSITION

The lifter stands erect with feet hip-width or slightly wider apart. The feet are flat on the floor and the weight is on the mid-foot and heel areas. The toes point forward or slightly to the outside. The head is upright and the gaze is forward. The barbell rests on the front of the shoulders (a). The lifter grasps the barbell with an overhand grip and palms facing upward. The elbows are rotated forward and upward so that the weight of the barbell rests on the shoulders and is not supported by the hands and arms. The hands are shoulder-width apart or slightly wider. The lifter removes the barbell from a power rack or squat rack to get into the start position.

MOVEMENT AND END POSITION

The lifter bends her knees and hips in a controlled manner until the tops of the thighs are parallel to the floor (b). As they bend, the knees should move forward and stay in line with the toes. The lifter returns to the start position in a controlled manner. The elbows remain rotated forward and upward so that the barbell rests on the front of the shoulders at all times. The torso will lean forward more than during the barbell back squat but should remain as upright as possible at all times. The feet remain flat on the floor and the weight is on the mid-foot and heel area at all times. The head stays upright and the eyes look forward at all times. The shoulders stay back at all times.

MOVEMENT VARIATION

If knee discomfort or other physical problems contraindicate going to the thigh-parallel-to-the-floor position, partial repetitions can be performed.

RESISTIVE-BALL SQUAT

START POSITION

The lifter stands with a slight backward lean against a resistive ball that is against a wall. The ball is approximately at the height of the upper-hip and lower-back area (a). The feet are flat on the floor and far enough away from the wall so that when the lifter is in the end position his knees form a 90-degree angle and his lower legs are perpendicular to the floor. The feet are approximately hip-width apart. The feet are flat on the floor and point forward or slightly outward. The arms hang at the sides of the body. The head is upright and the gaze is forward.

MOVEMENT AND END POSITION

The lifter bends his knees and hips in a controlled manner until the thighs are parallel to the floor (b). When the thighs are parallel to the floor, the lower leg should be perpendicular to the floor. The lifter briefly holds the thigh-parallel-to-the-floor position, then straightens the legs and returns to the start position. During the exercise the resistive ball rolls up and down the wall and the lifter's back.

MOVEMENT VARIATION

The lifter can add resistance by holding a dumbbell in each hand with the palms facing the thighs.

LEG PRESS

START POSITION

The lifter lies on her back on the pad provided. The entire back, buttocks, and shoulders are in contact with the back pad (a). The knees are at a 90-degree angle and the feet are flat on the foot platform. The feet are slightly wider than hip-width apart. Adjust the distance of the back pad from the foot platform so that the lifter's knees are at a 90-degree angle. The lifter grasps the handles that are near her shoulders (if provided).

MOVEMENT AND END POSITION

The lifter straightens her legs in a controlled manner until her knees are straight but not locked (b). She briefly holds the straight-knee position, then returns to the start position in a controlled manner. The weight should be on the mid-foot and heel areas. The entire back, gluteal muscles, and shoulders are in contact with the back pad at all times. The feet remain flat on the foot platform at all times.

MOVEMENT VARIATIONS

The foot position on the foot plate can vary from high to low. Partial repetitions can be performed if full range of motion (starting from a 90-degree knee angle) is contraindicated due to knee pain or other knee problems.

HIP SLED

START POSITION

The lifter lies on her back with her buttocks in contact with the seat and back pad. The entire back and shoulders are in contact with the back pad, and shoulders are in contact with the shoulder pads (if provided). The head is in contact with the head pad (if provided). The feet are flat on the foot platform and slightly wider than hip-width apart (a). The lifter grasps the handles located near the hips (if provided). She straightens both legs and moves the handles located on the sides of the machine so that the sled carrying the weight moves downward.

MOVEMENT AND END POSITION

The lifter bends her legs in a controlled manner until her knees are at an approximately 90-degree angle (b). She then straightens her legs in a controlled manner until the knees are straight but not locked. The weight is on the mid-foot and heel areas at all times. After completing the desired number of repetitions, the lifter swivels the handles located near her hips so that the sled carrying the weight rests on the stops and cannot come

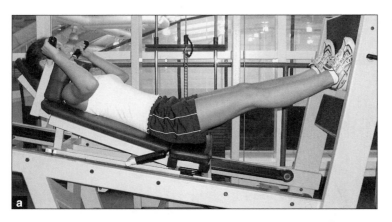

downward. The buttocks remain in contact with the seat and back pad at all times. The entire back and shoulders remain in contact with the back pad at all times, and the shoulders remain in contact with the shoulder pad at all times (if provided). The feet remain flat on the foot platform at all times.

MOVEMENT VARIATIONS

The foot position on the foot plate can vary from high to low. Partial repetitions can be performed if full range of motion (achieving a 90-degree knee angle) is contraindicated due to knee pain or other knee problems.

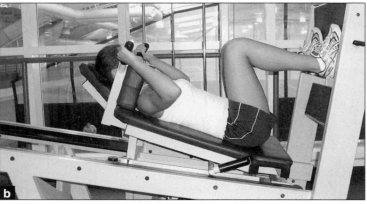

BARBELL LUNGE

START POSITION

The lifter stands erect with feet flat on the floor and hip-width or slightly wider apart. The torso and head are upright and the gaze is forward. The barbell rests on the spines of the shoulder blades, identical to the barbell position during a back squat (a). The lifter grasps the barbell with an overhand grip with her hands wider than shoulder-width apart and palms facing forward. The lifter removes the barbell from a power rack or squat rack to get into the start position.

MOVEMENT AND END POSITION

The lifter steps straight forward with one leg in a controlled manner so that the feet are still hip-width apart after the step (b). The step should be long enough so that the knee of the stepping leg is above the mid-foot area after the knee is bent, not in front of the toes or behind the heel. The lifter bends the knee of the stepping leg in a controlled manner until the knee of the rear leg almost touches the floor. The foot of the stepping leg remains flat on the floor at all times. The rear foot can rise up onto the toes as the front leg bends. After bending the front leg, the lifter straightens it

in a controlled manner but does not lock the knee. The lifter repeats this motion for the desired number of repetitions. After completing the desired number of repetitions, the lifter pushes off the floor with the front leg and returns to the start position with two short backward steps of the front leg. The lifter repeats the exercise motion with the opposite leg for the desired number of repetitions. The torso remains as upright as possible throughout the exercise motion.

DUMBBELL LUNGE

START POSITION

Similar to the barbell lunge except the lifter holds a dumbbell in each hand with an overhand grip and palms facing the thighs (a). The arms hang straight down from the shoulders at the sides of the body.

MOVEMENT AND END POSITION

Similar to the barbell lunge except the dumbbells hang straight down at the sides with the palms facing the thighs at all times (b)

Single-Joint Upper-Body Exercises

There are probably more single-joint upper-body exercises than any other type of exercise, in part due to the large number of upper-body movements that are possible. These exercises strengthen all those individual movements, and many can be performed using free weights and several different types of machines, which increases the total number of exercises possible. The exercises in this chapter are divided into the major muscle groups that they train.

UPPER BACK AND NECK

The trapezius muscle is located in the upper back and neck areas. Its major movement is to raise or shrug the shoulders. Shrugging the shoulders involves raising the shoulders as high as possible as if trying to touch the ears with the tips of the shoulders. These exercises use a barbell or dumbbells to train the trapezius muscle.

Common Technique Errors

- Tilting the head backward and looking straight up during the exercise movement limit the shrugging range of motion.
- Using the legs, back, or other muscles to start the lifting movement

Spotting and Safety

- No spotting is normally required.

SHOULDERS

The single-joint shoulder-area exercises predominantly train the deltoid muscle, which covers the front, back, and outside aspects of the shoulder area. Several types of dumbbell shoulder raises emphasize various aspects of the shoulder. One variation applicable to all dumbbell shoulder-raise exercises is to perform them in an alternate-arm fashion, raising one dumbbell at a time while lowering the other. The lateral shoulder raise exercise can also be performed using a machine. You should also train the rotator cuff. The rotator cuff is a group of muscles that rotate and stabilize the upper arm, or humerus, in the shoulder joint. The rotator cuff and surrounding muscles are frequently the source of pain in common shoulder-overuse injuries such as Little League shoulder. These exercises can be part of the treatment program for such injuries or used to help prevent injury. Normally, shoulder rotator cuff exercises are not performed for low numbers of repetitions; generally there are at least 10 repetitions per set. The muscles trained in rotator cuff exercises are the subscapularis, the infraspinatus, and the teres minor. The shoulder internal-rotation exercise emphasizes the subscapularis, while the shoulder external-rotation exercise emphasizes the infraspinatus and teres minor. The shoulder horizontal abduction exercise also trains the upper-back musculature (major and minor rhomboids) and shoulder area (posterior deltoid).

The muscles trained with shoulder raises include the entire deltoid (dumbbell lateral shoulder raise) and the anterior deltoid (dumbbell front shoulder raise).

Common Technique Errors

All Dumbbell Shoulder Raises and Machine Lateral Shoulder Raise

- Using the legs, back, or other muscles to start the lifting movement

Dumbbell Lateral Shoulder Raise and Machine Lateral Shoulder Raise

- Rotating the shoulders so that the palms face forward instead of toward the thighs; this places more training stress on the front of the shoulder (anterior deltoid) and less on the middle of the shoulder area.

Shoulder Rotator Cuff

- Failing to perform the exercise's full range of motion
- Using too much resistance

Spotting and Safety

- No spotting is normally necessary.

Resistive-Ball Exercise Variation (For All Shoulder Raise Exercises)

- All of the dumbbell shoulder-raise exercises can be performed with the lifter seated on a resistive ball.
- The lifter sits on a resistive ball with his torso upright.
- The feet are flat on the floor and approximately hip-width apart.
- The knees are at an approximately 90-degree angle.

CHEST

These single-joint exercises predominantly train the chest. The major muscles of the chest area are the pectoralis major and the pectoralis minor. However, these exercises also train other muscles, such as the anterior deltoid.

Dumbbell Chest Exercises

The muscles in the entire chest area are trained in the dumbbell fly flat bench, decline bench, and incline bench exercises. The dumbbell fly decline bench and incline bench exercises emphasize the lower-chest and upper-chest areas respectively.

Common Technique Errors

- Rotating the shoulders so that the palms face forward during the exercise motion increases the use of the anterior deltoid
- Raising the head or back off the bench

Spotting and Safety

- A spotter can hand the dumbbells to the lifter once he is in the starting position or take the dumbbells from him after completion of a set. We recommend having one spotter on either side of the lifter with each spotting an arm.

Resistive-Ball Exercise Variation

Dumbbell flys can be performed with the lifter lying on a resistive ball. The lifter lies on a resistive ball with the ball supporting the upper back. The feet are flat on the floor and approximately hip-width apart. The knees are at an approximately 90-degree angle.

Pec Deck Machine Exercises

The pec deck machine trains the entire chest. The lifter must be careful to apply force with the elbows, not the hands, which uses more of the anterior deltoid (the front of the shoulder).

Common Technique Errors

- On machines with elbow pads, applying force with the hands instead of the elbows allows more use of the anterior deltoid, which is located on the front of the shoulder.
- Moving the head or back off the seat back

Spotting and Safety

- No spotting is normally needed.

TRICEPS

Many single-joint exercises train the triceps, located on the back of the upper arm.

Standing Triceps Extensions

These exercises use a dumbbell, an EZ curl bar, high pulley, or machine to train the triceps while the lifter is in a standing position. Some of these exercises train one arm at a time while others train both arms at the same time.

Common Technique Errors

- Using the legs, back, or other muscles to lift the weight from the behind-the-neck position
- Moving the upper arm during the lowering or lifting phase of the exercise

Spotting and Safety

- A spotter may stand behind the lifter and assist if needed.

Resistive-Ball Exercise Variation

- All of the standing triceps extension exercises can be performed with the lifter seated on a resistive ball. The lifter sits upright on a resistive ball. The feet are flat on the floor. The knees are at an approximately 90-degree angle.

Free-Weight Lying Triceps Extensions

These exercises use a free weight as resistance and are performed while the lifter lies on his back on a bench. The focus is on training the triceps.

Common Technique Errors

- Moving the shoulders or upper arms during the lowering or lifting phase of the exercise
- Moving the shoulders in an attempt to help lift the weight from the almost-touching-the-forehead position

Spotting and Safety

- A spotter may stand behind the lifter's head and assist if needed.

Resistive-Ball Exercise Variation

All free-weight lying triceps extension exercises can be performed using a resistive ball. The lifter lies on his back on a resistive ball. The ball is underneath the lifter's upper-back area. The feet are flat on the floor. The knees are at an approximately 90-degree angle.

Miscellaneous Exercises

These exercises utilize free weights and machines to train the triceps. Some are performed while standing and others while seated.

ARM CURLS

Arm-curl exercises can be performed using a barbell, dumbbells, or a machine. All of these exercises predominantly train the arm flexors (biceps, brachialis) located on the front of the upper arm. Some also train muscles found on the thumb side of your lower arm (especially the brachioradialis).

Free-Weight Standing Arm Curls

These exercises utilize free weights to train the elbow-flexor muscle groups, including the biceps muscle group, located on the front of the upper arm, and the brachioradialis, a muscle located on the thumb side of the forearm. All free-weight standing arm curls train the biceps.

The barbell wide grip, EZ curl bar, dumbbells-palms-facing-forward, and standing arm curls emphasize the medial head of the biceps, located on the inside of the upper arm. The dumbbells-palms-facing-thighs (or hammer curl) standing arm curls emphasize the lateral head of the biceps, located on the outside of the upper arm, and the brachioradialis. The reverse standing arm curl also emphasizes the brachioradialis.

Common Technique Errors

- Using the legs, back, or shoulders to start the lifting movement
- Moving the elbows excessively during the exercise movement

Spotting and Safety

All Free-Weight Standing Arm Curls

- No spotting is normally needed.

Barbell Wide Grip and Barbell Narrow Grip Standing Arm Curls

- Some people cannot rotate the wrist (supinate) sufficiently so that the palm of the hand is completely parallel to the floor. If they cannot rotate the wrist enough, the bar will not rest across the entire palm of the hands, which can result in wrist and elbow pain.

Low Pulley Standing Arm Curls

These exercises are very similar to free-weight standing arm curls except that the resistance is supplied by a low pulley. All low pulley standing arm curls work the biceps. The reverse curl low pulley emphasizes the brachioradialis.

Common Technique Errors

- Using the legs, back, or shoulders to start the lifting movement
- Moving the elbows excessively during the exercise movement

Spotting and Safety

- No spotting is normally needed.

Free-Weight Seated Arm Curls

These arm-curl exercises are performed with the lifter seated and utilize either dumbbells, a barbell, or an EZ curl bar. All free-weight seated arm curls emphasize the biceps. The hammer curl emphasizes the lateral head of the biceps, located on the outside of the upper arm, and the brachioradialis, located on the thumb side of the forearm.

Common Technique Errors

- Using the back or shoulders to start the lifting movement
- Moving the elbows excessively during the exercise movement

Spotting and Safety

All Free-Weight Seated Arm Curls

- No spotting is normally needed.

Barbell and EZ Curl Bar Preacher Curl

- A spotter may stand or kneel in front of and facing the lifter to assist as needed.

Barbell Preacher Curl

- Some people are unable to rotate the wrist (supinate) sufficiently so that the palm of the hand is completely parallel to the floor. If this is the case, the bar cannot rest across the entire palm, which can result in wrist and elbow pain.

Machine Arm Curls

Most machine arm curls are performed in a seated position and train the biceps. The lifter grasps handles so that his elbow joints are aligned with the machine's center of rotation. (Most machines are adjustable.)

Common Technique Errors

- Using the torso, legs, or shoulders to start the lifting movement

Spotting and Safety

- No spotter is normally needed.

WRIST

Wrist exercises involve training either the muscles on the palm side of the forearm (wrist flexors) or the muscles found on the top of the forearm (wrist extensors). Many of the wrist flexors also flex the fingers and many of the wrist extensors also extend the fingers.

Free-Weight Wrist Flexions and Extensions

These exercises use either a barbell or dumbbells to train the wrist-flexor (wrist curl) or wrist-extensor (reverse wrist curl) muscles.

Common Technique Errors

- Using the torso or shoulders to help lift the weight from the lowest position
- Moving the forearms to help lift the weight from the lowest position
- Rising up on the toes to help lift the weight from the lowest position

Spotting and Safety

- No spotting is normally needed.

Resistive-Ball Exercise Variation

- All free-weight wrist-flexion and wrist-extension exercises can be performed with the lifter seated on a resistive ball. The lifter sits on a resistive ball with his torso upright, with feet flat on the floor and approximately hip-width apart. The knees are at an approximately 90-degree angle.

Grips

Gripping exercises can be performed using a portable hand-grip exerciser or a tennis ball. These exercises train the wrist and finger flexors located on the palm side of the forearm.

Spotting and Safety

- No spotting is normally needed.

Wrist Rollers

During this exercise both the wrist extensors and wrist flexors can be trained. All of these exercises involve performing a rolling motion or movement with the wrists.

Common Technique Errors

- Moving the elbows or forearms to help roll the wrists

Spotting and Safety

- No spotting is normally needed.

Single-Joint Upper-Body Exercises

Upper back and neck
Dumbbell and barbell shoulder shrug (page 151)
Machine shoulder shrug (page 152)

Shoulders
Dumbbell lateral shoulder raise (page 153)
Dumbbell front shoulder raise (page 154)
Machine lateral shoulder raise (page 155)

Rotator cuff
Shoulder internal rotation (page 156)
Shoulder external rotation (page 157)
Shoulder horizontal abduction (page 158)

Chest
Dumbbell fly flat bench (page 159)
Dumbbell fly decline bench (page 160)
Dumbbell fly incline bench (page 161)
Pec deck machine (page 162)

Standing triceps
Two-arm triceps push-downs (page 163)
One-arm dumbbell standing triceps extension (page 165)
Two-arm dumbbell standing triceps extension (page 166)
EZ curl bar standing triceps extension (page 167)

Lying triceps
Straight bar and EZ curl bar lying triceps extension (page 168)
Dumbbell lying triceps extension (page 169)

Miscellaneous triceps
Dumbbell triceps kickback (page 170)
Bench dip (page 171)
Machine triceps extension (page 172)

Standing arm curl
Barbell wide grip, barbell narrow grip, and EZ curl bar standing arm curl (page 173)
Dumbbells-palms-facing-forward and dumbbells-palms-facing-thighs (hammer
    curl) standing arm curl (page 174)
Reverse curl standing arm curl (page 175)
Wide and narrow grip straight bar/EZ curl bar low pulley standing arm curl (page 176)
Reverse curl low pulley standing arm curl (page 177)

Seated arm curl
Dumbbells-palms-facing-forward and dumbbells-palms-facing-thighs (hammer
    curl) incline seated arm curl (page 178)
Barbell and EZ curl bar preacher curl (page 179)
Concentration curl (page 180)

Machine arm curl
Machine arm curl (page 181)

Wrist
Barbell and dumbbell seated wrist curl (page 182)
Portable hand grip or tennis ball gripping (page 183)
Barbell or dumbbell reverse wrist curl (page 184)
Wooden handle wrist roller (page 185)

Most weight-training sessions involving the upper body include both multi-joint and single-joint exercises, as do weight-training sessions involving the lower body. The subject of the next chapter is proper technique of single-joint lower-body exercises.

DUMBBELL AND BARBELL SHOULDER SHRUG

START POSITION

The lifter stands with feet flat on the floor and hip-width apart. The knees bend slightly. The head is upright and the gaze is straight ahead. The lifter holds a dumbbell in each hand with an overhand grip (a). The palms can face either the side or front of the thighs.

MOVEMENT AND END POSITION

The lifter shrugs both shoulders at the same time, raising them as high as possible in a controlled manner (b). She briefly holds the highest shrug position and returns to the start position in a controlled manner. The elbows and wrists are straight throughout the entire exercise movement. The head is stationary throughout the exercise movement.

MOVEMENT VARIATIONS

- The exercise can be performed with a barbell: The lifter holds the barbell with an overhand grip and palms facing the thighs. The hands are approximately shoulder-width apart.
- In a circular or rolling motion, the lifter rotates the shoulders as far forward as possible while shrugging them; then, when lowering the shoulders, she circles them as far backward as possible.
- She reverses the direction of the circular motion (moving the shoulders back during the shrug, then forward when lowering them).

MACHINE SHOULDER SHRUG

This exercise requires a shoulder shrug machine. With some machines, the exercise is performed in a seated position, and, with others, in a standing position, as shown in figures.

START POSITION

If performed seated, adjust the seat height so that the lifter's shoulders hang down as far as possible. The lifter grasps the handles with an overhand grip (a). Depending on the type of machine, the palms may face backward or toward the sides of the thighs. The elbows and wrists are straight. The head is upright and the gaze is forward. The knees are at a 90-degree angle and the feet are flat on the floor.

MOVEMENT AND END POSITION

Same as for the barbell shoulder shrug (b)

DUMBBELL LATERAL SHOULDER RAISE

START POSITION

The lifter stands with feet flat on the floor, hip-width apart. The knees are bent slightly. The head is upright and the gaze is straight ahead. The lifter holds a dumbbell in each hand with an overhand grip (a). The arms hang straight down from the shoulders. The palms face the outside aspects of the thighs. The elbows are slightly bent and the wrists are straight.

MOVEMENT AND END POSITION

The lifter raises both dumbbells to the sides in a controlled manner, until his arms are parallel with the floor (b). He briefly holds the dumbbells parallel to the floor. He then returns to the start position in a controlled manner. The palms face the thighs at all times. When the arms are parallel to the floor, the palms face the floor. The elbows are almost straight at all times. The head remains stationary and the eyes look forward at all times.

DUMBBELL FRONT SHOULDER RAISE

START POSITION

Same as for the dumbbell lateral shoulder raise except the palms face backward (a)

MOVEMENT AND END POSITION

Similar as for the dumbbell lateral shoulder raise except the lifter raises the dumbbells to the front in a controlled manner (b). He raises the dumbbells until his arms are parallel to the floor. He briefly holds the arms parallel to the floor. He then returns to the start position in a controlled manner. The hands are in the palm-facing-backward position at all times, which means that the palm faces the floor when the arm is parallel to the floor.

MOVEMENT VARIATIONS

The lifter begins the exercise movement with the palms facing the outside aspect of the thighs, and he maintains this position throughout the exercise movement. This means that the thumb side of the hand will be higher than the little-finger side throughout the exercise. This variation places more emphasis on the front of the shoulder (anterior aspect of the deltoid).

MACHINE LATERAL SHOULDER RAISE

Several types of lateral shoulder raise machines exist, and the exercise technique varies slightly depending on the type of machine used. This exercise trains the entire shoulder area (deltoid).

START POSITION

Adjust the seat height so that the lifter's shoulders are centered on the middle of the cam or pulley. The lifter places the upper arm and/or elbow on the pads provided (a). The palms face the torso. The elbows are bent at a 90-degree angle. The feet are flat on the floor. The head is upright and the gaze is straight ahead. The torso is upright.

MOVEMENT AND END POSITION

The lifter raises the upper arms to the sides in a controlled manner, until they are parallel to the floor (b). He raises the upper arms by pushing on the pads with the upper arm or elbow, not with the hands. He briefly holds the upper arms parallel to the floor. He then returns to the start position in a controlled manner. The palms face the torso at all times. The elbows are at a 90-degree angle at all times.

MOVEMENT VARIATION

The lifter alternates the arms, raising one at a time while lowering the other.

SHOULDER INTERNAL ROTATION

START POSITION

The lifter lies on her back on the floor or on a bench. She grasps a light dumbbell with one hand. The elbow of the arm with which the dumbbell is held is at a 90-degree angle and the upper arm is at the side of the body (a). The back of the forearm touches the floor or is parallel to the floor if the lifter is lying on a bench.

MOVEMENT AND END POSITION

The lifter raises the dumbbell by rotating at the shoulder until the forearm is perpendicular to the floor (b). In a controlled manner, she returns to the start position. After completing the desired number of repetitions, the lifter performs the exercise with the opposite arm.

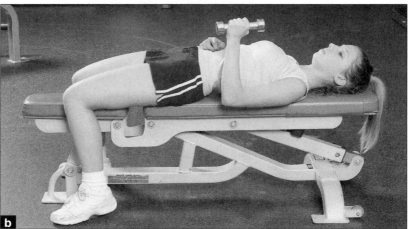

SHOULDER EXTERNAL ROTATION

START POSITION

The lifter lies on her side on the floor or on a bench. She grasps a dumbbell with one hand. The upper arm of the arm with which the dumbbell is held is along the side of the body (a). The elbow is bent to approximately 90 degrees. The dumbbell almost touches the floor or the top of the bench.

MOVEMENT AND END POSITION

The lifter slowly raises the forearm by rotating the shoulder (b). She rotates the shoulder as far as possible or until she feels discomfort. She then returns the dumbbell to the start position by rotating the shoulder. After completing the desired number of repetitions, the lifter performs the exercise with the opposite arm.

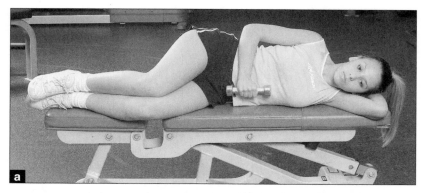

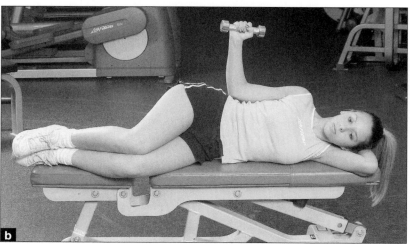

SHOULDER HORIZONTAL ABDUCTION

START POSITION

The lifter lies on his abdomen on the bench or table. He grasps a dumbbell with one hand (a). The arm is almost straight, with a slight bend in the elbow, and hangs down toward the floor. Ideally the arm hangs straight down from the shoulder toward the floor.

MOVEMENT AND END POSITION

The lifter slowly raises the working arm directly out to the side until it is parallel to the floor (b). He then returns to the start position. The elbow should remain slightly bent at all times. After completing the desired number of repetitions, the lifter performs the exercise with the opposite arm.

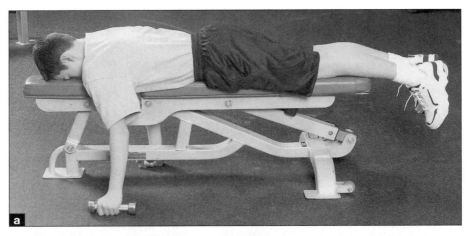

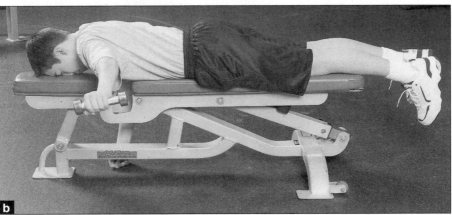

DUMBBELL FLY FLAT BENCH

START POSITION

The lifter lies on his back on a flat bench. The back of the head is in contact with the bench. The feet are flat on the floor and about shoulder-width apart. The lifter holds a dumbbell in each hand with an overhand grip (a). The dumbbells are directly above the chest. The palms face each other. The elbows are slightly bent.

MOVEMENT AND END POSITION

The lifter moves only at the shoulder, lowering both dumbbells to the side in a controlled manner, until the arms are parallel to the floor (b). He returns to the start position in a controlled manner. The palms face upward when the arms are parallel to the floor. The elbows should remain slightly bent at all times. The back and head maintain contact with the bench at all times. The feet remain flat on the floor at all times.

DUMBBELL FLY DECLINE BENCH

START POSITION

Same as for the dumbbell fly flat bench except the lifter lies on his back on a decline bench (a). The ankles and/or shins are hooked on pads, if provided.

MOVEMENT AND END POSITION

Same as for the dumbbell fly flat bench (b)

DUMBBELL FLY INCLINE BENCH

START POSITION

Same as for the dumbbell fly flat bench except the lifter lies on his back on an incline bench (a)

MOVEMENT AND END POSITION

Same as for the dumbbell fly flat bench (b)

PEC DECK MACHINE

START POSITION

The lifter is seated with his back and head in contact with the seat back. With most machines, the feet are flat on the floor (a). Adjust the seat height, if possible, so that the middle of the lifter's shoulders, as viewed from the top, are in line with the center of rotation of the machine's cams or pulleys. The correct seat height places the upper arm parallel to the floor in the start position. On machines with only handles the lifter grasps the handles with an overhand grip so the palms face forward. On machines with elbow pads the elbows should be touching the pads provided; with the hands, loosely grip the handles, if provided. On machines with elbow pads the elbows form an approximately 90-degree angle.

MOVEMENT AND END POSITION

On machines with only handles the lifter pushes the handles forward until they meet directly in front of the mid-chest area (b). On machines with elbow pads the lifter pushes the elbow pads forward until they meet directly in front of the mid-chest. With both types of machines he returns to the start position in a controlled manner. The back and head maintain in contact with the seat back at all times. The feet remain flat on the floor at all times.

TWO-ARM TRICEPS PUSH-DOWNS

These exercises train the triceps of both arms at the same time by using a high pulley. They include the rope, angled bar, and straight bar with narrow grip triceps push-downs. The rope and angled bar push-downs train the entire triceps muscle, while the straight bar emphasizes its lateral and long heads.

Common Technique Errors
- Moving the elbows, upper arms, or shoulders during the exercise movement
- Using the shoulder muscles to assist in straightening the elbows

Spotting and Safety
- No spotting is normally needed.

START POSITION

The exercise is shown using a rope handle. The lifter stands erect, facing the handle of a high pulley or lat pull-down machine. With an overhand grip, she grasps the handle. If it's a rope, the palms face each other (a); with an angled bar, the little fingers are lower than the thumbs; with a narrow-grip straight bar, it's an overhand grip with the hands approximately 6 inches apart. The upper arms are at the sides of the body. The elbows are completely bent.

(continued)

(continued)

MOVEMENT AND END POSITION

The exercise is shown using a rope handle. Moving only at the elbows, the lifter extends her arms in a controlled manner until the elbows are completely straight (b). Keeping the elbows, upper arms, and shoulders stationary the lifter allows her elbows to bend in a controlled manner and return to the starting position. The elbows, upper arms, and shoulders remain stationary at all times.

ONE-ARM DUMBBELL
STANDING TRICEPS EXTENSION

START POSITION

With an overhand grip, the lifter grasps a dumbbell with one hand with the palm facing toward the head. He holds the dumbbell directly overhead with his elbow fully extended. He places the opposite hand on the upper arm right above the elbow to assist in keeping it still (a). He stands erect with feet approximately hip-width apart. The head is upright and the gaze is straight ahead.

MOVEMENT AND END POSITION

Bending only at the elbow, the lifter lowers the dumbbell as far as possible behind his head in a controlled manner (b). Again moving only at the elbow, he straightens the arm and returns to the start position in a controlled manner. The elbow, shoulder, and upper arm remain stationary at all times.

MOVEMENT VARIATION

The lifter begins with his palm facing forward in the start position, and as the elbow bends to lower the dumbbell the lifter rotates the wrist so that the palm faces toward the head when the elbow is completely bent. When returning to the start position, he rotates the wrist so that the palm once again faces forward when the elbow is completely straight.

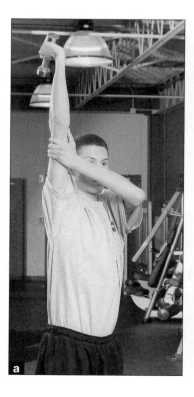 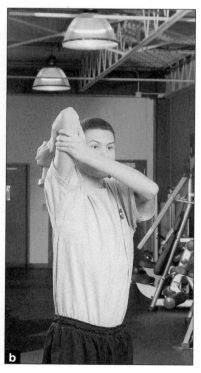

TWO-ARM DUMBBELL
STANDING TRICEPS EXTENSION

START POSITION

Similar to the one-arm dumbbell standing triceps extension except the lifter grasps a dumbbell at one end with both hands (a). He grasps the dumbbell by cupping both of his hands around the weight at one end.

MOVEMENT AND END POSITION

Similar to the one-arm dumbbell standing triceps extension except by bending only at both elbows in a controlled manner, the lifter lowers the dumbbell as far as possible behind his head (b). Then moving only at the elbows, the lifter straightens his arms and returns to the start position.

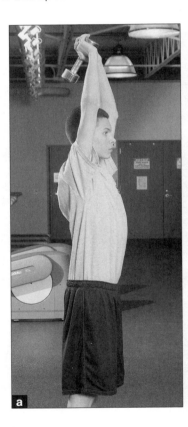

EZ CURL BAR
STANDING TRICEPS EXTENSION

START POSITION

Similar to the one-arm dumbbell standing triceps extension except the lifter grasps an EZ curl bar in the middle with an overhand grip (a). The little fingers are higher than the thumb and the palms face forward when the bar is overhead; the hands are narrower than shoulder-width apart.

MOVEMENT AND END POSITION

Similar to the one-arm dumbbell standing triceps extension except by bending only at the elbows in a controlled manner, the lifter lowers the EZ curl bar as far as possible behind his head (b). Then, moving only at the elbows in a controlled manner, the lifter straightens his arms and returns to the start position.

STRAIGHT BAR AND EZ CURL BAR LYING TRICEPS EXTENSION

START POSITION

The exercise is shown using an EZ curl bar. The lifter lies on a flat bench on his back. He grasps a straight bar or an EZ curl bar with an overhand grip so that the little fingers are higher than the thumbs when the bar is held above the chest (a). The palms face upward and the hands are approximately 6 inches apart. The lifter holds the bar above his chest with his elbows fully extended. The feet are flat on the floor.

MOVEMENT AND END POSITION

Moving only at the elbows, the lifter bends the elbows and lowers the bar toward his forehead in a controlled manner. He lowers the bar until it almost touches his forehead or passes over the top of his head (b). He pauses briefly with the bar almost touching the forehead. Moving only at the elbows, the lifter returns to the start position by straightening the elbows in a controlled manner. The elbows, shoulders, and upper arms remain stationary at all times.

DUMBBELL LYING TRICEPS EXTENSION

START POSITION

Similar to the straight bar or EZ curl bar lying triceps extension except the lifter cups the weights on one end of a dumbbell with both hands (a)

MOVEMENT AND END POSITION

Similar to the straight bar or EZ curl bar lying triceps extension except the lifter lowers the dumbbell until it almost touches his forehead or passes over the top of his head (b), then returns to the start position by straightening the elbows

DUMBBELL TRICEPS KICKBACK

Common Technique Errors
- Moving the shoulder or upper arm in an attempt to start lifting the dumbbell from the 90-degree-angle elbow position

Spotting and Safety
- No spotting is normally necessary.

START POSITION

With an overhand grip, the lifter grasps a dumbbell in one hand with the palm facing the thigh. The upper arm is parallel to the floor. The elbow is bent at 90 degrees. The opposite hand and knee are on a bench (a). This position should place the back in a position that is roughly parallel to the floor. The head is upright and the gaze is slightly forward.

MOVEMENT AND END POSITION

Moving only at the elbow in a controlled manner, the lifter straightens it completely (b). She briefly holds the straightened-elbow position; then, again moving only at the elbow in a controlled manner, she returns to the start position. The upper arm remains parallel to the floor at all times. The elbow, shoulder, and upper arm remain stationary throughout the exercise movement.

BENCH DIP

The bench dip trains the muscles of the upper arm (triceps), front of the shoulder (anterior deltoid), chest (pectoralis group), and upper back (latissimus dorsi, rhomboids). However, it is normally thought of as a triceps exercise.

Common Technique Errors

- Using the legs to assist in raising the body from the buttocks-almost-touching-the-floor position

Spotting and Safety

- No spotting is normally needed.
- For shorter individuals, attempting to touch the buttocks to the floor results in too much range of motion. Placing a box or other object between the benches for their buttocks to touch limits the movement to an appropriate degree.
- One spotter can stand behind the lifter and assist by placing his hands in the lifter's armpits.
- This exercise does require substantial movement at the shoulder joint, so if the lifter experiences shoulder pain she should stop the exercise.
- The benches must be sturdy and must not slide.

START POSITION

Adjust the distance between two flat benches so that the lifter's heels are on one bench and the palms of her hands are on the other (a). The palms are flat on one bench with the fingers pointing forward. The hands are slightly wider than shoulder-width apart. The elbows are straight. The torso is upright and forms a 90-degree angle with the legs. The head is upright and the gaze is straight ahead.

MOVEMENT AND END POSITION

Bending at the elbows and moving at the shoulders, the lifter lowers her body until her buttocks touch or almost touch the floor in a controlled manner (b). She straightens her elbows and returns to the start position in a controlled manner. The lower arms remain perpendicular to the floor at all times.

MACHINE TRICEPS EXTENSION

Common Technique Errors
- Using the shoulders, back, or other muscles to assist in straightening the elbows
- Moving the shoulders, upper arms, or elbows during the exercise movement

Spotting and Safety
- No spotting is needed.

START POSITION

The lifter sits on the seat provided. The upper arms rest on the pad provided. Adjust the seat height, if possible, so that the lifter's upper arms are in the position recommended by the manufacturer of the equipment; normally this means the shoulders are slightly higher than the elbows so that the upper arms are not quite parallel to the floor (a). The elbows are aligned with the machine's cam or pulley center of rotation. The lifter grasps the handles with an overhand grip or places her hands on the pad(s) provided. The elbows are completely bent. The back is straight and the feet are flat on the floor or on the foot plates provided. The head is upright and the gaze is straight ahead.

MOVEMENT AND END POSITION

Moving only at the elbows, the lifter straightens them completely in a controlled manner (b). She then returns to the start position by allowing her elbows to bend in a controlled manner. The shoulders, upper arms, and elbows remain stationary at all times.

BARBELL WIDE GRIP, BARBELL NARROW GRIP, AND EZ CURL BAR STANDING ARM CURL

START POSITION

The exercise is shown using a barbell with a wide grip. The lifter grasps a barbell with an underhand grip so that the palms face forward when the bar rests on the thighs (a). The hands are shoulder-width or slightly wider apart when using a wide grip, and approximately 6 inches apart when using a narrow grip. When using an EZ curl bar the thumbs are slightly higher than the little fingers due to the bends in the bar, and the hands are approximately shoulder-width apart or slightly narrower. The bar rests on the thighs. The lifter stands erect with feet hip-width apart. The feet are slightly staggered front to back for balance. The knees are slightly bent. The head is upright and the gaze is straight ahead.

MOVEMENT AND END POSITION

Keeping the upper arms stationary, the lifter raises the bar to shoulder height by bending the elbows in a controlled manner (b). He briefly holds the shoulder-height position. Moving only at the elbows, he returns to the start position in a controlled manner. The elbows are close to the body and stationary at all times. The shoulders, lower back, and head remain stationary at all times.

DUMBBELLS-PALMS-FACING-FORWARD AND DUMBBELLS-PALMS-FACING-THIGHS (HAMMER CURL) STANDING ARM CURL

START POSITION

Similar to the barbell wide grip standing arm curl except with the palms-facing-forward position, the lifter grasps a dumbbell in each hand using an underhand grip and the palms face forward (a). With the palms-facing-thighs position (hammer curl), the lifter grasps a dumbbell in each hand using an underhand grip and the palms face the outside aspect of the thighs.

MOVEMENT AND END POSITION

Similar to the barbell wide grip standing arm curl except keeping the elbows stationary, the lifter raises the dumbbells to shoulder height in a controlled manner by bending the elbows (b). She briefly holds the shoulder-height position. Then, moving only at the elbows, the lifter returns to the start position in a controlled manner. When using the palms-facing-forward position, the wrist and forearm should not rotate; the palms remain in the facing-forward position at all times. (This means in the end position the palms face the chest.) When using the palms-facing-the-thighs position (hammer curl), the wrist and forearm should not rotate; the palms remain facing the thighs at all times. (This means in the end position the palms face each other.)

MOVEMENT VARIATION

Both the palms-facing-forward and palms-facing-the-thighs exercises can be performed by lifting both dumbbells at the same time or in an alternating-arm fashion.

REVERSE CURL STANDING ARM CURL

START POSITION

Similar to the barbell wide grip standing arm curl except the lifter grasps a barbell with an overhand grip (a). The palms face the front of the thighs. The hands are approximately shoulder-width or slightly wider apart.

MOVEMENT AND END POSITION

Similar to the barbell wide grip standing arm curl except the exercise is performed with an overhand grip (b)

WIDE AND NARROW GRIP STRAIGHT BAR/EZ CURL BAR LOW PULLEY STANDING ARM CURL

START POSITION

The lifter grasps a bar handle attached to a low pulley with an underhand grip so that the palms face forward. For the straight bar wide-grip position, the hands are shoulder-width or slightly wider apart; for the straight bar narrow-grip position, the hands are approximately 6 inches apart (a); for the EZ curl bar version, the little fingers are slightly lower than the thumbs due to the bends in the handle. The handle rests on the lifter's thighs. The lifter stands at a distance from the low pulley that allows the cable to be pulled almost directly upward. He stands erect with feet hip-width apart. The feet are slightly staggered front to back for balance. The knees are slightly bent. The head is upright and the gaze is straight ahead.

MOVEMENT AND END POSITION

Keeping the elbows stationary, the lifter raises the handle to shoulder height in a controlled manner by bending the elbows (b). He briefly holds the shoulder-height position. Then, bending only at the elbows, he returns to the start position in a controlled manner. The elbows are close to the body and remain stationary at all times. The shoulders, lower back, and head remain stationary at all times.

REVERSE CURL LOW PULLEY
STANDING ARM CURL

START POSITION

Similar to the wide grip low pulley standing arm curl except the lifter grasps a straight bar attached to a low pulley with an overhand grip (a). The palms face the front of the thighs. The hands are approximately shoulder-width or slightly wider apart.

MOVEMENT AND END POSITION

Similar to the wide grip low pulley standing arm curl except the exercise is performed with an overhand grip (b)

DUMBBELLS PALMS-FACING-FORWARD AND DUMBBELLS PALMS-FACING-THIGHS (HAMMER CURL) INCLINE SEATED ARM CURL

START POSITION

The lifter sits on an incline bench with her back and head flat against the seat back. She grasps a dumbbell in each hand using an underhand grip (a). In the palms-facing-forward position, the palms face forward (shown in figures), and in the palms-facing-the-thighs position (hammer curl), the palms face the thighs or each other. The feet are flat on the floor.

MOVEMENT AND END POSITION

Bending only at the elbows, the lifter raises the dumbbells to shoulder height in a controlled manner. (b) The wrists or forearms do not rotate at any time; the palms stay in the facing-forward position or facing-the-thighs (or each other) position at all times. When the palms face each other the thumbs are slightly higher than the little fingers during the exercise movement. The lifter briefly holds the shoulder-height position. Then, moving only at the elbows, the lifter returns to the start position in a controlled manner. The shoulders, back, and head are stationary at all times.

MOVEMENT VARIATIONS

Both versions can be performed by lifting both dumbbells at the same time or in an alternating-arm fashion.

Resistive-Ball Exercise Variation

- The exercise can be performed with the lifter seated on a resistive ball. The lifter sits on a resistive ball with her torso upright, feet are flat on the floor, and knees are at an approximately 90-degree angle.

BARBELL AND EZ CURL BAR PREACHER CURL

START POSITION

The lifter sits on a preacher curl bench with her torso upright and her feet flat on the floor. Adjust the elbow-pad height so that it supports the lifter's upper arms when she sits upright (a). She grasps a barbell or EZ curl bar (shown in figures) with an underhand grip and palms facing forward and slightly upward. If using an EZ curl bar the bends in the bar will position the little fingers slightly lower than the thumbs. The hands and elbows are approximately shoulder-width apart. The head is upright and the gaze is straight ahead.

MOVEMENT AND END POSITION

Bending only the elbows, the lifter raises the bar or EZ curl bar to shoulder height in a controlled manner (b). She briefly holds the shoulder-height position. Then, moving only at the elbows, the lifter lowers the bar or EZ curl bar to the start position in a controlled manner. Do not allow the lifter to rest the bar on the supports between repetitions. The elbows, shoulders, torso, and head remain stationary at all times.

CONCENTRATION CURL

START POSITION

The lifter sits on a flat bench. He grasps a dumbbell with an underhand grip and palm facing forward. The elbow of the working arm is straight and rests on the inside of the thigh (a). The hand not grasping the dumbbell rests on the knee on the same side of the body. The torso and head are upright. The feet are flat on the floor.

MOVEMENT AND END POSITION

Bending only at the elbow, the lifter raises the dumbbell in a controlled manner until it touches the chest (b). He briefly holds the dumbbell in the chest-touch position. Then, moving only at the elbow, he lowers the dumbbell to the start position in a controlled manner. The wrist and forearm should not rotate. The palm remains facing forward at all times. The torso, shoulders, and head remain stationary at all times.

MACHINE ARM CURL

START POSITION

The lifter sits on the machine's seat. He aligns both elbows with the machine's center of rotation. Adjust the seat height, if possible, so that on most machines the lifter's upper arms are positioned so that the elbows are lower than the hands (a). Using an underhand grip, the lifter grasps the handles so that the palms face upward. The torso is upright and the feet are flat on the floor. The head is upright and the gaze is straight ahead.

MOVEMENT AND END POSITION

Bending only at the elbows, the lifter pulls the handles upward in a controlled manner as far as possible or until they touch the shoulder area (b). He briefly holds the highest position. Then, moving only at the elbows, the lifter returns to the start position in a controlled manner. Both elbows remain stationary at all times. The torso, shoulders, and head stay stationary at all times.

BARBELL AND DUMBBELL SEATED WRIST CURL

START POSITION

The lifter sits on a flat bench with feet flat on the floor. The backs of both forearms rest completely flat on the top of the thighs. The lifter grasps a barbell with both hands or a dumbbell in each hand with an underhand grip so that the palms face up (a). The hands are approximately shoulder-width apart. The forearms are positioned so that the wrists extend just beyond the knee, allowing free up-and-down movement of the wrists. Both wrists are bent (flexed) so that the barbell or dumbbells are as high as possible.

MOVEMENT AND END POSITION

The lifter lowers the barbell or dumbbells as far as possible by extending first the wrist, then the fingers, in a controlled manner. At the end of this movement the barbell or dumbbells are held only by the fingertips (b). The lifter briefly holds the barbell or dumbbells in the lowest position. She then flexes the fingers and then the wrists, raising the barbell or dumbbells as high as possible back to the start position in a controlled manner. The forearms remain stationary and in contact with the thighs at all times. The torso and head remain stationary at all times. The feet remain stationary and flat on the floor at all times.

MOVEMENT VARIATIONS

The dumbbell seated wrist curl can be performed with both arms at the same time or in an alternating-arm fashion.

PORTABLE HAND GRIP
OR TENNIS BALL GRIPPING

START POSITION

The lifter stands upright. She grasps the portable hand-grip exerciser with one hand or a tennis ball in the palm of each hand (a).

MOVEMENT AND END POSITION

The lifter grips the exerciser or squeezes the balls as far as possible by flexing the fingers (b). She relaxes the fingers, then repeats the gripping action for the desired number of repetitions. She changes hands and repeats the exercise with the other hand if using an exerciser.

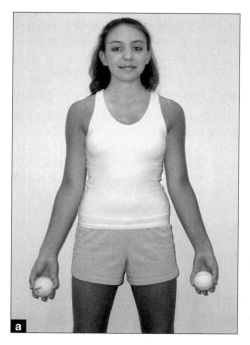
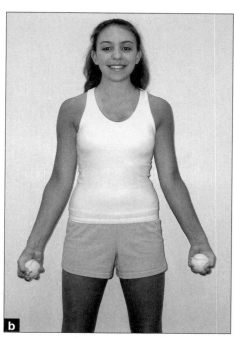

BARBELL OR DUMBBELL REVERSE WRIST CURL

START POSITION

The lifter is seated on a flat bench with feet flat on the floor. The palm sides of both forearms rest completely flat on the top of the thighs. The lifter grasps a barbell with both hands or a dumbbell in each hand (shown in figures) with an overhand grip so that the palms face downward (a). The hands are approximately shoulder-width apart. The forearms are positioned so that the wrists extend just beyond the knees, allowing free up-and-down movement of the wrists. Both wrists are bent (extended) so that the barbell or dumbbells are as high as possible.

MOVEMENT AND END POSITION

The lifter lowers the barbell or dumbbells as far as possible by allowing the wrists to flex in a controlled manner (b). She briefly holds the barbell or dumbbells in the lowest position. She then extends the wrists in a controlled manner, raising the barbell or dumbbells as high as possible back to the start position. The forearms remain stationary and in contact with the thighs at all times. The torso and head remain stationary at all times. The feet remain stationary and flat on the floor at all times.

MOVEMENT VARIATIONS

The dumbbell reverse wrist curl can be performed with both arms at the same time or in an alternating-arm fashion.

WOODEN HANDLE WRIST ROLLER

START POSITION

The lifter stands erect with feet hip-width apart. He holds the handle with an overhand grip and palms facing downward. The rope hangs down from the handle (a). The upper arms are at the sides of the body. The elbows are bent at a 90-degree angle so that the forearms are parallel to the floor. The torso and head are upright.

MOVEMENT AND END POSITION

The lifter flexes or extends the wrists one at a time, in a controlled manner, so that the cord wraps around the wooden handle (b). Clockwise rotation trains the wrist flexors. Counterclockwise rotation trains the wrist extensors. After the cord is completely wrapped around the wooden handle, the lifter unwraps it by moving the wrists in the opposite direction. The forearms remain parallel to the floor and the elbows are stationary at all times. The torso and head remain upright and the feet are flat on floor at all times.

10

Single-Joint Lower-Body Exercises

The majority of single-joint lower-body exercises require some type of weight-training machine. Although there are fewer single-joint exercises for the lower body than for the upper body, they are still an important part of weight training. The exercises in this chapter are divided according to the major muscle groups they train.

OUTER THIGH

These exercises train the hip abductors located on the outside aspect of the thighs and buttocks. To train the hip abductors the thigh must move away from the body's midline.

Common Technique Errors

- Rocking the hips or moving the lower back in an attempt to start the exercise movement

Machine Hip Abduction

- Failing to spread the legs as far as possible

Lying Hip Abduction

- Failing to keep the toes pointing forward throughout the exercise motion

Spotting and Safety

All Hip-Abduction Exercises

- No spotting is normally needed.

Lying Hip Abduction

- Placing a heavy weight around the ankle can result in knee strain.

INNER THIGH

These exercises train the hip adductors located on the buttocks and the inside of the thigh. To train the hip adductors, the thigh must move toward the body's midline, so the exercise motion must begin with the legs spread.

Common Technique Errors

All Hip-Adductor Exercises

- Rocking the hips or moving the lower back in an attempt to start the exercise movement

Machine Hip Adduction

- Spreading the legs too far, which can result in overstretching of the inner-thigh muscles

Lying Hip Adduction

- Failing to keep the toes pointing forward at all times

Spotting and Safety

All Hip-Adductor Exercises

- No spotting is normally needed.

Lying Hip Adduction

- Placing a heavy weight around the ankle can result in knee strain.

QUADRICEPS

The quadriceps muscle group is located on the front of the thigh. Its major action is to straighten, or extend, the knee. However, a weak hip flexor (rectus femoris) is also part of the group. The common single-joint exercises for the quadriceps muscle group involve extending the knee.

The knee extension, which involves straightening the knee while the lifter is in a seated position, is by far the most common single-joint quadriceps exercise. This exercise trains the front of the thigh (entire quadriceps muscle group).

Common Technique Errors

- Rocking the hips to start the lifting movement
- Excessively arching the lower back to start the lifting movement

Spotting and Safety

- No spotting is normally needed.

HAMSTRINGS

The hamstrings are located on the back of the thigh. This muscle group flexes (bends) the knee and also extends (straightens) the hip. Knee-curl exercises involve only the knee-bending action of the hamstrings with the lifter in a lying, seated, or standing position.

Common Technique Errors

All Knee-Curl Exercises

- Rocking the hips in an attempt to start the lifting movement
- Excessively arching the lower back in an attempt to start the exercise movement

Lying Knee Curl

- Failing to touch the ankle pad(s) to the buttocks at the end of the lifting motion

Standing Knee Curl

- Failing to touch the ankle pad(s) to the buttocks or raise the ankle pad(s) as far as possible at the end of the lifting motion

Spotting and Safety

All Knee-Curl Exercises

- No spotting is normally needed.

Movement Variation

Seated and Lying Knee Curls

- The exercise can be performed with one leg at a time.
- If one leg is stronger than the other, it will not be noticeable because the machine will still move freely.
- When the exercise is performed with one leg at a time, the training leg lifts the resistance, whereas if it is performed with both legs at the same time, one leg may develop more force than the other.

CALVES

All single-joint calf exercises involve pointing the toes, or plantarflexion. Calf raises can be performed in both standing and seated positions. All calf single-joint exercises train the entire calf musculature (which is composed of the medial and lateral heads of the gastrocnemius) and the soleus, but the seated calf raise especially emphasizes the soleus.

Common Technique Errors

- Failing to start from as low a heel position as possible at the start of the lifting motion

- Failing to rise as high as possible onto the toes at the end of the lifting motion

Spotting and Safety

- No spotting is normally needed.
- The lifter must position his feet so that they will not slip off the foot platform at any time.

Single-Joint Lower-Body Exercises

Outer thigh
Machine hip abduction (page 190)
Lying hip abduction (page 191)

Inner thigh
Machine hip adduction (page 192)
Lying hip adduction (page 193)

Quadriceps
Knee extension (page 194)

Hamstrings
Seated knee curl (page 195)
Lying knee curl (page 196)
Standing knee curl (page 197)

Calves
Machine standing calf raise (page 198)
Seated calf raise (page 199)
One-legged body-weight standing calf raise (page 200)

Strength of the lower-body musculature is important for many sporting, recreational, and daily life activities. Equally important to these activities is strength and training of the lower-back and abdominal musculature, which is the subject of the next chapter.

MACHINE HIP ABDUCTION

START POSITION

The lifter sits on the seat provided. The legs and feet are close together. The leg pads are above and on the outside of the knees, and the ankle pads (if provided) are on the outside of and slightly above the ankles (a). The toes point upward or forward. The head, lower back, and upper back are in contact with the seat back. The hands grasp the handles (if provided) near the hips.

MOVEMENT AND END POSITION

The lifter spreads her legs as far as possible in a controlled manner. She briefly holds the widest leg position (b). She then returns to the start position in a controlled manner. The toes point upward or forward at all times. The head, lower back, and upper back maintain contact with the seat back throughout the exercise motion. The buttocks remain in contact with the seat throughout the exercise motion.

LYING HIP ABDUCTION

START POSITION

The lifter lies on his side on the floor. The head is supported by the arm nearest the floor. The legs are together and the toes point forward (a).

MOVEMENT AND END POSITION

In a controlled manner, the lifter raises the top leg until it is at a 45-degree angle to the floor (b). She briefly holds the highest leg position. She then returns to the start position in a controlled manner. The toes remain pointing forward at all times. The head, lower back, and upper back remain stationary at all times. After completing the desired number of repetitions, the lifter switches legs.

MOVEMENT VARIATIONS

Resistance can be added by attaching a light ankle weight or a weight just above the knee. With the leg in its highest position, the lifter rotates the leg in small clockwise or counterclockwise circular motions before returning to the start position.

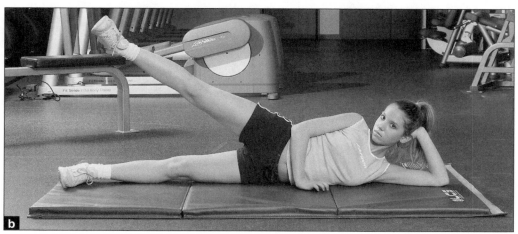

MACHINE HIP ADDUCTION

START POSITION

The lifter sits on the seat provided. The head, lower back, and upper back are in contact with the seat back. The legs are comfortably spread as wide apart as possible. The knee pads are on the inside of the leg and just above the knee (a). The ankle pads (if provided) are just above the inner aspect of the ankle. The toes point straight up or forward. The hands grasp the handles (if provided) near the hips. If possible, adjust how wide the lifter's legs will be allowed to spread.

MOVEMENT AND END POSITION

The lifter brings her legs together in a controlled manner (b). She briefly holds her legs together. In a controlled manner, she returns to the start position. The toes remain pointing straight up or forward at all times. The lower back, upper back, and head remain in contact with the seat back at all times.

LYING HIP ADDUCTION

START POSITION

The lifter lies on her side on the floor. The head is supported by the arm nearest the floor. The legs are together, but the top leg is slightly in front of the bottom leg (a). The toes point straight forward.

MOVEMENT AND END POSITION

In a controlled manner, the lifter raises the bottom leg as far as possible or until she feels discomfort (b). She briefly holds the leg in the highest position. She then lowers the bottom leg in a controlled manner until it almost touches the floor. The toes remain pointing forward at all times. The head, lower back, and upper back remain stationary at all times. The lifter completes the desired number of repetitions, then switches legs.

MOVEMENT VARIATIONS

Resistance can be added by attaching a light ankle weight or a weight just above the knee. With the leg in the highest position, the lifter can rotate it with small clockwise or counterclockwise circular motions before returning to the start position.

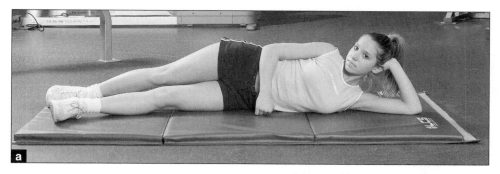

KNEE EXTENSION

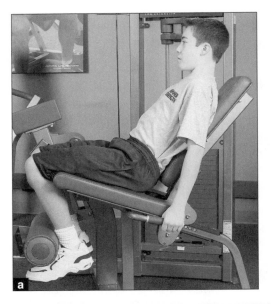

START POSITION

The lifter sits on the seat provided. The back is flat against the seat back. The fronts of the ankles are hooked under the ankle pads provided (a). The toes point straight forward and the knees are bent at approximately a 90-degree angle. Adjust the ankle pads so that they are just above the lifter's ankles and allow the toes to be pulled upward (dorsiflexion). The lifter aligns the center of the knee with the machine's center of rotation. He grasps the handles (if provided) near the hips. Adjust the machine's range of motion, if possible, to allow full knee extension and approximately a 90-degree bent-knee angle.

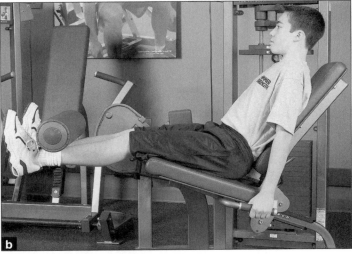

MOVEMENT AND END POSITION

The lifter straightens his knees in a controlled manner (b). He briefly holds his knees in the fully extended position. In a controlled manner, he then returns to the start position. The toes then point straight forward at all times.

MOVEMENT VARIATION

The exercise can be performed with one leg at a time. If one leg is stronger than the other it will not be noticeable on many machines because they will still move freely. When the exercise is performed with one leg at a time, the training leg lifts the resistance, whereas if it is performed with both legs at the same time, it is possible that one leg will develop more force than the other.

SEATED KNEE CURL

START POSITION

The lifter sits on the seat provided. The backs of the ankles are hooked over the ankle pad(s). The ankle pad(s) are just above the heel. The knees are straight (a). The lifter aligns the center of the knee with the machine's center of rotation. Adjust the thigh pad, if possible, so that it fits snugly across the lifter's thighs. Adjust the range of motion, if possible, to allow for full knee extension and a knee angle of 90 degrees when the lifter is in the end position. The lifter grasps the handles (if provided) near her hips.

MOVEMENT AND END POSITION

In a controlled manner, the lifter bends her knees to a 90-degree angle or slightly less (b). She briefly holds the greatest knee-bend position. In a controlled manner, she then returns to the start position. The buttocks are against the seat and the back is against the seat back at all times.

LYING KNEE CURL

START POSITION

The lifter lies on her abdomen on the bench provided. The backs of the ankles are hooked under the ankle pad(s) provided (a). Adjust the ankle pad(s), if possible, so that they are just above the lifter's heels. The lifter aligns her knee with the machine's center of rotation. She grasps the handles provided. Adjust the range of motion, if possible, to allow for full knee extension and for the lifter's heels to touch her buttocks when in the end position.

MOVEMENT AND END POSITION

In a controlled manner, the lifter bends her knees until the ankle pad(s) touch or almost touch the buttocks (b). She briefly holds the ankle pad(s) against or almost touching her buttocks. In a controlled manner, she returns to the start position. The abdomen and thighs are in contact with the machine's bench at all times.

STANDING KNEE CURL

START POSITION

The lifter stands on one foot. Place the ankle pad(s) just above the heel(s). The thigh pads are above the knees (a). Adjust the height of the ankle pad(s) and thigh pads if possible. The lifter aligns the center of her knee with the machine's center of rotation, if possible. The lifter grasps the handles provided. On some machines the knee that will not be performing the exercise is placed on a knee pad and the knee bent (flexed) so the foot is off of the floor (shown in figure).

MOVEMENT AND END POSITION

In a controlled manner, the lifter bends the knee of one leg while standing on the other leg (b). She bends the knee until the ankle pad touches her buttocks (or as far as possible). She briefly holds the greatest knee-bend position. In a controlled manner, she returns to the start position. The thighs are in contact with the thigh pads at all times. The lifter performs the desired number of repetitions, then switches legs.

MOVEMENT VARIATION

All repetitions with one leg can be performed consecutively or the exercise can be performed in an alternating-leg fashion on some machines.

MACHINE STANDING CALF RAISE

START POSITION

The lifter stands erect with her feet hip-width or slightly wider apart. The ball of the foot rests on the platform provided and the heels hang off it as low as possible (a). The toes point directly forward. The shoulder pads are on the shoulders. The knees are straight but not locked. The lifter grasps the handles provided. The head is upright and the gaze is straight ahead. If possible, adjust the height of the shoulder pads to allow for a full range of motion, with the heels as low as possible in the start position and the lifter standing as high as possible on her toes in the end position.

MOVEMENT AND END POSITION

The lifter rises up onto the toes as high as possible in a controlled manner (b). She briefly holds the highest position. She then returns to the start position, with the heels as low as possible, in a controlled manner. The back remains erect, the head is upright, and the legs are straight at all times.

SEATED CALF RAISE

START POSITION

The lifter is seated with her feet about hip-width or slightly wider apart. The balls of the feet are on the platform provided and the heels are as low as possible (a). The toes point directly forward. The knees are at an approximately 90-degree angle. The thigh pads rest on the thighs just above the knees. The lifter grasps the handles provided. The torso and head are upright (a). If possible, adjust the height of the thigh pads to allow a full range of motion so that the lifter's heels can be as low as possible in the start position and she can rise up on the toes as high as possible in the end position. Most machines have a mechanism, usually a lever of some type, to apply the weight at the start of a set and remove the weight at the end.

MOVEMENT AND END POSITION

The lifter rises onto the toes as high as possible, in a controlled manner (b). She briefly holds the highest position. She returns to the start position, with the heels as low as possible, in a controlled manner.

ONE-LEGGED BODY-WEIGHT STANDING CALF RAISE

START POSITION

The lifter stands erect on one leg. The ball of her foot is on a platform (such as a step) with the heel hanging off it as low as possible (a). The knee of the standing leg is straight but not locked. With one or both hands, the lifter grasps a handle, such as a staircase handrail or another machine, for balance. The head is upright and the gaze is forward.

MOVEMENT AND END POSITION

The lifter rises as high as possible onto the toes in a controlled manner (b). She briefly holds the highest position. In a controlled manner, she returns to the start position, with the heel as low as possible. After completing the desired number of repetitions, the lifter switches legs.

MOVEMENT VARIATION

The lifter can add resistance by holding a weight, such as a dumbbell, in one hand with the arm hanging straight down at the side of the body.

11

Single-Joint Abs, Lower-Back, and Shoulder Exercises

These exercises train the abdominal muscles, lower-back area, or shoulder rotator cuff. The abdominal and lower-back musculature are important for overall strength and to support the heavy weights used during some multi-joint lower-body exercises, such as squats, and total-body-type exercises, such as dead lifts.

SINGLE-JOINT ABDOMINAL EXERCISES

Although abdominal exercises are classed as single-joint exercises, they actually involve movement at all the joints of the lower-back vertebrae. Abdominal exercises train the front of the abdomen (rectus abdominis muscle) and both sides of the abdomen (the obliques). All abdominal exercises train all of these muscle groups, but some emphasize either the front or sides of the abdomen.

Crunches

Crunch-type exercises are normally performed with the lifter lying on his back on the floor. There are many variations, including the normal crunch and twisting crunch. Resistance can be added in several ways to make the exercise more challenging. Crunches train the entire abdominal area; twisting crunches emphasize the obliques.

Common Technique Errors

- Moving the arms to start the exercise motion
- Clasping the hands behind the head by interlacing the fingers and then pulling with the arms to help raise the torso can place stress on the neck.
- Rocking the hips to help start the exercise motion

Spotting and Safety

- No spotting is normally needed.

Resistive Ball for Abs

Use of resistive balls has become quite popular, including for variations of the crunch and twisting crunch. Resistive-ball crunches are very similar to normal crunches except that they are performed while the lifter lies on his back on a resistive ball. They train the entire abdominal area, while twisting resistive-ball crunches emphasize the oblique abdominal musculature.

Common Technique Errors

- Moving the arms to start the exercise motion
- Clasping the hands behind the head by interlacing the fingers and pulling with the arms to help raise the torso can place stress on the neck.
- Rocking the hips to help start the exercise motion

Spotting and Safety

- No spotting is normally needed.

Ab Machines

Abdominal machines are available in two major types. One type allows performance of an abdominal flexion exercise resembling a crunch or sit-up. The second type allows a twisting, or rotary, abdominal exercise. Both machines train the entire abdominal area, but the rotary abdominal machine targets the oblique musculature.

Common Technique Errors

- Moving the arms or rocking the head in an attempt to start the exercise motion
- Rocking the hips to help start the exercise motion

Spotting and Safety

- No spotting is normally needed.

LOWER-BACK EXTENSIONS

Back-extension exercises train the lower-back musculature, or lumbar extensors. Many varieties of exercises and several varieties of machines exist. The muscles trained include the lower-back area and, to some extent, the hamstrings.

Common Technique Errors

- Resting excessively between each repetition
- Swinging the arms, legs, or torso in an attempt to start the exercise motion

Spotting and Safety

- No spotting is normally needed.

- If the lifter adds resistance by holding a weight plate behind the head, the plate should rest on the lower-neck and upper-back area.
- Holding the plate directly behind the head can place strain on the neck.

Resistive Ball for Lower Back

Resistive-ball back-extension exercises are very similar to other lower-back exercises except they are performed while the lifter lies on the abdomen on a resistive ball.

Lower-Back Machines

Several types of back-extension machines are available. On one type the lifter performs a back-extension exercise while lying with his hips supported on a benchlike piece of equipment. On another, a back extension is performed from a seated position. The lower-back area and hamstrings are the primary muscles trained when performing the lying back-extension machine.

Common Technique Errors

- Resting excessively between each repetition
- When using the lying back-extension machine, swinging the torso in an attempt to start the exercise motion

Spotting and Safety

- No spotting is normally needed.

Lower-Back Free Weight Exercises

These exercises use a barbell to provide added resistance. As with all barbell exercises, proper technique is necessary to ensure a safe training environment. These exercises train the hamstrings as well as the lower-back area (lumbar extensors).

Common Technique Errors

- Failing to keep the back straight and stiff at all times
- Bending the lower back instead of bending straight forward at the hips so that a stretch of the hamstrings is felt during the lifting motion

Straight-Legged Dead Lift
- Bouncing the barbell off the floor to help start the next repetition

Good Morning
- Going past the parallel-to-floor position, which can place excessive stress on the lower back
- Placing the barbell too high on the shoulders, thereby placing strain on the neck
- Failing to have the barbell centered on the shoulders

Spotting and Safety

- No spotting is normally needed for the straight-legged dead lift.

- The good morning exercise uses two spotters, one at each end of the barbell.

- The good morning exercise can be performed inside a power rack with the pins set just below the barbell's lowest position during the exercise.

Single-Joint Abs, Lower-Back, and Shoulder Exercises

Abdominal
Crunch (page 205)
Twisting crunch (page 206)
Resistive-ball crunch (page 207)
Resistive-ball twisting crunch (page 208)

Abdominal machine
Flexion abdominal machine (page 209)
Rotary abdominal machine (page 210)

Lower back
Lying-on-the-floor back extension (page 211)
Superhero (page 212)
Resistive-ball back extension (page 213)
Resistive-ball twisting back extension (page 214)

Lower-back machine
Lying back-extension machine (page 215)
Seated back-extension machine (page 216)

Lower-back free weight
Straight-legged dead lift (page 217)
Good morning (page 218)

Sufficient abdominal and lower-back muscular strength is needed for successful performance of many sport and daily life activities, while strengthening the shoulder rotator cuff should help prevent shoulder injury. All of these muscle groups are important for proper exercise technique and injury prevention during total-body weight training, which is the subject of the next chapter.

CRUNCH

START POSITION

The lifter lies on his back on the floor. The knees are at a 90-degree angle (a). The feet are flat on the floor. The fingers of each hand touch the mid-thigh areas.

MOVEMENT AND END POSITION

Keeping the hips on the floor, the lifter raises the torso toward the knees in a controlled manner. As the torso rises, the fingers slide up the thighs until they touch the kneecaps (b). The lifter briefly holds the position where the fingers touch the kneecaps, then returns to the start position in a controlled manner.

MOVEMENT VARIATIONS

The crunch can be made more difficult by using these exercise variations. The lifter must keep his arms stationary at all times and not move or jerk them to help start the exercise movement.

- Crossing the arms over the abdominal area
- Crossing the arms over the chest area
- Interlacing the fingers behind the head
- Holding a light weight plate on the chest
- Placing the lower legs on a bench with the back flat on the floor so that the knees and hips both form 90-degree angles

TWISTING CRUNCH

START POSITION

Same as for a crunch (a)

MOVEMENT AND END POSITION

Similar to a crunch except after raising the torso to the highest position, the lifter twists to the left and then to the right (b). After twisting the torso, the lifter returns to the start position in a controlled manner.

MOVEMENT VARIATIONS

The exercise can be made more difficult using the same variations as for the crunch. Many different combinations of twisting can be performed, such as twisting several times to each side or twisting only to one side before returning to the start position.

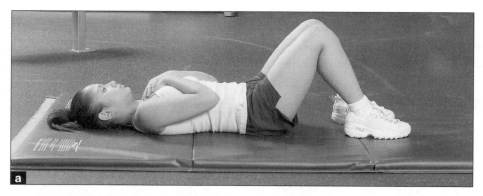

a

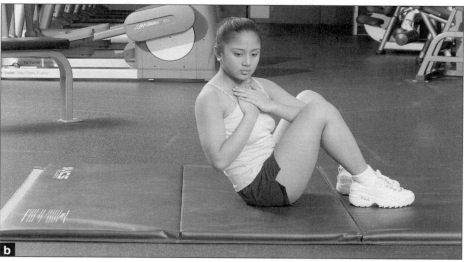

b

RESISTIVE-BALL CRUNCH

START POSITION

The lifter lies on his lower-back and hip area on a resistive ball. The ball is positioned so that its curvature supports the lower back (a). The knees are at a 90-degree angle. The feet are flat on the floor. The fingers of each hand touch the mid-thigh area of each leg.

MOVEMENT AND END POSITION

Keeping the hips on the resistive ball, the lifter raises his torso toward his knees in a controlled manner. As he raises the torso, the fingers slide up the thighs until they touch the kneecaps (b). He briefly holds the position where the fingers touch the kneecaps, then returns to the start position in a controlled manner.

MOVEMENT VARIATIONS

The resistive-ball crunch can be made more difficult by using these variations:

- Crossing the arms over the abdominal area
- Crossing the arms over the chest area
- Interlacing the fingers behind the head
- Holding a light weight plate on the chest

RESISTIVE-BALL TWISTING CRUNCH

START POSITION

Same as the resistive-ball crunch (a)

MOVEMENT AND END POSITION

Similar to the resistive-ball crunch except after raising the torso to the highest position, the lifter twists to the left and then to the right (b). After twisting the torso, the lifter returns to the start position in a controlled manner.

MOVEMENT VARIATIONS

- The exercise can be made more difficult using the same variations as for the resistive-ball crunch.
- Many different combinations of twisting can be performed, such as twisting several times to each side or twisting only to one side before returning to the start position.

FLEXION ABDOMINAL MACHINE

START POSITION

The lifter is seated on the machine's seat. The feet are flat on the floor, on a foot platform with the ankles/shins between the pads provided or the ankles/shins are hooked on a pad provided (a). The arms are crossed over the pad provided or the lifter grasps the handles provided. The lifter should adjust the machine for proper fit.

MOVEMENT AND END POSITION

The lifter pulls her ribs toward the thighs, in a controlled manner, so that the elbows approach the thighs (b). She briefly holds the position in which the elbows are closest to the thighs. In a controlled manner, she returns to the start position.

ROTARY ABDOMINAL MACHINE

START POSITION

The lifter sits on the machine's seat. She adjusts the machine for proper fit and desired range of motion. The chest touches the pads provided. The feet rest on the supports provided (a). Some machines have pads that the inner thighs should be in contact with. The lifter grasps the handles provided.

MOVEMENT AND END POSITION

The lifter rotates his torso in a controlled manner in the desired direction (b). She briefly holds the position at the end of the range of motion. She returns to the start position in a controlled manner. She adjusts the machine to perform the exercise in the opposite direction.

LYING-ON-THE-FLOOR BACK EXTENSION

START POSITION

The lifter lies on his abdomen on a floor mat. The fingers touch the ears or the hands are clasped behind the head with the fingers interlaced (a). The chin almost touches the floor. A partner may hold the lifter's lower body down by placing his hands just above the back of the lifter's knees.

MOVEMENT AND END POSITION

The lifter raises his torso several inches off the floor or as high as possible in a controlled manner (b). He briefly holds the highest position. In a controlled manner, he returns to the start position.

MOVEMENT VARIATION

To add resistance, the lifter can hold a weight plate behind the lower-neck and upper-back area.

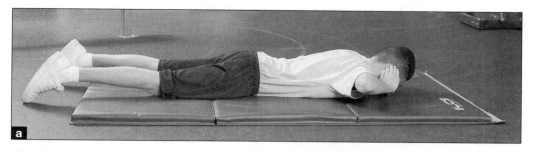

SUPERHERO

START POSITION

The lifter lies on his abdomen, flat on the floor. The arms are extended in front of the body (a).

MOVEMENT AND END POSITION

The lifter raises the torso and legs off the floor several inches or as high as possible, in a controlled manner (b). He briefly holds the highest position. In a controlled manner, he returns to the start position.

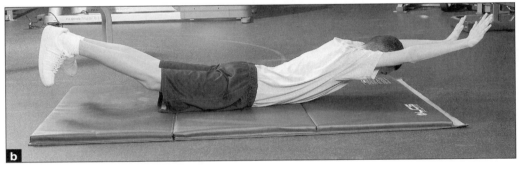

RESISTIVE-BALL BACK EXTENSION

START POSITION

The lifter lies on the abdomen and hip areas on a resistive ball (a). The lower back is flexed so that the torso follows the curvature of the resistive ball. The toes touch the floor. The hands are at the sides of the body, touching the outside of the thighs. The head is in line with the back. The exercise can be made more difficult by having the lifter place his hands so his fingers are touching his ears.

MOVEMENT AND END POSITION

The lifter raises his torso until the upper back is in line with the lower back (b), or as high as possible, in a controlled manner. He briefly holds the highest position. In a controlled manner, he returns to the start position.

MOVEMENT VARIATIONS

Resistance can be added in several ways to make the exercise more difficult:

- By crossing the arms over the chest
- By interlacing the fingers behind the head
- By holding a light weight plate on the chest
- By placing the hands so the fingers are touching the ears

RESISTIVE-BALL TWISTING BACK EXTENSION

START POSITION

Same as for the resistive-ball back extension (a)

MOVEMENT AND END POSITION

Same as for the resistive-ball back extension except after raising the torso, the lifter twists to one side and then the other (b)

MOVEMENT VARIATIONS

Resistance can be added in the same manner as for the resistive-ball back extension. Many variations of twisting patterns can be employed, such as twisting several times to each side or to only one side during each repetition.

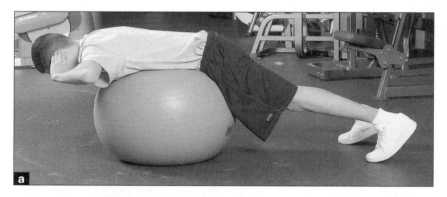

LYING BACK-EXTENSION MACHINE

START POSITION

The lifter lies face down with hips on the hip pad and ankles hooked below the ankle pads. The hips are just over the front edge of the hip pad (a). There is a slight bend in the knees. The torso hangs down so that it forms a 90-degree angle with the legs. The arms are crossed in front of the chest. If possible, the distance between the ankle and hip pads should be adjusted so that the hips are just off the hip pad.

Some equipment places the lifter in a position so the legs are parallel to the floor, while other machines place the lifter in a position so the legs form an angle to the floor (as shown in figures).

MOVEMENT AND END POSITION

In a controlled manner, the lifter raises the torso until it is parallel to the floor on some machines, or until the back is in line with the

legs (b). She briefly holds the torso in the parallel-to-floor position. She returns to the start position in a controlled manner.

MOVEMENT VARIATIONS

The exercise can be made more difficult by clasping the hands behind the head. Resistance can be added by holding a weight plate on the front of the chest.

SEATED BACK-EXTENSION MACHINE

START POSITION

The lifter sits on the seat provided. The upper back is in contact with the pad provided. The feet are flat on the floor or on the platform provided (a). The arms are crossed over the chest. The lifter should adjust the machine for proper fit and the desired range of motion, if possible.

MOVEMENT AND END POSITION

The lifter extends the lower back in a controlled manner (b). She briefly holds the most extended position. She returns to the start position in a controlled manner.

STRAIGHT-LEGGED DEAD LIFT

START POSITION

The lifter picks up a barbell as if doing a normal dead lift (see page 223). He stands erect with head upright and feet hip-width or slightly wider apart (a). He holds the barbell at arm's length with it touching the thighs. The hands are shoulder-width or slightly wider apart. The entire back is straight and stiff. The knees are slightly bent. The body weight is over the mid-foot area.

MOVEMENT AND END POSITION

Keeping the back straight, the lifter slowly bends over at the waist until the barbell almost touches the floor (approximately 1 to 2 inches). He does not bend the lower back, but bends forward from the hip joints (b). The knees remain only slightly bent at all times. If the movement is performed correctly, the buttocks will raise slightly and the lifter will feel a stretch of the hamstrings. The body weight remains over the mid-foot and heel areas at all times. The neck remains in line with the back at all times. After almost touching the floor with the barbell, the lifter returns to the start position in a controlled manner.

MOVEMENT VARIATIONS

The barbell can be gripped with two overhand grips, with both palms facing the thighs, or with a mixed grip (one palm facing the thigh and one facing forward); normally, if a mixed grip is used the dominant hand's palm faces forward.

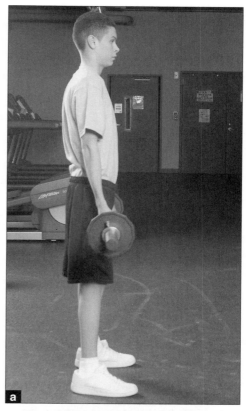

a

b

GOOD MORNING

START POSITION

The lifter stands erect with the barbell resting on the spines of the scapulae as if preparing to do a back squat (see page 135). The feet are hip-width or slightly wider apart, and there is a slight bend in the knees (a). The hands grasp the barbell with an overhand grip, with palms facing forward and hands wider than shoulder-width apart. The body weight is over the mid-foot and heel area. The head is upright.

MOVEMENT AND END POSITION

Keeping the lower back straight, the lifter bends forward from the hips in a controlled manner. He does not bend the lower back but bends forward from the hip joints (b). If done correctly, the buttocks will rise slightly and the lifter will feel a slight stretch of the hamstrings. The lifter bends forward until the torso is parallel to the floor.

He briefly holds the parallel-to-floor position. He then returns to the start position in a controlled manner. The body weight remains over the mid-foot and heel area at all times.

 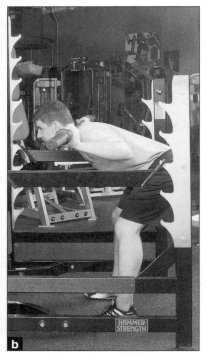

12

Total-Body Exercises

As the name indicates, total-body exercises involve the use of musculature throughout the body. In order to accomplish this, they must be multi-joint exercises. There are two major types: non-power-type exercises, such as dead lifts, which are performed at slower velocities, and total body-power exercises, such as power cleans, power snatches, and total-body overhead lifts. Proper exercise technique is difficult to master for total-body exercises, so a broomstick or light barbell can be used at first.

FREE-WEIGHT DEAD LIFTS

Dead lifts involve lifting a free weight from the floor to approximately waist or hip height. This exercise demands substantial strength in most of the body's major muscle groups. However, lifting ability in a dead lift is usually limited by lower-back strength. Strengthening the lower-back musculature and, in many instances, the abdominal musculature will aid the ability to perform a dead lift. The muscles trained in free-weight dead lifts include most major muscle groups: the front and back of the thigh (quadriceps, hamstrings), buttocks (gluteals), hip (abductors, adductors), upper back (back erectors, trapezius, rhomboids), lower back (back erectors), shoulder area (deltoids), wrist and finger flexors (palm side of forearm), and front of the upper arm (biceps).

Common Technique Errors

- Having the shoulders behind the bar or dumbbells in the start position
- Failing to have the feet flat on the floor in the start position
- Keeping the weight over the toes and not over the mid-foot and heel areas at all times
- Straightening the hips before the bar or dumbbells are higher than the knees

- Failing to lower the weight in a controlled manner, and bouncing the weight off the floor to help start the lifting motion of the next repetition
- Strengthening the abdominal muscles and lower back helps with correct exercise technique.

Spotting and Safety

- No spotting is normally needed.
- Leaning forward, which puts the body weight on the toes instead of on the mid-foot and heel areas, can result in lower-back strain.

POWER CLEANS

There are several variations of the power clean exercise. In order to be successfully completed all power cleans must be performed at a relatively fast velocity, which makes mastering exercise technique difficult. For safe performance of power cleans a lifting platform and bumper plates are recommended. The muscles trained in power cleans include most major muscle groups: the entire leg, hip, and back areas; buttocks (gluteals); front of the thigh (quadriceps); back of the thigh (hamstrings); lower back (back erectors); upper back (back erectors, trapezius, rhomboids); shoulder area (deltoids); wrist and finger flexors (palm side of forearm); and front of the upper arm (biceps).

Common Technique Errors

All Power Clean Variations

- Failing to assume a correct start position, most commonly having the shoulders in back of the barbell or the barbell too far in front of the lifter instead of above the balls of the feet
- Having the weight on the toes and not over the mid-foot and heel areas in the start position
- Assuming an upright position too early in the lifting motion, resulting in the barbell hitting or rubbing excessively against the thighs

Power Clean and Clean Partial Pull—Second Pull

- Not rotating the elbows underneath and then to a position in front of the barbell when catching the barbell at shoulder height

Spotting and Safety

- No spotting is normally needed; if the lifter cannot complete the lift he returns the barbell to the floor.
- Bumper plates (rubber-coated weight plates) should be used to prevent damage to the floor.
- These exercises should be performed on a lifting platform to help prevent damage to the floor.

POWER SNATCHES

Like the power clean, the power snatch exercise has several variations, and in order to be successfully completed, all must be performed at a relatively fast velocity. The power snatch differs from the power clean in that the barbell is held overhead instead of at shoulder height in the end position. The muscles trained with the power snatch include the entire leg, hip, and back areas: buttocks (gluteals), front of the thigh (quadriceps), back of the thigh (hamstrings), lower back (back erectors), and upper back (back erectors, trapezius, rhomboids). It also trains the shoulder area (deltoids), wrist and finger flexors (palm side of forearm), and back (triceps) and front (biceps) of the upper arm.

Common Technique Errors

- Failing to assume a correct start position. Normally this means the shoulders are in back of the barbell or the barbell is too far in front of the lifter and not above the balls of the feet.
- In the start position, the body weight is not over the mid-foot and heel areas.
- Assuming an upright position too early in the lifting motion, resulting in the barbell hitting or rubbing excessively against the thighs.

Spotting and Safety

- No spotting is normally needed; if the lifter cannot complete the lift he returns the barbell to the floor.
- Bumper plates (rubber-coated weight plates) should be used to prevent damage to the floor.
- These exercises should be performed on a lifting platform to help prevent damage to the floor.

TOTAL-BODY OVERHEAD LIFTS

These lifts involve moving a barbell from a shoulder-height position to an overhead position. However, since the legs supply much of the force to move the barbell, these lifts involve both the upper and lower body and are therefore classed as total-body lifts. The major difference between the push press and the push jerk is the amount of force produced by the legs to propel the barbell toward the overhead position. In the push press the legs produce enough force to propel the barbell to a position slightly higher than the top of the head. The lifter then presses the barbell to the complete overhead position. In the push jerk the legs produce enough force to propel the barbell to the complete overhead position. The muscles trained with overhead lifts include the entire leg, hip, and back areas: buttocks (gluteals), front of the thigh (quadriceps), back of the thigh (hamstrings), lower back (back erectors), and upper back (back erectors, trapezius, rhomboids). They also train the shoulder area (deltoids) and back of the upper arm (triceps). All total overhead body lifts can also be performed by holding a dumbbell in each hand.

Common Technique Errors

- Allowing the barbell to go out in front of the body instead of straight up from the shoulders
- From the overhead position, allowing the barbell to go forward instead of bringing it straight down to the shoulders
- Failing to keep the back upright and erect at all times

Spotting and Safety

- No spotting is normally needed.
- If the lifter cannot complete a repetition, the barbell can be returned to the shoulder-height position.
- If the lifter loses control of the barbell he can return it to the floor.
- The exercise can be performed in a power rack with the pins set slightly higher than the position during the knee-and-hip bend.
- Bumper plates (rubber-coated weight plates) should be used to prevent damage to the floor.
- These exercises should be performed on a lifting platform to help prevent damage to the floor.

Total-Body Exercises

Dead lifts
Barbell dead lift (page 223)
Dumbbell dead lift (page 224)

Power cleans
Power clean (page 225)
Power clean—clean high pull (page 228)
Power clean—clean partial pull—second pull (page 228)

Power snatches
Power snatch (page 229)
Power snatch—snatch high pull (page 232)
Power snatch—snatch partial pull—second pull (page 232)

Overhead lifts
Push press (page 233)
Push jerk (page 234)

With this knowledge of proper exercise technique, it is time to utilize it in implementing a complete weight-training program. The next chapter presents programs designed for specific sports and activities.

BARBELL DEAD LIFT

START POSITION

The lifter stands with feet hip-width or slightly wider apart. The feet are flat on the floor and the toes point straight forward or slightly to the outside. The bar of the barbell is directly above where the toes meet the foot (a). The lifter bends the knees and hips just far enough to grasp the barbell. The knees are directly above or slightly in front of the bar of the barbell. The lifter grasps the barbell with hands slightly wider than shoulder-width apart. The shoulders are directly above or slightly in front of the bar of the barbell. The elbows are straight. The back is straight and the head is upright. The body weight is on the mid-foot and heel areas.

MOVEMENT AND END POSITION

The lifter lifts the bar to knee height by only straightening the knees. He does not straighten the hips to lift the bar to knee height; the angle of the back to the floor remains the same when lifting the bar from the floor to knee height (b). Once the bar is past the knees, the lifter straightens the hips and the back, gradually moving to an upright position. The lifter straightens the knees, hips, and back until he stands erect with the shoulders back and the barbell resting on the thighs. He briefly holds the erect standing position, then returns to the start position in a controlled manner. The head remains upright and the back is straight and arched at all times. The body weight remains over the mid-foot and heel areas at all times. The elbows remain straight at all times.

MOVEMENT VARIATION

The bar may be gripped with two overhand grips, both palms facing backward, or with a mixed grip (one palm facing backward and one forward); if a mixed grip is used, normally the palm of the dominant hand faces forward.

DUMBBELL DEAD LIFT

START POSITION

Similar to the barbell dead lift except the lifter holds a dumbbell in each hand with an overhand grip (a)

MOVEMENT AND END POSITION

Similar to the barbell dead lift except the dumbbells are held at arm's length with the elbows straight at all times (b)

MOVEMENT VARIATIONS

The dumbbells can be held so that the palms face either backward or toward the legs.

POWER CLEAN

START POSITION

The lifter stands with feet hip-width or slightly wider apart and toes pointing straight forward or slightly to the outside. The bar of the barbell is over the balls of the feet (a). The shoulders are above or slightly in front of the bar. The feet are flat on the floor. The body weight is on the mid-foot and heel areas and evenly distributed between both feet. The lifter grasps the barbell with an overhand grip slightly wider than shoulder-width apart, thumbs wrapped around the bar, and palms facing backward. The back is arched. The thighs are approximately parallel to the floor. The shoulders are directly above or slightly in front of the barbell. The elbows are completely straight. The head is upright and the lifter looks at a point 2 to 3 yards in front of the barbell.

MOVEMENT AND END POSITION

The description of this exercise is separated into various positions and phases; however, it should be done in one complete fluid motion.

Pull to Knee Height

The pull to knee height is often referred to as the first pull. The lifter pulls the barbell to knee height by straightening the knees while keeping the barbell close to the shins. The angle of the back to the floor remains the same as it was in the start position. This means that the pull to knee height is performed by straightening the knee joints (b). The shoulders remain above or slightly in front of the bar. The body weight remains over the mid-foot and heel areas. The speed of the pull to knee height is moderate and controlled.

Pull Above Knee Height

The pull above knee height to the end of the lift is often referred to as the second pull. Once the barbell is past the knees, the hips are driven forward and the torso starts to assume an upright position (c). The barbell is now at approximately the height of the middle third of the thighs. From this position the lifter performs a rapid movement similar to a vertical jump. The hips and knees straighten rapidly as the torso assumes a

(continued)

(continued)

completely upright position (d). The shoulders remain over the bar. The barbell is now near the top of the thighs. The lifter now straightens the ankles as if jumping and shrugs the shoulders as if trying to touch them to the ears (e). The elbows are still straight. Once the lifter has shrugged the shoulders, the elbows begin to bend as she pulls the bar upward, keeping the elbows above the barbell (f). The barbell moves upward but is still close to the torso. The barbell is now at the level of the lower-chest area.

Catching the Barbell at Shoulder Height

The elbows now start to rapidly rotate underneath the barbell as the lifter catches it at shoulder height (g). The elbows continue to rotate until they are in front of the bar and the bar rests on the shoulders and upper chest. When catching the bar at shoulder height, the lifter's knees may bend slightly to absorb the force of catching the bar (h). The lifter should drop only far enough beneath the bar to catch it; if she drops too far the bar will crash into the shoulder area. The feet may leave the ground or the lifter may simply rise up onto the toes as she pulls the bar as high as possible and starts to drop underneath it to catch it. If the feet leave the ground, upon landing they should be slightly wider than hip-width apart and in a side-by-side position. If the feet leave the ground, they

should not land in front of or behind where they were during the pull. After catching the bar the lifter assumes an erect standing position (i).

Returning the Barbell to the Floor
The elbows are rotated downward and the lifting motion is performed in reverse order. Due to the height of the barbell it may hit the floor with some velocity; however, it should not be dropped.

POWER CLEAN—CLEAN HIGH PULL

All photos refer to power clean photos on pages 225-227.

START POSITION

Same as for the power clean (a).

MOVEMENT AND END POSITION

Same as for the power clean except after pulling the barbell as high as possible (power clean photos b-f, pages 225-227) , the lifter does not rotate the elbows to catch it at shoulder height. After pulling the barbell as high as possible, the lifter returns it to the floor in the same manner as in a power clean.

POWER CLEAN—CLEAN PARTIAL PULL—SECOND PULL

All photos refer to power clean photos on pages 225-227.

START POSITION

The same as if starting the lift from the pull-above-knee-height position the barbell can be held in the above-knee-height position or be supported on blocks, or a power rack can hold the barbell at this height (c).

MOVEMENT AND END POSITION

The same as if starting the power clean from the above-knee-height position (refer to power clean photos c-i, pages 225-227).

MOVEMENT VARIATIONS

The barbell may be caught at shoulder height in the same manner as in a power clean. The barbell may be pulled as high as possible and then returned to the floor, blocks, or a power rack without catching it at shoulder height.

POWER SNATCH

START POSITION

To determine the lifter's approximate grip width, she stands erect with the right arm straight out to the side of the body, parallel to the floor (see figure). With the right hand clenched in a fist, the distance from the acromion process (the lateral bony projection of the spine of the shoulder blade) of the left shoulder to the knuckles of the right hand is the approximate correct grip width. The lifter grasps the bar with an overhand grip, with both palms facing backward (a). The elbows are straight. The barbell is above the balls of the feet and close to the shins. The barbell may be resting on the floor if normal-sized 45 pound plates are on the bar, or it can be held in this position by the lifter, or blocks can be used to hold the barbell in this position if smaller plates are on the barbell. The back is arched and stiff. The head is upright. The shoulders are above the bar or slightly in front of the bar. The feet are flat on the floor approximately hip-width or slightly wider apart. The toes point forward or slightly to the outside. The body weight is over the mid-foot and heel areas and evenly distributed between both feet.

MOVEMENT AND END POSITION

The description of this exercise is separated into various positions and phases; however, it should be done in one complete fluid motion.

Pull to Knee Height

The pull to knee height is often referred to as the first pull (b). The lifter pulls the barbell to knee height by straightening the knees and keeping the barbell close to the shins. The angle of the back to the floor remains the same as it was in the start position, which means the pull to knee height is performed by straightening the knee joints. The body weight remains over the mid-foot and heel areas. The shoulders remain above the barbell. The speed of the pull is moderate and controlled.

Pull Above Knee Height

The pull above knee height to finish the lift is often referred to as the second pull. Once the barbell is past the knees, the hips are driven forward and the torso starts to assume an upright position (c). The shoulders remain above the bar. The barbell is now at thigh height. The hips and knees straighten rapidly and the torso assumes an upright position as if performing a vertical jump. The body weight moves toward the front of the feet and the lifter rises up onto the toes and shrugs the shoulders as if trying to touch them to the ears (d). The elbows are still completely straight. Once the shoulders have been shrugged the elbows begin to bend as the lifter pulls the bar upward, keeping her elbows above the barbell (e). The lifter pulls the barbell as high as possible, usually to lower- or mid-chest height.

(continued)

(continued)

Catching the Barbell

After pulling the barbell as high as possible, the lifter rapidly bends at the knees, not the waist, dropping below the barbell. At the same time she rapidly rotates the elbows down and to the front until they are below the barbell (f). The lifter should only bend the knees far enough to get underneath the barbell and catch it overhead with the elbows straight; normally the knees do not bend more than 90 degrees. The lifter then pushes with the arms and shoulders to support the barbell overhead in a position approximately above the ears (g). During the catching movement, the lifter's feet may leave the floor or she may simply rise up onto the toes. If the feet leave the floor, upon landing they

should be slightly wider than hip-width apart and in a side-by-side position. Once the barbell is overhead the lifter straightens the knees and hips and assumes an erect standing position (h). The lifter then lowers the barbell to the floor in a controlled manner by reversing the lifting motion. The barbell may hit the floor with some velocity, but it should not be dropped.

POWER SNATCH—SNATCH HIGH PULL

All photos refer to power snatch photos on pages 230-231.

START POSITION

Same as for the power snatch (a).

MOVEMENT AND END POSITION

Same as for the power snatch except once the barbell is pulled as high as possible, it is not caught overhead but returned to the floor in a controlled manner (refer to power snatch photos b-e, pages 230-231).

POWER SNATCH—SNATCH PARTIAL PULL—SECOND PULL

START POSITION

The same as if starting the lift from the pull-above-knee-height position (b). The barbell can be held in the above-knee-height position or supported on blocks, or a power rack can hold it at this height.

MOVEMENT AND END POSITION

The movement is the same as if starting the exercise from the above-knee-height position (refer to photo c-h, pages 230-231).

MOVEMENT VARIATION

Instead of catching the barbell overhead, the lifter can pull it as high as possible (e) and then return it to the floor, blocks, or power rack without catching it overhead.

PUSH PRESS

START POSITION

The lifter stands erect. The feet are approximately hip-width apart and the toes point straight forward or slightly out to the sides. The barbell is supported on the front of the shoulders, upper chest, and collarbones. The lifter grips the barbell with an overhand grip slightly wider than shoulder-width and palms facing upward. The elbows are rotated forward and slightly upward (a).

MOVEMENT AND END POSITION

Keeping the barbell resting on the shoulders and the back upright, the lifter slightly bends the knees and hips (b). He extends the knees and hips and rises up onto the toes, thrusting the barbell straight up from the shoulders to a position slightly higher than the top of the head (c). From the slightly-higher-than-the-head position, the lifter presses the barbell to a completely overhead position (d). He briefly holds the barbell overhead, then in a controlled manner returns it to the shoulder-height position. The knees and hips may bend slightly to cushion the barbell returning to the shoulder-height position.

PUSH JERK

START POSITION

The lifter stands erect. The feet are approximately hip-width apart and the toes point straight forward or slightly out to the sides. The barbell is supported on the front of the shoulders, upper chest, and collarbones. The lifter grips the barbell with an overhand grip slightly wider than shoulder-width and palms facing upward. The elbows are rotated forward and slightly upward (a).

MOVEMENT AND END POSITION

Keeping the barbell resting on the shoulders and the back upright, the lifter slightly bends the knees and hips (b). He extends the knees and hips maximally and rises up onto the toes, thrusting the barbell straight up overhead from the shoulders (c). After extending the lower body, the lifter bends the knees and hips slightly so that the barbell can be

caught overhead with the elbows completely straight (d). The knees may bend again slightly to cushion the force of catching the barbell overhead. After catching it, the lifter straightens the knees and hips completely and assumes an erect standing position (e). He briefly holds the barbell overhead, then returns it to the shoulder-height position in a controlled manner. He can bend the knees and hips slightly to cushion the back as the barbell returns to the shoulder-height position.

13

Sport-Specific Regimens

The development of training programs for young athletes involves the design approach outlined in this textbook. It starts with a needs analysis and ends with the design of the workout and a plan for progression over time. All programs should be individualized for each athlete. An emphasis on exercise technique is mandatory for a safe training environment. The development of a workout is related to the governing principles of specificity, progressive overload, and exercise progression (i.e., periodized training). For young athletes a total conditioning program that addresses cardiovascular aerobic exercise along with flexibility, speed, agility, and power training is vital to overall success. Emphasis should be placed on those areas related to the sport or sports in which each athlete participates. Finally, guidelines for proper nutrition, to ensure optimal growth and recovery of muscles, bones, and other bodily tissues, are needed.

SAMPLE RESISTANCE-TRAINING PROGRAMS

These programs act as a starting point for the resistance-training component of a conditioning program. These examples address the important aspects that need to be considered at the onset of a sport-specific or fitness program for young children or athletes. Implementation of these concepts and progression is vital to the successful development of a high-quality resistance-training program. The following samples are meant to stimulate your thinking about various sports and activities and give you a starting point for a program design that guards against too much specialization too early in a young athlete's career. All resistance-training programs for young athletes should include exercises for all the major muscle groups of the body.

This chapter contains sample programs for children who are interested in improving physical fitness and performance in various sports. It begins with a basic program, followed by descriptions of sport-specific programs. Following the basic program for each sport are additional exercises that you can add as the children mature and their needs change. Also included are exercises for the older, more experienced young athlete (approximately 15 years of age or older) who is ready for more advanced resistance-training programs for sports. These advanced exercises require a greater emphasis on exercise technique; therefore, before you introduce them, be sure the lifter understands the basic concepts of resistance exercise. Although we can provide basic guidelines, one program will not fit all children; individualization is ultimately the only way to address the diversity among children. These programs are starting points from which you can make appropriate reductions or advancements. For example, a resistance that is too heavy for a child needs to be lightened the next day, or if a child is too tired the day after a workout that increased the total number of sets (i.e., volume increases), then the volume has to be lowered the next day. Changing the characteristics of the workout in response to the child's ability to tolerate the exercise or improve is an important part of the art of individualizing the program. One cannot just grind out the same old sets and repetitions day after day. Successful monitoring of the training program can lead to more optimal, and thus productive, training manipulations. Keeping track of what is being done and how the child feels is vital to making the right choices about the workout plan day to day and week to week.

When a child performs advanced exercises (e.g., power clean), the amount of resistance used should always allow six or more repetitions, even though the lifter may not perform this many. For example, a program may specify five repetitions with a 6- to 8RM load. Although the resistance is light enough to allow six to eight repetitions, the lifter performs five. This is appropriate since the technique must be perfect, because the repetitions cannot be performed properly if fatigue becomes a factor. Thus, the loading reference is given in terms of an RM range that should allow more repetitions than actually performed.

Body-Weight and Partner-Resisted Exercise Program

This program can be used for beginners, when minimal equipment is available, or when you are training large groups. As with all exercise programs, care must be taken not to overwork the trainees during the initial sessions. This can be ensured by having them perform only one set of each exercise during the first two or three training sessions, then increasing to two sets of each exercise during the next two or three sessions. Thereafter, the program should be performed as outlined, with three sets of each exercise.

The program can be performed in either a circuit or a set-repetition format. With a circuit format, the lifter performs one set of an exercise, then moves to the next exercise after a short, predetermined rest period. If two or three sets are to be performed, the lifter repeats the entire circuit two or three times. With a set-repetition format, the lifter performs all sets of a particular exercise before moving on to the next one. The sets and exercises in a set-repetition format are separated by predetermined rest periods. Note: This program can be used year round. All programs should include a warm-up consisting of jogging or cycling for 5 to 10 minutes, followed by a general stretching routine. Initially, always have the lifters perform the exercises in the order listed.

Schedule this workout two or three times per week for 25 to 45 minutes, with at least one day separating the sessions. Start with one set and work up to three sets of 10 to 15 repetitions (reps) at 10- to 12RM. Abdominal exercises should include 15 to 30 reps per set. Rest periods should be 2 minutes initially, then decrease to 1 minute. The lifter should move through the full range of motion for each exercise.

Core Exercises	Injury Prevention	Replacement	Advanced
Push-up Body-weight squat Partner-resisted arm curls One-legged calf raise Partner-resisted triceps extension Lying back extension Crunches	Shoulder adduction Shoulder extension Shoulder rotator cuff	Progress to resistance-equipment exercises	Progression to resistance-equipment exercises. Note that not all body-weight exercises are simple or beginning exercises. Push-ups and pull-ups may be very difficult for some trainees to perform because body weight for these exercises is a significant resistance. If this is the case, using exercise equipment will allow the lifter to progress to body-weight exercises. Some body-weight exercises, such as push-ups, can be altered to make them more or less difficult to perform (see chapter 7).

Resistance-Equipment Program

Several factors concerning the safety of children when using resistance-training equipment cannot be overemphasized. These factors, which are discussed in detail in chapter 5, include proper equipment fit, correct exercise technique, correct spotting technique, proper resistance progression, and the need for proper supervision. Finally, the program must be individualized for each child.

A child's age and resistance-training experience will affect the program design. A 16- to 17-year-old may be able to perform the entire program as described, while some of the exercises may have to be altered or substitutions found for a 10- to 11-year-old due to equipment fit, current strength level, and other safety factors. It may also be necessary initially to decrease the total number of exercises performed until the lifter's tolerance of the exercise stress increases. Initially, an alternating exercise order (not performing exercises for the same muscle group in succession) should be utilized to reduce the exercise stress. Either free weights or resistance-training machines can be used.

Additional or replacement exercises and changes in the number of sets and repetitions can make the program more advanced or individualized or provide exercise variety. Note: This program may be used year round. Schedule this workout two or three times per week for 25 to 55 minutes, with at least one day separating the sessions. Start the lifter with one set of each exercise for the first six to nine sessions, working up to two, then three sets at 12- to 15RM. Abdominal exercises should include 20 to 25 reps per set. Rest periods should be 2 minutes initially, decreasing to 1 minute. The lifter can choose half of the listed exercises initially, then add one exercise per training session until all are included. An undulating periodized training format (chapter 3 can be utilized with high-school-age lifters after several months of training, once they have mastered correct exercise and spotting techniques.

Core Exercises	Replacement	Advanced
Shoulder press Leg press or back squat Bench press Arm curl Knee curl (using one leg at a time or both legs together) Overhead press Knee extension (using one leg at a time or both legs together) Lat pull-down Calf raise Crunches	Substitute an exercise that trains the same muscle group.	Dead lift Clean pull from thigh or knee level (perform no more than 5 repetitions per set)

ALPINE SKIING

Alpine skiing is a speed sport that involves the ability to turn and function on a one-legged base of support. Events such as slalom and giant slalom require different skills and physical abilities. The program presented is designed to help all young skiers regardless of the event in which they specialize.

Off-Season Program

Schedule this as a set-rep workout three times per week for 35 to 45 minutes with at least one day separating sessions, with two to three sets of nonlinear periodization or a mix of 8- to 10RM, 6- to 8RM, and 12- to 15RM for the multi-joint exercises (in italics). Always use 8- to 10RM for the single-joint exercises. Abdominal exercises should include 20 to 25 reps per set, adding twisting movements in the sit-up variations used. The lifter should rest for 2 to 3 minutes between sets of large-muscle-group exercises and 1 to 2 minutes between sets of single-joint exercises.

Monday and Friday	Wednesday	Injury Prevention	Replacement	Advanced
Squat *Bench press* Power clean-clean Partial pull-second pull Lying-on-the-floor back extension Leg press *Stiff-legged dead lifts* *Seated row* Crunches with twist Resistive ball sit-ups	*Dead lift* Triceps push-down Crunches with twist Wrist rollers Shoulder front raises Shoulder lateral raises Upright rows Triceps press-down *Lunges* Dumbbell fly	Overhead dumbbell press Wrist rollers Lower-back machine	Wrist curls Hammer arm curl Dumbbell bench press Knee curl Barbell overhead press Power clean-clean high pull	These exercises can be periodized with the nonlinear method for resistance in this phase. Cleans and pulls can be performed from the knee or thigh level. Perform pulls and cleans with 3-5 repetitions using 6- to 8RM loading for maximal acceleration.

Pre-Season Program

Schedule this as a set-rep workout two to three times per week for 30 to 45 minutes with at least one day separating sessions, with two to three sets of 8- to 10RM. Abdominal exercises should include 20 to 30 reps per set. The lifter should rest for 2 to 3 minutes between sets.

Core Exercises	Injury Prevention	Replacement	Advanced
Power clean-clean high pull Bench press Standing calf raises Leg press Hip adductor/ abductor exercises Crunches with twist Upright row Push press Triceps push-downs Lying-on-the-floor back extension	Hand-grip exercise Wrist rollers Rotator cuff exercises	Lat pull-down Lunges Seated leg curls	Perform only 6 repetitions with a light load in the pull and clean exercises.

In-Season Program

Schedule this as a set-rep workout one to two times per week for 30 to 45 minutes with at least one day separating sessions, with two or three sets of 8- to 10RM. Abdominal exercises should include 20 to 30 reps per set with twisting movements. The lifter should rest for 2 to 3 minutes between sets of large-muscle-group exercises and 1 to 2 minutes between sets of single-joint exercises. This program can also use the undulating periodization model for multi-joint, large-muscle-group exercises (in italics).

Core Exercises	Injury Prevention	Replacement	Advanced
Power clean-clean partial pull-second pull *Squats* *Bench press* Back extension Leg press Triceps extension Arm curl *Stiff-legged dead lifts* *Seated row* Shoulder front raise Shoulder lateral raise Bent-over row Crunches with twist	Wrist curls Shoulder rotator cuff exercises Medicine-ball push-ups	Incline dumbbell bench press Lunges Wrist exercises Power clean-clean high pull *Push press*	The trainee performs no more than 5 repetitions per set using 8- to 10RM resistances for advanced exercises. Pulls and cleans can be done from the knee or thigh levels.

BASEBALL

Baseball involves short periods of maximal power output from a player, such as swinging a bat, throwing the ball, and sprinting to a base. Maximal throwing velocity in adult baseball players has a significant relationship to shoulder adduction and elbow extension strength. Professional pitchers have been shown to have stronger shoulder muscles than players at other positions. Most sports-medicine professionals agree that resistance training can help prevent shoulder pain, commonly called pitcher's shoulder. In addition, most coaches agree that power and short-sprint ability are important characteristics for a baseball player.

The exercises listed are for players of all positions. The program stresses overall body strength with emphasis on the shoulder area. You may wish to have pitchers perform more shoulder exercises, such as those outlined in the shoulder rotator cuff exercises (chapter 9), to help prevent shoulder injury. The program includes abdominal and lower-back exercises so that power developed by the legs can be transferred to the upper body during throwing and hitting. As the program progresses, the lifter performs the abdominal and lower-back exercises with a twisting motion to strengthen the muscles involved in rotating the hips, an action that occurs in throwing and hitting.

Off-Season Program

The lifter performs the exercises in the order listed. Italics indicate exercises that can be periodized (strength/power or undulating periodization) within this phase. Schedule this workout in a set-rep fashion where all the sets of an exercise are done before moving to the next exercise. Schedule training two to three times per week for 30 to 50 minutes with at least one day separating sessions, starting the lifter with one set and working up to three sets of 8- to 15RM. Abdominal exercises should include 20 to 25 reps per set. The lifter should rest for 2 minutes between sets for large-muscle-group exercises and for 90 seconds for small-muscle-group exercises.

Shoulder adduction can be performed using a high pulley or as a partner exercise. To perform it with a high pulley the lifter grasps the handle with one hand and stands with that side of the body toward the pulley. Then he adjusts his position so that the arm is slightly below parallel to the floor. Keeping the elbow slightly bent, he pulls the arm toward his body until the hand touches the upper thigh; then, in a controlled manner, he returns the handle to the start position. After completing the desired number of repetitions, the trainee performs the exercise with the opposite arm. To perform partner-resisted shoulder adduction, the lifter stands with one arm held out to the side, slightly below parallel to the floor. A partner stands behind him and places her hand below the lifter's elbow. As he moves his arm toward his body, the partner resists. The exercise is performed with both arms.

Core Exercises	Injury Prevention	Replacement	Advanced
Shoulder press *Leg press or back squat* *Bench press* Calf raise Triceps extension Knee curl Lat pull-down Knee extension Abdominal exercise	Shoulder adduction Shoulder extension Shoulder rotator cuff	Seated row Lower-back exercise Wrist curl Reverse wrist curl Gripping exercise	Dead lift Power snatch

Pre-Season Program

Schedule this workout in a set-rep fashion two or three times per week for 30 to 50 minutes with at least one day separating sessions, starting the lifter with two to three sets of 10RM, then use 6- to 8RM resistance near the end of the phase. Abdominal exercises should include 20 to 30 reps per set. The lifter should rest for 1.5 to 2 minutes initially, then for 2 to 3 minutes near the end of the phase.

Core Exercises	Injury Prevention	Replacement	Advanced
Dumbbell incline bench press Lunge Upright row Knee extension Lat pull-down Knee curl Abdominal exercise with a twist	Shoulder adduction Shoulder extension Shoulder rotator cuff	Wrist curl Reverse wrist curl Gripping exercise	None

In-Season Program

Schedule this workout in set-rep fashion two times per week for 25 to 30 minutes with at least one day separating sessions, starting the lifter with two to three sets of 8- to 10RM. Abdominal exercises should include 20 to 30 reps per set. The lifter should rest for 1.5 to 2 minutes between sets and exercises. This program can also use the undulating periodization model for multi-joint, large-muscle-group exercises.

Core Exercises	Injury Prevention	Replacement	Advanced
Seated row Lunge Triceps extension Calf raise Upright row Abdominal exercise with a twist	Internal and external rotation for rotator cuff exercises Wrist roller Wrist curl	None	None

BASKETBALL

In basketball, the abilities to jump, rebound, change direction, and shoot are important. Resistance training can improve a player's ability to jump vertically, grasp a ball, change direction, and pass. It may also improve a player's shooting range by strengthening the upper-body muscles. As players get older, adequate body size and muscle mass for the physical style of play used today can also be enhanced with a resistance-training program.

For many years, basketball players and coaches were afraid of lifting weights because they did not want to become muscle-bound, which they thought would affect their ability to shoot the ball. Today, however, it is clear that resistance training is an important part of a basketball player's development. Lack of sufficient leg strength has been shown to make basketball players susceptible to knee injury; thus, exercises to strengthen the muscles of the knee joint are important. This is especially true for female players because their knee-injury rate is significantly higher than that of their male counterparts. Exercises for the ankle should also be a part of the sport-specific program for basketball.

Off-Season Program

The exercises are performed in the order listed. Italics indicate exercises that can be periodized strength/power or undulating model in this phase. Perform this workout in a set-rep fashion two to three times per week for 35 to 45 minutes with at least one day between sessions, starting the lifter with two to three sets of 10- to 12RM. Abdominal exercises should include 20 to 25 reps per set. The lifter should rest for 2 to 3 minutes between sets. This program can also use the undulating periodization model for multi-joint, large-muscle-group exercises (exercises in italics).

Core Exercises	Injury Prevention	Replacement	Advanced
Bench press *Back squat or leg press* Lat pull-down Knee curl Overhead press Calf raise Abdominal exercise	Knee extension	Lunge Seated row Wrist curls or wrist roller	Power clean or clean pull from the knee or thigh level No more than 5 repetitions per set using 8- to 10RM for advanced exercises should be performed. If an advanced exercise is used, it should be performed at the beginning of the training session. These exercises can be periodized (strength/power) for resistance in this phase.

Pre-Season Program

Perform this workout in a set-rep fashion or circuit two to three times per week for 30 to 45 minutes with at least one day between sessions, starting the lifter with one set and progressing up to three sets of 8- to 10RM. Abdominal exercises should include 20 to 30 reps per set. The lifter should rest 1 to 1.5 minutes between sets; reduce the rest periods after the trainee can perform three circuits or sets. This program can also use the undulating periodization model for multi-joint, large-muscle-group exercises (in italics).

Core Exercises	Injury Prevention	Replacement	Advanced
Narrow-grip bench press Lunge Knee curl *Overhead dumbbell press* Knee extension *Lat pull-down* Calf raise Reverse arm curl Abdominal or twisting abdominal exercise	None	Seated row Wrist curl or wrist roller	Push press Power snatch or snatch pull from thigh or knee level Power clean or clean pull from thigh or knee level The trainee performs no more than 5 repetitions per set using 8- to 10RM resistances for advanced exercises. If an advanced exercise is used, it should be performed at the beginning of the training session.

In-Season Program

Schedule this workout as a circuit two to three times per week for 25 to 30 minutes with at least one day between sessions, starting the lifter with one set and progressing up to three sets of 8- to 10RM. Abdominal exercises should include 20 to 30 reps per set. The lifter should rest for 1 minute between sets. This program can also use the undulating periodization model for multi-joint, large-muscle-group exercises (in italics).

Core Exercises	Injury Prevention	Replacement	Advanced
Back squat or leg press *Dumbbell overhead press* *Lat pull-down* Knee curl *Bench press* Knee extension Reverse elbow curl Calf raise Abdominal exercise (with or without a twist)	None	*Incline dumbbell press* *Lunge* Wrist exercise Seated row	Push press or push jerk Power snatch or snatch pull from thigh or knee level Power clean or clean pull from thigh or knee level The trainee performs no more than 5 repetitions per set using 8- to 10RM resistances for advanced exercises. If an advanced exercise is used, it should be performed at the beginning of the training session.

CYCLING

Strength in the major muscle groups of the buttocks (gluteus maximus) and the hamstrings, which produce hip extension, is of vital importance in cycling. Many types of cycling events, including road and track, are addressed in this section. Each event differs but for younger athletes a general program for each of these would be similar, using a greater endurance-training component for the road cycling events. The important training benefits for cycling are to gain strength and power, which are vital components in this sport. Remember that strength plays a major role in the power equation and needs to be addressed along with exercises that build power, which increases the rate of force development and is needed for hills in road cycling and bursts of speed in track cycling events.

Off-Season Program

Alternate between the circuit and the set-rep format. **Circuit:** Perform two to three circuits of 10- to 12RM and 15- to 17RM, alternating the resistances (RM ranges) used on different days. Abdominal exercises should include 20 to 25 reps per set. The lifter should rest for 1 to 2 minutes between sets. **Set-Rep Format:** Perform two to three sets of 6- to 8RM for those exercises denoted with italics and 10- to 12RM for all others. Abdominal exercises should include 20 to 25 reps per set. The lifter should rest for 2 to 3 minutes between sets.

Circuit	Set	Injury Prevention	Replacement	Advanced
Leg press	*Squat*	Low-back machine	Reverse arm curls	Perform power clean-clean high pull from the knees or mid-thigh
Back extensions	*Power clean-clean high pull*	*Dead lift*	*Seated row*	
Seated dumbbell press	*Bench press*	Bent-over row	*Lunges*	
Sit-ups	Crunches	Wrist curls or wrist roller		
Lat pull-down	*Seated row*			
Incline bench press	*Stiff-legged dead lift*			
Arm curls	Shrugs			

Pre-Season Program

Schedule two to three circuits of 10- to 12RM. Abdominal exercises should include 20 to 25 reps per set. The lifter should rest for 1 to 2 minutes between sets.

Core Exercises	Injury Prevention	Replacement	Advanced
Power clean-clean partial pull-second pull	None	Lunges	Perform only 3-5 repetitions in the high pulls, using 8- to 10RM for resistance
Leg press		Squat jumps	
Back extension			
Seated shoulder dumbbell press			
Sit-ups			
Lat pull-down			
Bench press			
Stiff-legged dead lift			
Upright row			
Single leg curl			
Arm curl			
Seated rows			
Calf raises			

In-Season Program

Schedule two to three circuits of 8- to 10RM. Abdominal exercises should include 20 to 30 reps per set. The lifter should rest for 1 minute with lighter resistances and for 2 to 3 minutes with heavier resistances. This program can also use the undulating periodization model for multi-joint, large-muscle-group exercises (in italics).

Core Exercises	Injury Prevention	Replacement	Advanced
Back squat or leg press Power clean *Dumbbell overhead press* Back extensions *Lat pull-down* *Stiff-legged dead lift* *Bench press* Knee extension Reverse elbow curl Calf raise Abdominal exercise with a twist	None	Incline dumbbell bench press *Lunge* Wrist exercise *Seated row* Clean pull from thigh or knee level	The trainee performs no more than 5 repetitions per set using 8- to 10RM resistances for power clean-clean partial pull-second pull

DISTANCE RUNNING

The major goals of a resistance-training program for distance runners are to prevent injury and increase local muscular endurance, which in turn increases endurance performance. Injury prevention is in part a product of increased bone density and tendon and ligament strength. Weight training has been shown to increase distance-running performance without increasing endurance capabilities (peak oxygen consumption). The increase in performance appears to be related to an increased lactate threshold, or the running velocity at which blood lactate elevates significantly. Blood lactate is a by-product of anaerobic metabolism.

To meet the goals of distance-running athletes, resistances of approximately 10RM and short rest periods between sets and exercises can be used for the majority of the program. However, heavier resistances of 6- to 8RM can also be used. Increasing strength and local muscular endurance of the trunk muscles helps the runner maintain proper running form. Improved leg strength helps in hill running and in the "kick" at the end of a race. Thus weight training should be a part of a distance runner's total training program.

Off-Season Program

Schedule this workout as a circuit beginning with one circuit and progressing up to three circuits two to three times per week of 10- to 12RM. Abdominal exercises should include 20 to 30 reps per set. The lifter should rest for 2 minutes initially; reduce the rest periods after the trainee can perform three circuits. This program can also use the undulating periodization model for multi-joint, large-muscle-group exercises (in italics).

Core Exercises	Injury Prevention	Replacement	Advanced
Back squat or leg press *Dumbbell incline press* Knee curl *Overhead press* Bent-over row Calf raise Shoulder shrug Abdominal exercise	Knee extension	*Lat pull-down* *Lunge*	None

Pre-Season Program

Schedule this workout in a circuit format performing two to four circuits, two times per week for 20 to 30 minutes with at least one day between sessions, using 6- to 12RM. Abdominal exercises should include 20 to 30 reps per set. The lifter should rest for 1 minute or less for lighter resistances or smaller-muscle-group exercises and generally, for 2 minutes for large-muscle-group exercises when heavy resistances (6- to 8RM) are used. This program can also use the undulating training plan (exercises in italics). Include twisting abdominal and lower-back exercises in the program. Dumbbells may be used for the exercises whenever possible.

Core Exercises	Injury Prevention	Replacement	Advanced
Lunge *Overhead press* Knee curl Bent-over row Calf raise *Shoulder shrug* Lower-back exercise Shoulder lateral raise Abdominal exercise	Knee extension	*Lat pull-down* *Seated row* Arm curl	None

In-Season Program

Schedule this workout in a circuit format performing two to four circuits, one to two times per week for 15 to 25 minutes with 8- to 15RM. Abdominal exercises should include 20 to 30 reps per set. The lifter should rest for .5 to 1 minute. Include twisting abdominal exercises in the program; dumbbells may be used whenever possible.

Core Exercises	Injury Prevention	Replacement	Advanced
Lunge Shoulder shrug Calf raise Overhead press Knee curl Bent-over row Abdominal exercise Arm curl	Knee extension	Lat pull-down Narrow-grip bench press	None

FENCING

The sport of fencing includes several events, all of which require agility, speed, balance, and timing. The modern foil is a light implement with a rectangular blade that tapers from a relatively thick, inflexible section at the guard to a slimmer, more flexible section at the end. The tip of the foil is flattened into a small button-like end for practice, then fitted with an electric point for official competition. In foil fencing, the target area is confined to the trunk. Valid hits are those that reach the target area. The modern épée is triangular in cross-section and lacks any cutting edges; it has the ability to flex up and down but not to the sides. Unlike the foil, the épée target area includes the fencer's whole body. Finally, the modern saber is both a thrusting and cutting implement. In the past saber fencing was exclusively nonelectric, meaning that all bouts required a referee and side judges; now an electrical scoring apparatus can be used. The target consists of all parts of the body above the horizontal line between the top folds formed by the thighs and the trunk of the fencer when in the on-guard position.

Fencing involves full-body movement that begins with the athlete in an upright standing position and culminates in a lunge position. Lunging is an important part of fencing and the explosive, quick movement of the lunge requires power and agility as well as balance. Wrist actions are also important in blocking the opponent's movements.

Off-Season Program

Schedule this as a set-rep workout three times per week for 35 to 45 minutes with at least one day between sessions, including two to three sets of nonlinear periodized exercises or mixing 8- to 10RM, 6- to 8RM, and 12- to 15RM (exercises in italics). Abdominal exercises should include 20 to 25 reps per set; be sure to add the twisting movements in abdominal exercise variations. The lifter should rest for 2 to 3 minutes for large muscle groups.

Monday and Friday	Wednesday	Injury Prevention	Replacement	Advanced
Squat	Dead lift	Shoulder dumbbell press	Wrist curls or hammer exercise	These exercises can be periodized for resistance in this phase. Cleans and pulls can be performed from the knee or thigh level. Perform pulls and cleans with 3-5 repetitions using 6- to 8RM loading for maximal acceleration.
Bench press	Triceps push-down	Wrist rolls	Side lateral raises	
Power clean-clean partial pull-second pull	Sit-ups with a twist	Lower-back machine	Front squats	
Lying-on-the-floor back extensions	Wrist rolls		Dumbbell bench press	
Barbell lunges	Dumbbell front and lateral raises		Leg press	
Stiff-legged dead lifts	Upright row		Knee curl	
Seated row	Triceps cable press-down		*Overhead press*	
Crunch with twist	*Lunges*		Power clean-clean high pull	
	Flys			

Pre-Season Program

Schedule this as a set-rep workout two to three times per week for 30 to 45 minutes with at least one day between sessions, with two to three sets of 8- to 10RM. Abdominal exercises should include 20 to 30 reps per set. The lifter should rest for 2 to 3 minutes between sets.

Core Exercises	Injury Prevention	Replacement	Advanced
Front squats Dumbbell bench press Stiff-legged dead lift Dumbbell front raises Lunges Abdominal exercises with twists Standing calf raises Push press Arm curls Back extension	Hand-grip exercises Wrist roller Rotator cuff exercises	Lat pull-down Seated calf raises Seated leg curls Incline bench press Power clean-clean high pull	Perform only 6 repetitions with a light load in the power clean exercises.

In-Season Program

Schedule this as set-rep workout one or two times per week for 30 to 45 minutes with at least one day between sessions, with two to three sets of 8- to 10RM. Abdominal exercises should include 20 to 30 reps per set with twisting movements. The lifter should rest for 2 to 3 minutes for large muscle groups. This program can also use the undulating periodization model for multi-joint, large-muscle-group exercises (in italics).

Core Exercises	Injury Prevention	Replacement	Advanced
Front squats *Bench press* Lying-on-the-floor back extensions *Lunges* Tricep extensions with biceps curl Triceps extensions *Stiff-legged dead lifts* *Seated row* Shoulder front raise Shoulder lateral raise Bent-over row Twisting sit-ups Power clean-clean partial pull-second pull	Wrist curls Medicine-ball push-ups	*Incline dumbbell bench press* *Lunges* Wrist exercises Power clean-clean high pull Push press	The trainee performs no more than 5 repetitions per set using 8- to 10RM resistances for advanced exercises. If an advanced exercise is used, it should be performed at the beginning of the training session. Pulls and cleans can be done from the knee or thigh levels.

GIRLS' FIELD HOCKEY

Girls' field hockey is a fast-paced sport with body position being very demanding for each player during practice and games. The crouch or partially bent-over body position and the interface with the stick and its movements make for a demanding sport based in skill and conditioning. Injury prevention is also important, with knee and ankle joints particularly susceptible. It is a "burst-like" sport consisting of sprinting followed by continuous movement. Upper-body position is also important for the optimal use of stick mechanics.

Off-Season Program

Schedule this as a set-rep workout three times per week for 35 to 45 minutes, with at least one day between sessions, using two or three sets of nonlinear periodized exercises or mixing 8- to 10RM, 6- to 8RM, and 12- to 15RM. Abdominal exercises should include 20 to 30 reps per set, adding twist movements to the abdominal exercise variations. The lifter should rest for 2 to 3 minutes between sets of large-muscle-group exercises (in italics).

Monday and Friday	Wednesday	Injury Prevention	Replacement	Advanced
Squat	*Dead lift*	Shoulder dumbbell press	Wrist curls or hammer exercise	These exercises can be periodized for resistance in this phase. Cleans and pulls can be performed from the knee or thigh level. Perform pulls and cleans with 3-5 repetitions using 6- to 8RM loading for maximal acceleration.
Bench press	Triceps push-down	Wrist rolls	Side lateral raises	
Power clean- clean partial pull-second pull	Sit-ups with a twist	Lower-back machine	Front squats	
Lying-on-the- floor back extensions	Wrist rolls		Dumbbell bench press	
Lunges	Reverse curls		Leg press	
Stiff-legged dead lifts	Dumbbell front lateral raises		Overhead press	
Seated row	Upright rows		Power clean-clean high pull	
Abdominal exercise with twist and side raises	Triceps cable press-down			
	Lunges			
	Flys			

Pre-Season Program

Schedule this workout in a set-rep fashion two to three times per week for 30 to 45 minutes with at least one day between sessions, with two to three sets of 8- to 10RM. Abdominal exercises should include 20 to 30 reps per set. The lifter should rest for 2 to 3 minutes between sets.

Core Exercises	Injury Prevention	Replacement	Advanced
Front squat Bench press Stiff-legged dead lift Dumbbell front raises Lat pull-down Abdominal exercises with twists Standing calf raises Push press Arm curl Back extensions Power clean-clean partial pull-second pull	Hand-grip exercise Wrist rollers Shoulder rotator cuff exercises	Lunges Seated calf raise Seated leg curls Incline bench press Snatch	Perform only 6 repetitions with a light load in the snatch and clean exercises.

In-Season Program

Schedule this as a set-rep workout one or two times per week for 30 to 45 minutes with at least one day between sessions, with two to three sets of 8- to 10RM. Abdominal exercises should include 20 to 30 reps per set with twisting movement. The lifter should rest for 2 to 3 minutes for large muscle groups. This program can also use the undulating periodization model for multi-joint, large-muscle-group exercises (in italics).

Core Exercises	Injury Prevention	Replacement	Advanced
Power clean-clean partial pull-second pull Front squats *Bench press* Lying-on-the-floor back extensions *Lunges* Triceps extensions with biceps curl Triceps extension *Stiff-legged dead lifts* *Seated row* Shoulder front raise Shoulder lateral raise Bent-over row Abdominal exercise with a twist	Wrist curls Medicine-ball push-ups	Incline dumbbell bench press Lunges Wrist exercises Power clean-clean high pull Push press	The trainee performs no more than 5 repetitions per set using 8- to 10RM resistances for advanced exercises. If an advanced exercise is used, it should be performed at the beginning of the training session. Pulls and cleans can be done from the knee or thigh levels.

FOOTBALL

Playing football requires speed, strength, and power. The requirements for each position are somewhat different, yet improving these three factors with resistance training can contribute to enhanced sport performance and prevent injury. In this sport the young athlete must be physically prepared to play in order to prevent injury. Quarterbacks need to stress exercise for the shoulders. All players need to perform exercises for the neck, shoulders, knees, and ankles, which are areas in which injury frequently occurs.

Off-Season Program

Schedule this as a set-rep workout three times per week for 60 to 70 minutes with at least one day between sessions, with two to three sets of 10- to 12RM. Abdominal exercises should include 20 to 30 reps per set. The lifter should rest for 2 to 3 minutes between sets. Quarterbacks and offensive linemen should perform supplemental shoulder-girdle exercises.

Core Exercises	Injury Prevention	Replacement	Advanced
Bench press Squat or leg press Overhead press Knee curl Seated row Knee extension Arm curl Abdominal exercise	Neck exercise Shoulder rotator cuff exercise Calf raise	Dead lift Lat pull-down Lunge Front squat Narrow-grip bench press	The lifter should perform no more than 5 repetitions per set using 8- to 10RM resistances for advanced exercises. If an advanced exercise is used, it should be performed at the beginning of the training session. Power clean or clean pull from knee or thigh level Power snatch or snatch pull from knee or thigh level

Pre-Season Program

Schedule this workout in a set-rep fashion three times per week for 30 to 45 minutes with at least one day separating sessions, with three sets of 8- to 10RM. Abdominal exercises should include 20 to 30 reps per set. The lifter should rest for 1 to 1.5 minutes between sets.

Core Exercises	Injury Prevention	Replacement	Advanced
Incline bench press Back squat Lat pull-down Knee curl Reverse arm curl or arm curl Abdominal exercise Shoulder internal rotation and shoulder external rotation (especially for quarterbacks)	Calf raise Additional shoulder rotator cuff exercises Neck exercise Knee extension	Narrow-grip bench press Seated row or bent-over row Bench press Wrist curl Dead lift	The lifter should perform no more than 5 repetitions per set using 8- to 10RM resistances for advanced exercises. If an advanced exercise is used, it should be performed at the start of the training session. Power clean or clean pull from knee or thigh level Power snatch or snatch pull from knee or thigh level

In-Season Program

Schedule this as a set-rep or circuit workout one or two times per week for 25 to 45 minutes with at least one day separating sessions, with two to three sets or circuits of 8- to 10RM. Abdominal exercises should include 20 to 30 reps per set. The lifter should rest for 1 to 2 minutes between sets; reduce the rest periods once the trainee can perform three circuits or sets. This program can also use the undulating periodization model for multi-joint, large-muscle-group exercises (in italics).

Core Exercises	Injury Prevention	Replacement	Advanced
Overhead press *Back squat* *Bench press* Knee curl Neck exercise Knee extension Shoulder internal rotation and shoulder external rotation Abdominal exercise	None	*Incline bench press* *Seated row* *Lat pull-down* Lunge *Front squat* Calf raise *Narrow-grip bench press*	The lifter should perform no more than 5 repetitions per set using 8- to 10RM resistances for advanced exercises. If an advanced exercise is used, it should be performed at the beginning of the training session. Power clean or clean pull from knee or thigh level Power snatch or snatch pull from knee or thigh level

GOLF

Golf has become one of the most popular games around the world. With the game being played by younger and younger athletes and the need for full range of motion, physical preparation beyond the practice of the skills themselves has began to emerge. Early attempts at muscle-building programs met with little success because they were not designed to be golf-specific, and for many years golfers were concerned that they would bulk up, which would hinder their golf swing (e.g., Johnny Miller's case in the '70s), giving resistance training for golfers a bad name. Not until those involved in the sport saw that other players, such as Gary Player and more recently Tiger Woods, had used resistance training in their golf-fitness programs did they start to take another look at it. Other concerns were that resistance training would cause a decrease in flexibility and change the feel of the shots. But again, these have not been shown to be problems with a balanced resistance-training program, especially one that's golf-specific. The ability to feel a shot is typically based on joint stability, and resistance training strengthens joint integrity. (As with tennis, if practice is ongoing such changes will not be so dramatic.) In addition, by starting a resistance-training program with the younger athlete, such concerns will most likely never occur.

The need for resistance training was further fueled by the need for injury prevention, especially in the lower back. The key to any program for golf is injury prevention, rotational power, solid stability for single-leg positioning, and ultimately good core muscle strength. Thus, while extreme muscle hypertrophy is not the primary goal in training for golf, adequate muscle fitness and physical capabilities to enhance ball strike and provide neural control of all the musculature are vital to success. Flexibility training, along with core stability, strength, and power, play vital roles in a successful golf-specific resistance-training program. Specialty exercises need to supplement a solid base program of normative body movements (e.g., exercises for each of the major muscle groups balanced around each joint).

Off-Season Program

Golf-stroke practice must continue in the off-season so that stroke feel and skills are ingrained into a recognizable motor pattern by the young athlete. The exercises are performed in the order listed. Schedule this as a set-rep workout two to three times per week for 30 to 45 minutes with at least one day separating the sessions, starting the lifter with one set and progressing up to three sets of 10- to 12RM initially, then proceeding to undulating periodization with heavy (6- to 8RM), light (15- to 17RM), and moderate (10- to 12RM) loads on different days for the multi-joint, large-muscle-group exercises. Abdominal exercises should include 20 to 30 reps per set. The lifter should rest for 2 to 3 minutes between sets; reduce the rest periods after the trainee can perform three circuits or sets. This program can also use the undulating periodization model for multi-joint, large-muscle-group exercises (in italics).

Core Exercises	Injury Prevention	Replacement	Advanced
Bench press	Lying-on-the-floor back extensions	One-quarter squats (i.e., perform a regular squat but only lower yourself a quarter way down from the standing position allowing more weight to be lifted in the upper range of motion)	Make sure that adequate rest is utilized between sets for the dead lift during a heavy day.
Squat	Calf raises in various foot positions		
Seated row	*Dead lift*		
Stiff-legged dead lift	Rotator cuff exercises		
Resistive ball twisting sit-ups		*Lunge*	
Arm curls		Knee extension	
Standing calf raises		*Leg press*	
Sit-ups with twist		Triceps extension	
Lateral raises		Dips	
Front raises		*Incline bench press*	
Wrist curls and wrist extensions			
Dumbbell shoulder press			

Pre-Season Program

Schedule this as a set-rep workout two times per week for 20 to 30 minutes with at least one day between sessions, with two to three sets of 10- to 12RM. Abdominal exercises should include 20 to 30 reps per set. The lifter should rest for 2 minutes between sets; reduce the rest periods after the trainee can perform three sets. This program can also use the undulating periodization model for multi-joint, large-muscle-group exercises (in italics).

Core Exercises	Injury Prevention	Replacement	Advanced
Bench press Lunge Bent-over row Power clean-clean partial pull-second pull *Stiff-legged dead lift* Resistive ball twisting sit-ups Arm curls Standing calf raises Sit-ups with twist Lying-on-the-floor back extensions Wrist curls and wrist extensions *Overhead press*	Knee extension *Front squats*	*Lat pull-down* *Seated row* Reverse arm curls	For power clean-clean partial pull-second pull make sure technique has been taught during the off-season program and allow 2-3 minutes of rest between sets.

In-Season Program

Schedule this as a set-rep workout one or two times per week for 15 to 25 minutes with at least one day between sessions, with one or two sets of undulating periodization with heavy (6- to 8RM), light (15- to 17RM), and moderate (10- to 12RM) loads on different days for the multi-joint core exercises (in italics). Abdominal exercises should include 20 to 30 reps per set. The lifter should rest for 2 to 3 minutes for 6- to 8RM loads; 2 minutes for 10- to 12RM loads; and one minute for 15- to 17RM loads.

Core Exercises	Injury Prevention	Replacement	Advanced
Bench press *Squat* *Seated row* Lying-on-the-floor back extensions Stiff-legged dead lift Resistive ball twisting crunches Arm curls Standing calf raises Crunches with twist Lateral raises Front raises Wrist curls and wrist extensions *Dumbbell shoulder press*	Knee extension Rotator cuff exercises	*Lat pull-down* *Narrow-grip bench press* *Leg press*	None

GYMNASTICS

Gymnastics requires control of the body through various strength and balance moves. A gymnast needs high levels of strength/power and local muscular endurance to complete movements, retain body positions, and perform winning routines. Resistance training complements the practice of gymnastics by improving strength and endurance and thus helping to prevent injury.

Off-Season Program

Schedule this as a set-rep workout three times per week for 20 to 60 minutes with at least one day between sessions, with two to four sets of 10- to 12RM. Abdominal exercises should include 20 to 30 reps per set. The lifter should rest for 2 to 3 minutes for large-muscle-group exercises and 1 to 2 minutes between sets of small-muscle-group or single-joint exercises. Periodize large-muscle-group exercises (in italics).

Core Exercises	Injury Prevention	Replacement	Advanced
Power clean *Bench press* *Squat or leg press* Shoulder front raise Knee curl Abdominal exercise Shoulder lateral raise Stiff-legged dead lift Push press Lat pull-down	Shoulder internal rotation and shoulder external rotation Wrist curl or wrist roller	Triceps extension *Incline press* Lunge *Narrow-grip bench press* Bent-over row *Overhead press*	The lifter should perform no more than 5 repetitions per set at 8- to 10RM resistances for advanced exercises. Power clean, clean pull, power snatch, or snatch pull from knee or thigh level

Pre-Season Program

Schedule this as a set-rep workout two to three times per week for 15 to 45 minutes with at least one day between sessions, with one to three sets of 8- to 10RM. Abdominal exercises should include 20 to 30 reps per set. The lifter should rest for 1 to 1.5 minutes between sets.

Core Exercises	Injury Prevention	Replacement	Advanced
Power clean or power-clean partial pull-second pull Lunge Overhead dumbbell press Stiff-legged dead lift Lat pull-down Calf raise Incline or bench press using dumbbells Front shoulder raise Abdominal exercise with twist Shoulder lateral raise	Shoulder rotator cuff exercises	Knee extension Seated row Lower-back exercise	The lifter should perform no more than 5 repetitions per set at 8- to 10RM resistances for advanced exercises. Power clean, clean pull, power snatch, or snatch pull from knee or thigh level

In-Season Program

Schedule this workout as a circuit one or two times per week for 25 to 30 minutes with at least one day between sessions, with two to three circuits of 8- to 10RM. Abdominal exercises should include 20 to 30 reps per set. The lifter should rest for 1 to 1.5 minutes between sets; reduce the rest periods after the trainee can perform three circuits.

Core Exercises	Injury Prevention	Replacement	Advanced
Push press Power clean-clean partial pull-second pull Lunge Bench press Calf raise Seated row Abdominal exercises	Shoulder rotator cuff exercises Wrist curl or wrist roller	Front squat Shoulder anterior, posterior, and lateral dumbbell raises Lat pull-down Knee curl Knee extension Narrow-grip bench press	The lifter should perform no more than 5 repetitions of power clean, push press, or power snatch exercises per set using 8- to 10RM resistances for advanced exercises. Push press Power clean, clean pull, power snatch, or snatch pull from knee or thigh level

ICE HOCKEY

Ice hockey is a high-speed, anaerobic sport that requires skating and stick-handling ability for successful performance. As a contact sport, its physical demands are great. Resistance training can provide the strength/power and high-intensity local muscular endurance of the legs, back, and arms needed for successful hockey performance and can help prevent injuries of the ankles, knees, back, and shoulders. Resistance exercise can also help improve speed and control of movement during skating. Adequate local muscular endurance of the legs and back is especially important for young hockey players who are trying to improve their toleration of long periods of play on the ice. In addition, core-stability exercises can also be a part of a supplemental training program.

Off-Season Program

Schedule this as a set-rep workout three times per week for 55 to 60 minutes with at least one day between sessions, with three sets of 10- to 12RM. Abdominal exercises should include 20 to 30 reps per set. The lifter should rest for 1 to 1.5 minutes between sets.

Core Exercises	Injury Prevention	Replacement	Advanced
Bench press Squat or leg press Overhead press Knee curl Seated row Calf raise Arm curl Abdominal exercise	Knee extension	Dead lift Reverse arm curl Lunge Lat pull-down Wrist roller or wrist curl Reverse wrist curl	The lifter should perform no more than 5 repetitions per set using 8- to 10RM resistances for advanced exercises. Power clean, clean pull, power snatch, or snatch pull from knee or thigh level

Pre-Season Program

Schedule this workout as a set-rep (near the end of the phase a circuit format can be used) three times per week for 25 to 36 minutes with at least one day between sessions, with three sets of 8- to 10RM. Abdominal exercises should include 20 to 30 reps per set. The lifter should rest for 1 to 1.5 minutes between sets.

Core Exercises	Injury Prevention	Replacement	Advanced
Lunge Reverse arm curl Dead lift Knee curl Abdominal exercises with twists Calf raise	Wrist curl or roller Shoulder rotator cuff exercises	Arm curl Bent-over row Overhead press Dumbbell bench press Lower-back exercise Reverse wrist curl	The lifter should perform no more than 5 repetitions per set using 8- to 10RM resistances for advanced exercises. Power clean, clean pull, power snatch, or snatch pull from knee or thigh level

In-Season Program

Schedule this workout as a circuit one or two times per week for 15 to 30 minutes with at least one day separating the sessions, with two circuits of 8- to 10RM. Abdominal exercises should include 20 to 30 reps per set. The lifter should rest for 1 minute; for variation use rest periods of 0.5, 1, and 1.5 minutes between sets and exercises in the circuit.

Core Exercises	Injury Prevention	Replacement	Advanced
Overhead press Single-leg knee extension Dumbbell fly Single-leg knee curl Bench press Calf raise Abdominal exercise Seated row	Wrist curl or roller Shoulder rotator cuff exercises	Lower-back exercise Lunge Incline bench press Reverse wrist curl	The lifter should perform no more than 5 repetitions per set using 8- to 10RM resistances for advanced exercises. Power clean, clean pull, power snatch, or snatch pull from the knee or thigh level

ROWING

The sport of rowing can take place in a variety of different competitions, including one-person boats to multiple-person boats. The sport demands both power and, at the same time, endurance, making training for this sport a challenge. The distances can also vary depending on the event. A resistance-training program should address three aspects: strength, power, and local muscular endurance.

Off-Season Program

Schedule this as a set-rep workout three times per week for 35 to 45 minutes with at least one day separating sessions, with two to three sets of nonlinear periodization or a mix of 8- to 10RM, 6- to 8RM, and 12- to 15RM. Abdominal exercises should include 20 to 25 reps per set, adding twisting movement in the crunch variations used. The lifter should rest for 2 to 3 minutes between sets of large-muscle-group exercises and 1 to 2 minutes between single-joint exercises.

Monday and Friday	Wednesday	Injury Prevention	Replacement	Advanced
Close-stance, high-bar squats Bench press Lying-on-the-floor back extension Leg press Triceps extension arm curl Stiff-legged dead lifts Seated row Shoulder front raise Shoulder lateral raise Bent-over row Abdominal exercises	Power clean-clean partial pull-second pull Dumbbell incline bench press Crunches with twist Reverse arm curls Upright rows Stiff-legged dead lifts Medicine ball: side toss, chest press	Shoulder dumbbell press Wrist rollers Lower-back machine	Wrist curls or wrist roller Knee curl Overhead barbell press Power clean-clean high pull	These exercises can be periodized (strength/power) for resistance in this phase. Cleans and pulls can be performed from the knee or thigh level. Perform pulls and cleans with 3-5 repetitions using 10- to 12RM loading for maximal acceleration.

Pre-Season Program

Schedule this as a circuit workout two to three times per week for 30 to 45 minutes with at least one day separating sessions, starting the lifter with one circuit and progressing up to two circuits at 12- to 15RM. Abdominal exercises should include 20 to 30 reps per set. The lifter should rest for 1 to 1.5 minutes between sets; reduce the rest periods once the trainee can perform three circuits.

Core Exercises	Injury Prevention	Replacement	Advanced
Close-stance, high-bar squats Bench press Lying-on-the-floor back extension Dumbbell lunges Triceps extension with biceps arm curl Power clean-clean partial pull-second pull Stiff-legged dead lifts Seated row Shoulder front raise Shoulder lateral raise Bent-over row Crunches Dumbbell incline bench press Crunches with twist Reverse arm curls Upright row Knee curl	Hand-grip squeeze Wrist rollers	Lat pull-down Lunges Seated leg curls	Perform only 6 repetitions with the light load in the pulls and clean exercises.

In-Season Program

Schedule this as a set-rep workout one or two times per week for 30 to 45 minutes with at least one day separating sessions, with two to three sets of 8- to 10RM. Abdominal exercises should include 20 to 30 reps per set with twisting movements. The lifter should rest for 2 to 3 minutes between sets of large-muscle-group exercises and 1 to 2 minutes between single-joint exercises. This program can also use the undulating periodization model for multi-joint, large-muscle-group exercises (in italics).

Core Exercises	Injury Prevention	Replacement	Advanced
Power clean Close-stance, high-bar squats *Bench press* Lying-on-the-floor back extension *Leg press* Triceps extensions with arm curl *Stiff-legged dead lift* *Seated row* Shoulder front raise Shoulder lateral raise Bent-over row Abdominal crunches Power clean	Wrist curls Medicine-ball push-ups	*Incline dumbbell bench press* Lunges Wrist exercises Power clean-clean high pull *Push press*	The trainee performs no more than 5 repetitions per set using 8- to 10RM resistances for advanced exercises. Advanced exercise should be performed at the beginning of the training session. Pulls and cleans can also be done from the knee or thigh levels.

RUGBY

Rugby is a very popular game played by men and women of all ages in more than 100 countries. The basic game involves 15 players but using 7 on a side in a tournament is also popular. The object of the game is to score as many points as possible by carrying, passing, kicking, or grounding an oval ball into the scoring zone at the far end of the field, which is called the in-goal area. Grounding the ball, which must be done with downward pressure, results in a try (worth 5 points). After a try, a conversion may be attempted by a place kick or a drop kick. If the ball passes over the bar and between the goalposts, the conversion is good and results in 2 additional points. Points may also be scored from a drop kick in a general play, which is worth 3 points. In addition, many youth leagues use a form of "touch" rugby to eliminate some of the contact in the sport. Core stability is crucial for all players and each position requires a high level of lower-body strength and power.

Off-Season Program

Schedule this as a set-rep workout three times per week for 35 to 45 minutes with two to three sets on Monday and Friday and one to two sets on Wednesday of nonlinear periodized exercises or a mix of 8- to10RM, 6- to 8RM, and 12- to 15RM. Abdominal exercises should include 20 to 25 reps per set, adding twisting movements in the sit-up variations used. The lifter should rest for 2 to 3 minutes between sets for large-muscle-group exercises and 1 to 2 minutes between sets of single-joint exercises.

Monday and Friday	Wednesday	Injury Prevention	Replacement	Advanced
Squat	Dead lift	Shoulder dumbbell press	Wrist curls or hammer exercise	These exercises can be periodized with the nonlinear method for resistance in this phase.
Bench press	Shrugs	Wrist rolls	Shoulder lateral raises	
Power clean-clean partial pull-second pull	Triceps push-down	Lower-back machine	Front squats	
Bent-over rows	Crunches with twist		Dumbbell bench press	Cleans and pulls can be performed from the knee or thigh level at the beginning of the workout.
Lying-on-the-floor back extension	Wrist rollers		Leg press	
Lateral lunge	Incline bench press		Knee curl	
Stiff-legged dead lifts	Reverse curls		Overhead dumbbell press	
Seated row	Dumbbell front lateral raises		Power clean-clean high pull	Perform pulls and cleans with 3-5 repetitions using 6- to 8RM loading for maximal acceleration.
Crunches with twist	Push press			
	Arm curls/ reverse curl			
	Dumbbell fly			
	Standing calf raises			

Pre-Season Program

Schedule this as a set-rep workout two to three times per week for 30 to 45 minutes with at least one day separating sessions, with two to three sets of 8- to 10RM. Abdominal exercises should include 20 to 30 reps per set. The lifter should rest for 1 to 2 minutes between sets.

Core Exercises	Injury Prevention	Replacement	Advanced
Squat Power clean-clean high pull Bench press Stiff-legged dead lift Seated dumbbell press Lat pull-down Abdominal exercises with twists and side raises Standing calf raises Push press Arm curls Lying-on-the-floor back extension	Hand-grip exercise Wrist rollers Rotator cuff exercises	Lunges Seated calf raises Seated leg curls Incline bench press Snatch exercise Leg press	Perform only 6 repetitions with the light load in the snatch and clean exercises.

In-Season Program

Schedule this as a set-rep workout one or two times per week for 30 to 45 minutes with at least one day separating sessions, with two to three sets of 8- to 10RM. Abdominal exercises should include 20 to 30 reps per set with twisting movements. The lifter should rest for 2 to 3 minutes between sets of large-muscle-group exercises and 1 to 2 minutes between sets of single-joint exercises. This program can also use the undulating periodization model for multi-joint, large-muscle-group exercises (in italics).

Core Exercises	Injury Prevention	Replacement	Advanced
Squat Power clean-clean partial pull-second pull *Bench press* Lying-on-the-floor back extension Lunges Triceps extensions with biceps curl Upright row *Stiff-legged dead lift* *Seated row* Shoulder front raise Shoulder lateral raise Arm curls Crunch with twist	Wrist curls Arm curl	*Incline dumbbell bench press* Lunges Wrist exercises Power clean-clean high pull *Push press*	The trainee performs no more than 5 repetitions per set using 8- to 10RM resistances for advanced exercises. Snatch, clean, and pull exercises can be done from the knee or thigh levels.

SKATEBOARDING

Skateboarding has become one of the most popular activities and is part of the X Games. Types include street skating (on streets, curbs, benches, handrails, and other elements of urban and suburban landscapes), vert skating (on ramps and other vertical structures specifically designed for skating), half-pipe (a U-shaped ramp of any size, usually with a flat section in the middle), and vert ramp (a half-pipe, usually at least 8 feet tall, with steep sides that are perfectly vertical near the top).

With the many types of tricks that have been fashioned over the years, this sport requires balance, skill, coordination, and strength. There are five basic stance positions; normal (which can be either regular or goofy), fakie, switch, and nollie. Most athletes in this sport consider their "normal" stance to be regular, meaning the left foot is forward, or goofy, where the right foot is forward.

The following are some of the terms for tricks: air (riding with all four wheels off the ground), backside (when a trick or turn is executed with the skater's back facing the ramp or obstacle), and fakie (skating backward, which is not to be confused with "switch stance," which is switching to the opposite foot from your normal stance). Caballerial (a 360-degree turn performed on a ramp while riding fakie, named after skater Steve Caballero), grind (scraping one or both axles on a curb, railing, or other surface); and carve (to skate in a long, curving arc). These are just a few of the skills that have made their way into a complex sport where the ability to control one's body is paramount to success. This sport can benefit from a simple program designed to prevent injury, improve neuromuscular function, and improve body control. Using an undulating program, a skater can train year-round for this activity.

Schedule this as a set-rep workout three times per week for 35 to 45 minutes with at least one day separating sessions, with two to three sets of nonlinear periodization for the exercises in italics and always using 8- to 10RM for the other exercises or a mix of 8- to 10RM, 6- to 8RM, and 12- to 15RM. Abdominal exercises should include 20 to 25 reps per set, including twisting movements in the variations used. The lifter should rest for 2 to 3 minutes for large-muscle-group exercises (in italics).

Monday and Friday	Wednesday	Injury Prevention	Replacement	Advanced
Squat	*Lunges*	Shoulder dumbbell press	*Front squats*	These exercises can be periodized for resistance in this phase. Snatch, clean, and pull exercises can be performed from the knee or thigh level. Perform these exercises with 3-5 repetitions using 6- to 8RM loading for maximal acceleration.
Bench press	Arm curls/triceps push-down (super set)	Wrist rolls, wrist curls	Power clean-high pull	
Lying-on-the-floor back extension		Lower-back machine	Dumbbell bench press	
Leg press	Sit-ups (twisting)		Knee curl	
Stiff-legged dead lifts	Abdominal/ adductor exercise		*Push press*	
Seated row	Dumbbell front lateral raises			
Crunches with twist	*Upright rows*			
	Triceps cable press-down			
	Lunges			
	Flys			

SNOWBOARDING

Snowboarding is enjoyed by both recreational and competitive athletes. Snowboarders compete in slalom and half-pipe events. In the half-pipe, like skateboarders, they perform various tricks such as an "alley oop" or an "air to fakie." The snowboarder can ride on the board in the conventional manner, with the right foot in front, or in a stance called "goofy," with the left foot in front. The sport involves a great deal of athleticism with balance and coordination of moves in both the downhill runs and the tricks. The competitive snowboarder tries to remain in the center of the board (the "sweet spot") during all turns. Snowboarders are especially prone to anterior cruciate ligament (ACL) injuries due to the twists, fixed-foot positions, and landing dynamics of the sport; therefore sport technique and injury prevention for this area of the body are necessary for optimal training.

Off-Season Program

The exercises are performed in the order listed. The lifter should vary between workout protocols 1 and 2 and supplement the training program with balance exercises. Schedule this as a set-rep workout two to three times per week for 30 to 45 minutes with at least one day between sessions. Start the lifter with one set and progress to three sets of 10- to 12RM, using undulating variation for major muscle groups (exercises in italics). Abdominal exercises should include 20 to 30 reps per set. The lifter should rest for 2 to 3 minutes between sets. For jumping exercises use six sets of 2 to 3 repetitions for maximal power and three sets of 10 to 12 reps for development of endurance.

Adequate rest should be allowed between sets and exercises in workout 2 to optimize maximal power. If shorter rest periods are used, careful supervision is needed so that form in the whole-body exercises and landings is not lost. Landing in the proper crouched position after a jump is needed in order to limit stress on ACL positioning. Hamstring strength is especially important for girls.

Workout Protocol 1	Supplemental	Workout Protocol 2	Injury Prevention	Replacement	Advanced
Squats	Balance exercises	*Power clean*	Knee extension	One-quarter squats	
Knee extension	Elbow bridge	*Push press*	Wrist curls and wrist extensions	Lunge	
Leg curl	Push-up and hold	Lunges	Landing exercises and other jump and landing plyometrics	Seated row	
Bench press	Abdominal crunches on resistive ball	Standing long jumps		Lying on the floor back extension	
Dumbbell tricep extensions	Dumbbell bench press on resistive ball	Tuck jumps and landings (jump in the air as high as you can trying to bring your knees to your chest)	Calf raises in various foot positions		
Back extension	Standing stability board practice	Depth jumps	Dead lift		
Flys		Stiff-legged dead lift			
Preacher curl					
Calf raise					
Arm curls					
Abdominal exercises					

Pre-Season Program

Schedule this as a circuit workout two times per week for 20 to 30 minutes with at least one day between sessions, with two to three circuits of 10- to 12RM. Abdominal exercises should include 20 to 30 reps per set. The lifter should rest for 1 to 2 minutes between exercises. Include twisting abdominal and lower-back exercises in the program; dumbbells may be used whenever possible, and plyometrics and jumps can be done for 2 to 3 repetitions for maximal power and 10 to 12 reps for power-endurance development.

Core Exercises	Injury Prevention	Replacement	Advanced
Power clean-clean partial pull-second pull Lunge Knee curl Bent-over row Calf raises Stiff-legged dead lift Lying-on-the-floor back extension Abdominal exercises	Knee extension Good morning exercise Front squats	Lat pull-down Seated row Arm curls Overhead press	The trainee performs no more than 5 repetitions per set using 8- to 10RM resistances for advanced exercises. Pulls and cleans can be done from the knee or thigh levels.

In-Season Program

Schedule this as a circuit workout one or two times per week for 15 to 25 minutes with at least one day separating sessions, starting the lifter with one set and progressing up to three sets of 8- to 15RM. Abdominal exercises should include 20 to 30 reps per set. The lifter should rest for .5 to 1 minute between exercises. Include plyometric jumping and landing drills and twisting abdominal exercises in the program; dumbbells may be used with the exercises whenever possible.

Core Exercises	Injury Prevention	Replacement	Advanced
Squat Bench press Calf raises with different toe positions Push press Knee curl Bent-over row Abdominal exercise Arm curls Seated rows	Knee extension	Lat pull-down Narrow-grip bench press	None

SOCCER

Soccer presents a unique set of physical demands for the young athlete: cardiovascular endurance, sprint speed, ball-handling ability, and physical power to kick the ball for passing or shots on goal. Younger players must develop leg strength to perform soccer skills and improve performance; neck strength is also vital for absorbing and tolerating the forces involved with heading the ball. Resistance training can contribute to improved leg, neck, and total-body strength/power of the young soccer player. Furthermore, it can improve muscle and connective-tissue strength, which helps prevent injury. Youth soccer has one of the highest injury frequencies of any sport; being ready to take on the rigors of the game is vital to safe, effective play and competition. A total conditioning program, including resistance exercise, will help the young soccer player perform better and decrease injuries.

Off-Season Program

Schedule this as a circuit workout three times per week for 25 to 45 minutes with at least one day separating sessions, with two to three circuits of 12- to 15RM. Abdominal exercises should include 20 to 30 reps per set. The lifter should rest for 1 to 2 minutes between exercises.

Core Exercises	Injury Prevention	Replacement	Advanced
Back squat or leg press Bench press Knee curl Lat pull-down Abdominal exercise with twist Calf raise	Knee extension Neck exercise	Front squat Lunge Overhead press	The lifter should perform no more than 5 repetitions per set using 8- to 10RM resistances for advanced exercises. If an advanced exercise is used, it should be performed at the beginning of the training session. Clean pull and snatch pull from knee level

Pre-Season Program

Schedule this as a set-rep or circuit workout three times per week for 25 to 40 minutes with at least one day between sessions, with two to three circuits of 8- to 10RM. Abdominal exercises should include 20 to 30 reps per set. The lifter should rest for 1 to 1.5 minutes between exercises.

Core Exercises	Injury Prevention	Replacement	Advanced
Lunge Seated row Knee curl Dumbbell shoulder press Neck exercise Abdominal exercise with twist	Calf raise Knee extension	Dumbbell incline bench press Dumbbell bench press Front or back squat	The lifter should perform no more than 5 repetitions per set using 8- to 10RM resistances for advanced exercises. If an advanced exercise is used, it should be performed at the beginning of the training session. Clean pull or snatch pull from knee or thigh level.

In-Season Program

Schedule this as a circuit workout one or two times per week for 20 to 35 minutes with at least one day between sessions, with two to three circuits of 8- to 10RM. Abdominal exercises should include 20 to 30 reps per set. The lifter should rest for 1 minute between exercises.

Core Exercises	Injury Prevention	Replacement	Advanced
Lunge Dumbbell shoulder press Knee curl Bent-over row Calf raise Neck exercises Abdominal exercise	Knee extension	Bench press Narrow-grip bench press Incline bench press Dumbbell fly Arm curl	The lifter should perform no more than 5 repetitions per set using 8- to 10RM resistances for advanced exercises. If an advanced exercise is used, it should be performed at the beginning of the training session. Clean pull or snatch pull from knee or thigh level

SWIMMING

The power of the upper body—the chest, back of the arm, front of the arm, shoulder, and upper back—has a significant effect on swimming performance. In addition, during the crawl, backstroke, and fly, the legs supply some propulsive force through knee and hip flexion and extension. During the breaststroke, hip adduction and abduction are also important. Resistance training can help prevent the shoulder pain commonly referred to as swimmer's shoulder. Injury prevention for the shoulder is very important for swimmers, even for divers. A properly designed resistance program can improve swimming performance and aid in injury prevention.

The exercises presented are for swimming in general; you should modify them to meet the specific needs of a particular athlete. For example, for a child who swims the breast-stroke, add hip adduction and abduction exercises to the program. For a distance swimmer, keep the number of repetitions per set in the 12- to 15RM range during the pre-season and in-season programs. You can also reduce rest periods for distance swimmers in the pre-season and in-season training sessions to 1 minute or less, so that the body can develop and increase toleration to high-intensity exercise. For an in-season program, exercises can be performed in a circuit fashion to save time.

Off-Season Program

Schedule this as a set-rep workout three times per week for 30 to 50 minutes with at least one day between sessions, with three sets of 12- to 15RM. Abdominal exercises should include 20 to 30 reps per set. The lifter should rest for 2 minutes between sets.

Core Exercises	Injury Prevention	Replacement	Advanced
Bench press Back squat or leg press Lat pull-down Knee curl Shoulder lateral raise Seated row Abdominal exercise	Shoulder rotator cuff exercises	Dip Knee extension Elbow curl Pullover	The lifter should perform no more than 5 repetitions per set using 8- to 10RM resistances for advanced exercises. If an advanced exercise is used, it should be performed at the beginning of the training session. Power clean or clean pull from knee or thigh level (especially for sprinters)

Pre-Season Program

Schedule this as a circuit workout two to three times per week for 30 to 45 minutes with at least one day separating sessions, with three circuits of 8- to 10RM. Abdominal exercises should include 20 to 30 reps per set. The lifter should rest for 1 minute between circuits.

Core Exercises	Injury Prevention	Replacement	Advanced
Lat pull-down Back squat or leg press Seated row Knee curl Dumbbell fly Knee extension Arm curl Abdominal exercise	Shoulder side raise Shoulder front raise Shoulder rotator cuff exercises	Dip Incline dumbbell press	The lifter should perform no more than 5 repetitions per set using 8- to 10RM resistances for advanced exercises. If an advanced exercise is used, it should be performed at the beginning of the training session. Power clean, clean pull, or snatch pull from knee or thigh level

In-Season Program

Schedule this as a circuit workout one or two times per week for 25 to 40 minutes with at least one day between sessions, with two to three circuits of 8- to 10RM. Abdominal exercises should include 20 to 30 reps per set. The lifter should rest for .5 to 1 minute between exercises.

Core Exercises	Injury Prevention	Replacement	Advanced
Lat pull-down Knee extension Shoulder internal rotation and shoulder external rotation Knee curl Shoulder lateral raise Abdominal exercise Shoulder front raise Seated row Shoulder posterior raise	Shoulder rotator cuff exercises	Bench press Narrow-grip bench press Lunge Back squat or leg press	The lifter should perform no more than 5 repetitions per set using 8- to 10RM resistances for advanced exercises. If an advanced exercise is used, it should be performed at the beginning of the training session. Power clean, clean pull, or snatch pull from knee or thigh level

TENNIS

The sport of tennis has become a "power" game with the speed of the game increasing each year. Injury prevention is needed for the rotator cuff muscles of the shoulder along with adequate strength and endurance of the lower-back and abdominal muscles. Research has shown that strength training can improve the ball velocities in all tennis strokes. Since tennis is a racquet sport, one side of the body can dominate in its development. Therefore, resistance training can balance out potential strength and size asymmetries between sides of the body. In addition, injury prevention is vital with the long seasons and competitive demands of the sport. Care should be taken to periodize the training program because doing so has been found to be superior to nonperiodized programs. Supplemental conditioning related to speed, agility, and power (e.g., plyometrics and medicine-ball exercises) are important aspects of a total training program for tennis.

Off-Season Program

The exercises are performed in the order listed. Italics indicate exercises that can be periodized (strength/power or undulating model) in this phase. The Wednesday workout should be done in a circuit fashion in which a set of 10 repetitions is performed with 2 minutes of rest or less between exercises. Progressing up to three circuits allows for greater endurance. A hang pull is used to simulate the need for whole-body lifting under conditions of great fatigue in a match.

Schedule this as a set-rep workout two to three times per week for 35 to 45 minutes with at least one day separating sessions, with two to three sets of non-linear periodization resistance by mixing 6- to 8RM, 8- to 10RM, and 12- to 15RM resistances. Abdominal exercises should include 20 to 25 reps per set; be sure to add twisting movements in the sit-up variations used. The lifter should rest for 2 to 3 minutes between sets of large-muscle-group exercises and 1 to 2 minutes between sets of single-joint exercises.

Monday and Friday	Wednesday	Injury Prevention	Replacement	Advanced
Squat *Bench press* Single-leg knee curls *Dead lift* Seated dumbbell overhead press Standing calf raises Arm curls *Lat pull-down* *Seated row* Internal/external rotation Wrist curls Crunches with and without twists	Squat jumps/ Power clean-clean partial pull-second pull *Incline bench press* Dumbbell fly Lunges Reverse arm curls Upright row Stiff-legged dead lift	Knee extension Wrist rollers Lower-back machine Shoulder front raises Shoulder lateral raises	Wrist curls or wrist roller Leg press Knee curl Overhead press Power clean-clean high pull	These exercises can be periodized (strength/power) for resistance in this phase. Snatch, clean, and pull exercises can be performed from the knee or thigh level. Perform these exercises with 3-5 repetitions using 10- to 12RM loading for maximal acceleration in the early part of the workout.

Pre-Season Program

Schedule this as a circuit workout two to three times per week for 30 to 45 minutes with at least one day separating sessions, starting the lifter with one circuit and progressing up to three circuits of 8- to 10RM. Abdominal exercises should include 20 to 30 reps per set. The lifter should rest for 1 to 1.5 minutes between exercises; reduce the rest periods after the trainee can perform three circuits.

Core Exercises	Injury Prevention	Replacement	Advanced
Front squats Dumbbell fly Stiff-legged dead lift Overhead dumbbell press Twisting sit-ups Seated rows Calf raises Arm curls Rotator cuff exercises Shoulder lateral raises Lower-back machine Dumbbell bench press	Push-ups on medicine ball with one arm on ground, both arms on ball, alternating Hand-grip exercises Wrist rollers	Lat pull-down Wrist roller or wrist curl Seated leg curls	None

In-Season Program

Schedule this as a set-rep workout one to two times per week for 30 to 45 minutes with at least one day separating sessions, with two to three sets of 12- to 15RM. Abdominal exercises should include 20 to 30 reps per set with twisting movements. The lifter should rest for 2 minutes between sets (2 to 3 minutes for large-muscle group exercises). The undulating periodized model can also be used for multi-joint, large-muscle-group exercises (in italics).

Core Exercises	Injury Prevention	Replacement	Advanced
Back squat or leg press Dumbbell overhead press Power clean-clean partial pull-second pull *Bench press* *Lat pull-down* *Stiff-legged dead lift* Rotator cuff exercises *Seated rows* Single knee extension (30-degree arcs) Reverse arm curl Calf raises Abdominal or twisting abdominal exercise	Wrist curls Medicine-ball push-ups	Incline dumbbell bench press *Lunges* Wrist exercises Power clean-clean high pull *Push press*	The trainee performs no more than 5 repetitions per set using 8- to 10RM resistances for advanced exercises. If an advanced exercise is used, it should be performed at the beginning of the training session. Pulls and cleans can be done from the knee or thigh levels.

TRACK AND FIELD—JUMPS

The high jump, long jump, and pole vault each can be divided into two phases: the approach run and the actual jump or vault. Speed during the approach run is more important for the long jump and pole vault than for the high jump, but all events depend on leg strength for the jump or vault. Pole vaulters also need upper-body strength. The program presented stresses leg strength and power for performance of these events. In addition, upper-body exercises are included for the pole vaulter.

Off-Season Program

Schedule this as a set-rep workout three times per week for 40 to 60 minutes with at least one day separating sessions, with three sets of 10- to 12RM. Abdominal exercises should include 20 to 30 reps per set. The lifter should rest for 2 minutes between sets. Exercises in italics can be periodized (strength and power, or undulating) in this phase.

Core Exercises	Injury Prevention	Replacement	Advanced
Bench press *Back squat or leg press* Upright row Knee curl *Overhead press* Calf raise Arm curl	Knee extension	*Seated row* *Incline press* Triceps extension (for pole vaulters) Lunge	The lifter should perform no more than 5 repetitions per set using 8- to 10RM resistances for advanced exercises. If an advanced exercise is used, it should be performed at the beginning of the training session. Clean or snatch pulls from knee or thigh level

Pre-Season Program

Schedule this as a set-rep workout three times per week for 20 to 50 minutes with at least one day separating sessions, with one to three sets of 8- to 10RM. Abdominal exercises should include 20 to 30 reps per set. The lifter should rest for 2 minutes between sets.

Core Exercises	Injury Prevention	Replacement	Advanced
Dumbbell bench press Lunge Upright rowing Knee curl Overhead press Calf raise Pull-up or lat pull-down Abdominal exercise	Knee extension	Dumbbell incline press Seated row Arm curl Back squat	The lifter should perform no more than 5 repetitions per set using 8- to 10RM resistances for advanced exercises. If an advanced exercise is used, it should be performed at the beginning of the training session. Power snatch or snatch pull from knee or thigh level

In-Season Program

Schedule this as a set-rep workout one or two times per week for 30 to 50 minutes with at least one day separating sessions, with two to three sets of 7- to 9RM. Abdominal exercises should include 20 to 30 reps per set. The lifter should rest for 1.5 to 2 minutes between sets.

Core Exercises	Injury Prevention	Replacement	Advanced
Overhead press Front or back squat or leg press Pull-up or lat pull-down (especially for pole vaulters) Knee curl Seated row Calf raise Abdominal exercise with twist	Knee extension	Narrow-grip bench press Dead lift Upright row	The lifter should perform no more than 5 repetitions per set using 8- to 10RM resistances for advanced exercises. If an advanced exercise is used, it should be performed at the beginning of the training session. Power snatch or snatch pull from knee or thigh level

TRACK AND FIELD— SHOT PUT AND DISCUS

Because throws are short-term, high-powered events, increases in strength and power will improve an athlete's performance in these events. However, maximal bench-press ability does not have as strong a relationship to performance as power-oriented lifts, such as the power clean and snatch, do. Therefore, you should include these exercises in the resistance program as the child gets older and advances in these events, and you should de-emphasize the bench press. Overhead lifts should also be part of the program for these events. Emphasize technique and carefully monitor resistance for these exercises. These events are what the classic linear periodization models of training were designed for.

Off-Season Program

Schedule this as a set-rep workout three times per week for 40 to 60 minutes with at least one day separating sessions, with three sets of 10- to 12RM. Abdominal exercises should include 20 to 30 reps per set. The lifter should rest for 2 to 3 minutes between sets. Exercises in italics should be periodized (strength and power model) in this phase.

Core Exercises	Injury Prevention	Replacement	Advanced
Bench press *Back squat or leg press* *Overhead press* Knee curl *Lat pull-down* Calf raise Dumbbell fly Abdominal exercise	Wrist curl Wrist roller Shoulder rotator cuff exercises	Knee extension Lower-back exercise Triceps extension Pullover *Lunge* Seated row	The lifter should perform no more than 5 repetitions using 8- to 10RM resistances for advanced exercises. If an advanced exercise is, used, it should be performed at the beginning of the training session. Power clean pull from knee to thigh level

Pre-Season Program

Schedule this as a set-rep workout three times per week for 45 to 60 minutes with at least one day separating sessions, with three sets of 8RM. Abdominal exercises should include 20 to 30 reps per set. The lifter should rest for 1.5 to 3 minutes between sets. Exercises in italics can be periodized (strength and power model) in this phase.

Core Exercises	Injury Prevention	Replacement	Advanced
Front squat *Dumbbell press* *Dead lift* Dumbbell incline press Knee curl Calf raise Abdominal exercise with twist	Wrist curl Wrist roller Shoulder internal rotation and shoulder external rotation	*Lunge* Knee extension Arm curl *Bench press* *Narrow-grip bench press* *Back squat* *Leg press*	The lifter should perform no more than 5 repetitions per set using 8- to 10RM resistances for advanced exercises. If an advanced exercise is used, it should be performed at the beginning of the training session. Power clean and power snatch Clean and snatch pulls from floor, knee, or thigh level

In-Season Program

Schedule this as a set-rep workout one or two times per week for 35 to 60 minutes with at least one day separating sessions, with two to three sets of 6- to 8RM. Abdominal exercises should include 20 to 30 reps per set. The lifter should rest for 1.5 to 3 minutes between sets. Technique practice in throwing skills is necessary in order to successfully transfer strength and power gains to the events. In-season programs should stress maintenance of total-body power development and technique enhancement.

Core Exercises	Injury Prevention	Replacement	Advanced
Back or front squat Incline press Dead lift Dumbbell fly Knee curl Abdominal exercise	Wrist curl Wrist roller Shoulder internal rotation and shoulder external rotation	Leg press Bench press Dumbbell incline press Knee extension Calf raise Lunge	The lifter should perform no more than 5 repetitions per set using 8- to 10RM resistances for advanced exercises. If an advanced exercise is used, it should be performed at the beginning of the training session. Power snatch and power clean from the floor, knee, and thigh levels Snatch pull and clean pull from the floor, knee, or thigh level

TRACK—SPRINTS

Sprinting is a high-power-output, short-duration event (100 meters) as well as a high-power, local-muscular-endurance event (200 and 400 meters). A program for sprinting should be designed to meet the needs of a particular individual and a particular sprint event. For example, 200- and 400-meter sprinters may use shorter rest periods (30 seconds to 1 minute) between sets and exercises than 100-meter sprinters, especially during the pre-season and in-season programs. Because the 100-meter event requires higher power output than the 200- to 400-meter events, 100-meter sprinters may switch to 8RM resistances in the late pre-season.

Off-Season Program

Schedule this as a set-rep workout three times per week for 45 to 60 minutes with at least one day separating sessions, with one to three sets of 8- to 10RM. Abdominal exercises should include 20 to 30 reps per set. The lifter should rest for 1.5 to 3 minutes between sets. Exercises in italics may be periodized (strength and power, or undulating model) in this phase.

Core Exercises	Injury Prevention	Replacement	Advanced
Back squat or leg press *Bench press* Knee curl Upright row Knee extension *Lat pull-down* Calf raise Abdominal exercise	None	*Incline press* Lower-back exercise *Lunge*	The lifter should perform no more than 5 repetitions per set using 8- to 10RM resistances for advanced exercises. If an advanced exercise is used, it should be performed at the beginning of the training session. Power clean or clean pull from knee or thigh level

Pre-Season Program

Schedule this as a circuit for 200- and 400-meter sprinters and as a set-rep workout for 100-meter sprinters three times per week for 35 to 55 minutes with at least one day separating sessions, with one to three sets or circuits of 10- to 12RM for 200- and 400-meter sprinters and up to 6RM for 100-meter sprinters. Abdominal exercises should include 20 to 30 reps per set. The lifter should rest between exercises or sets for 0.5 seconds to 1 minute for 200- and 400-meter sprinters and 2 to 3 minutes for 100-meter sprinters.

Core Exercises	Injury Prevention	Replacement	Advanced
Lunge Dumbbell bench press or dumbbell incline press Single-leg knee curl Single-leg knee extension Calf raise Abdominal exercise with twist	None	Seated row Back squat or leg press Lat pull-down Dead lift	The lifter should perform no more than 5 repetitions per set using 8- to 10RM resistances for advanced exercises. If an advanced exercise is used, it should be performed at the beginning of the training session. Power clean or power snatch from floor, knee, or thigh level. Clean pull or snatch pull from floor, knee, or thigh level

In-Season Program

Schedule this as a set-rep or circuit workout one or two times per week for 20 to 45 minutes with at least one day separating sessions, with two to three sets or circuits of 10- to 12RM for 200- and 400-meter sprinters and 8RM for 100-meter sprinters. Abdominal exercises should include 20 to 30 reps per set. The lifter should rest between exercises for 30 seconds to 1 minute for 200- and 400-meter sprinters and 1 to 2 minutes for 100-meter sprinters and for sprints of less than 100 meters.

Core Exercises	Injury Prevention	Replacement	Advanced
Dumbbell bench press or dumbbell incline press Lunge Seated row or dumbbell bent-over row Calf raise Abdominal exercise with a twist Knee curl	Knee extension	Lat pull-down Shoulder shrug Dumbbell arm curl Dumbbell fly Front or back squat	The lifter should perform no more than 5 repetitions per set using 8- to 10RM resistances for advanced exercises. If an advanced exercise is used, it should be performed at the beginning of the training session. Clean pull and snatch pull from knee or thigh level

VOLLEYBALL

In volleyball, blocking, vertical jumping, passing (bumping), and spiking are skills crucial to success. By increasing leg and total-body strength and power, an athlete can enhance vertical jumping ability. Shoulder rotator cuff strength and upper-body and abdominal development are vital for spiking and serving. In addition, increased shoulder, leg, and hip strength will help prevent injury. Unilateral leg strength is vital for skills predominantly involving one leg. Resistance exercise can provide positive changes in these physical capabilities.

Off-Season Program

Schedule this as a set-rep workout three times per week for 45 to 60 minutes with at least one day separating sessions, with two to three sets of 10- to 12RM. Abdominal exercises should include 20 to 30 reps per set. The player should rest for 1 to 1.5 minutes between sets. Exercises in italics can be periodized (undulating model) in this phase.

Core Exercises	Injury Prevention	Replacement	Advanced
Back squat or leg press *Overhead press* *Dumbbell bench press or dumbbell incline press* Knee curl *Lat pull-down* Calf raise Abdominal exercise with twist	Shoulder internal rotation and shoulder external rotation Shoulder rotator cuff exercises	Knee extension Seated row Arm curl Front squat	The lifter should perform no more than 5 repetitions per set using 8- to 10RM resistances for advanced exercises. If an advanced exercise is used, it should be performed at the beginning of the training session. Power clean and clean pull from knee or thigh level

Pre-Season Program

Schedule this as a circuit workout three times per week for 25 to 45 minutes with at least one day separating sessions, with two to three circuits of 8- to 10RM. Abdominal exercises should include 20 to 30 reps per set. The lifter should rest for 1 to 2 minutes between circuits. Exercises in italics can be periodized (undulating model) in this phase.

Core Exercises	Injury Prevention	Replacement	Advanced
Lunge *Overhead press* Shoulder anterior raise Knee curl Shoulder lateral raise Calf raise Abdominal exercise with twist	Shoulder internal rotation and shoulder external rotation Shoulder rotator cuff exercises	Reverse elbow curl Dumbbell fly Lat pull-down Leg press Knee extension	The lifter should perform no more than 5 repetitions per set using 8- to 10RM resistances for advanced exercises. If an advanced exercise is used, it should be performed at the beginning of the training session. Power clean and clean pull from the knee or thigh level. Snatch pull from mid-thigh level

In-Season Program

Schedule this as a circuit workout one or two times per week for 20 to 35 minutes with at least one day separating sessions, with two to three circuits of 8- to 10RM. Abdominal exercises should include 20 to 30 reps per set. The lifter should rest for 1 minute between exercises.

Core Exercises	Injury Prevention	Replacement	Advanced
Overhead press or push press Single-leg knee extension Seated row Single-leg knee curl Abdominal exercise with twist Calf raise	Shoulder internal rotation and shoulder external rotation Shoulder rotator cuff exercises	Bench press Shoulder lateral raise Lat pull-down Arm curl Front squat Lunge	The lifter should perform no more than 5 repetitions per set using 8- to 10RM resistances for advanced exercises. If an advanced exercise is used, it should be performed at the beginning of the training session. Power clean, clean pull, or snatch pull from the knee or thigh level

WRESTLING

The sport of wrestling has a number of different components. First, it requires great strength and power. Moves depend on the wrestler's ability to lift an opponent off the mat in takedowns and throws. Isometric strength is also needed for gripping and holding various positions and therefore upper-body strength becomes very important. All of these strength and power demands take place within a metabolic scenario of anaerobic glycolysis or lactic acid metabolism. Thus, the wrestler must learn to tolerate such metabolic conditions and be able to physiologically buffer the acid that builds up during a match from the sustained muscular activity. Lactic acid levels can rise to more than 10-15 times resting concentrations, and since injury often occurs during periods of fatigue, allowing the wrestler to adapt to this type of competitive environment is important to a successful training program. A strength-training program must then address this type of metabolic need with workouts that simulate the buildup of lactic acid. Younger wrestlers must be taught that the extreme fatigue they feel is due to the buildup of lactic acid in their muscles and that with training they will be able to better tolerate it.

Despite the nationwide emergence of new weight-loss guidelines, young wrestlers should not limit their body mass to such a degree that future growth and development are hindered. Resistance training can help them attain optimal strength, power, and endurance at a given weight; starvation weight-loss practices and using exercise only to cut weight is not recommended for the optimal maturity and growth of the wrestler over time. A recent study shows that years of abusive weight-loss practices promote chronic dehydration and abnormal fluid regulatory systems in both high school and college wrestlers who have undertaken the practice of making dramatic weight cuts prior to each match. See the National Wrestling Coaches Association Web site (www.nwcaonline.com), the American College of Sports Medicine (www.acsm.org), the NCAA (www.ncaa.org), and your high school state organization for more information. The American Medical Association, the

American Academy of Pediatrics, and the American College of Sports Medicine have published position statements regarding weight control in wrestling starting more than 25 years ago. Guidelines for weight loss and avoiding hypohydration have been in the NCAA *Sports Medicine Handbook* since 1985.

Off-Season Program

Some whole-body exercises are done at the end of the workout to prepare the body for exerting effort under conditions of fatigue, which is a very common feature of wrestling. Strict attention to exercise technique is needed in such workouts. Spotters must be especially aware of this in these types of workout designs.

Schedule this as a set-rep workout three times per week for 40 to 60 minutes with at least one day separating sessions, with three sets of periodized resistances (undulating model) for the exercises denoted in italics; other exercises should use 10- to 12RM. Abdominal exercises should include 20 to 25 reps per set. The lifter should rest for 2 to 3 minutes for heavy lifts and for 1 to 2 minutes for lighter lifts of greater than 10 repetitions.

Monday and Friday	Wednesday	Injury Prevention	Replacement	Advanced
Bench press	Power cleans	Neck exercises	Front squats	The lifter should perform no more than 5 repetitions per set using 8- to 10RM resistances for advanced exercises. If an advanced exercise is used, it should be performed at the beginning of the training session. Power clean and clean pull from knee or thigh level.
Squat	*Dumbbell incline press*	Lower-back machine exercise	Plyometrics	
Shrugs	*Lunges*	Various wrist exercises	Exercises for power development	
4-way neck exercise	Knee curls	Shoulder rotator cuff exercises	Wrist curls or wrist rollers	
Crunches	*Seated row*			
Barbell overhead press	Crunches			
Arm curls	*Lat pull-down*			
Power clean-clean partial pull-second pull	Isometric grip exercises (6-second holds)			
Stiff-legged dead lift	Standing calf raises			
	Dead lift			
	Reverse arm curls			

Pre-Season Program

Schedule this as a circuit and set-rep workout where appropriate two times per week for 30 to 45 minutes with at least one day between sessions. Two days a week for six weeks prior to the season should be dedicated to developing the wrestlers' ability to tolerate and buffer lactic acid. The other day is used to maintain strength and power capabilities. Have the wrestler do two to three circuits of 10- to 12RM with 2 minutes or less between exercises. The Wednesday workout should be done in a set-rep fashion, in which a set of 10RM is performed with 2-3 minutes of rest between sets and exercises. Abdominal exercises should include 20 to 30 reps per set. The whole-body lift using a hang pull is used to simulate whole-body lifting under conditions of great fatigue in a match.

Monday and Friday	Wednesday	Injury Prevention	Replacement	Advanced
Circuit Squat Bench press Seated row Crunches Arm curls Upright row Hang pull from the ground Crunches Knee curls	Maintenance strength and power Bench press Squat Power cleans Dead lift Knee curls Isometric grip exercises (6-second hold) Crunches	Knee extensions Barbell lunges Front squats	Lat pull-down Seated row Arm curls Overhead press	The lifter should perform no more than 5 repetitions per set using 8- to 10RM resistances for advanced exercises. If an advanced exercise is used, it should be performed at the beginning of the training session. Power clean and clean pull from knee or thigh level.

In-Season Program

Schedule this as a circuit workout one or two times per week for 30 to 35 minutes with at least one day separating sessions, depending on the match schedule. Have the lifter do one or two circuits, based on the match schedule. Resistance varies (undulating model) for exercises denoted in italics from 6- to 8RM, 10- to 12RM, and 15- to 17RM. Small-group exercises, such as wrist curls, can be started at the 10- to 12RM resistance, then range to a lighter resistance of 15- to 20RM for variation. Abdominal exercises should include 20 to 30 reps per set. The lifter should rest for 2 minutes between sets.

Workout 1	Workout 2	Injury Prevention	Replacement	Advanced
Power clean-clean partial pull-second pull *Back squat* *Bench press* *Dumbbell overhead press* *Lat pull-down* Knee curl Reverse arm curl Calf raise Abdominal (regular or twisting)	Power cleans *Leg press* Neck exercises Isometric grip/wrist exercises *Seated rows* *Stiff-legged dead lift* Arm curls Abdominal (regular or twisting)	Shoulder rotator cuff exercises Shoulder internal/external rotation	*Incline dumbbell bench press* Lunge *Dead lift*	The lifter should perform no more than 5 repetitions per set using 8- to 10RM resistances for advanced exercises. If an advanced exercise is used, it should be performed at the beginning of the training session. Power clean and clean pull from knee or thigh level.

References

CHAPTER 1

1. Vrijens, J. 1978. Muscle strength development in the pre- and post-pubescent age. *Medicine and Sport* (Basel), 11: 152-158.

2. Kraemer, W.J., A.D. Faigenbaum, J.A. Bush, and B.C. Nindl. 1999. Resistance training and youth: Enhancing muscle fitness. In *Lifestyle Medicine*, ed. J.M. Rippe, 626-637. Cambridge, MA: Blackwell Scientific.

3. National Strength and Conditioning Association Position Stand. 1996. Faigenbaum, A.D., W.J. Kraemer, B. Cahill, J. Chandler, J. Dziados, L.D. Efrink, E. Forman, M. Gaudiose, L. Micheli, M. Nitka, S. Roberts. Youth resistance training: Position statement paper and literature review. *Strength and Conditioning*, 18(6): 62-75 (update of first stand, 1985).

4. Blimkie, C.J. 1989. Age- and sex-associated variation in strength during childhood: Anthropometric, morphologic, neurologic, biomechanical, endocrinologic, genetic, and physical activity correlates. In *Perspectives in Exercise Science and Sports Medicine: Vol. 2. Youth Exercise and Sport*, ed. C. Gisolfi and D. Lamb, 99-163. Indianapolis: Benchmark Press.

5. Malina, R. and C. Bouchard. 1991. *Growth, Maturation, and Physical Activity*. Champaign, IL: Human Kinetics.

6. Faigenbaum, A., L. Zaichkowsky, W. Westcott, L. Micheli, and A. Fehlandt. 1993. The effects of a twice-per-week strength-training program on children. *Pediatric Exercise Science*, 5: 339-346.

7. Sailors, M., and K. Berg, 1987. Comparison of responses to weight training in pubescent boys and men. *Journal of Sports Medicine*, 27(1): 30-37.

8. Kraemer, W.J., and N.A. Ratamess. 2000. Physiology of resistance training: Current issues. In *Orthopaedic Physical Therapy Clinics of North America: Exercise Technologies*, ed. C. Hughes, 9:4, 467-513. Philadelphia: Saunders.

9. Maffulli, N., and A.D. Baxter-Jones. 1995. Common skeletal injuries in young athletes. *Sports Medicine*, 19(2): 137-149.

10. Hejna, W.F., A. Rosenberg, D.J. Buturusis, and A. Krieger. 1982. The prevention of sports injuries in high school students through strength training. *National Strength Condition Association Journal*, 4(1), 28-31.

11. Micheli, L.J. 1986. Pediatric and adolescent sports injury: Recent trends. *Exercise and Sport Science Review*, 14, 359-374.

12. Gill, T.J., and L.J. Micheli. 1996. The immature athlete: Common injuries and overuse syndromes of the elbow and wrist. *Clinics Sports Medicine*, 15(2): 401-423.

13. Metcalf, J., and S. Roberts. 1993. Strength training and the immature athlete: An overview. *Pediatric Nursing*, 19(4): 325-332.

14. Micheli, L. 1988. Strength training in the young athlete. In *Competitive Sports for Children and Youth*, ed. E. Brown and C. Branta, 99-105. Champaign, IL: Human Kinetics.

15. Brady, T., B. Cahill, and L. Bodnar. 1982. Weight-training-related injuries in the high school athlete. *American Journal of Sports Medicine*, 10(1): 1-5.

16. Brown, E., and R. Kimball. 1983. Medical history associated with adolescent power lifting. *Pediatrics*, 72(5): 636-644.

17. Rains, C., A. Weltman, B. Cahill, C. Janney, S. Tippet, and F. Katch. 1987. Strength training for prepubescent males: Is it safe? *American Journal of Sports Medicine*, 15(5): 483-489.

18. Zaricznyj, B., L. Shattuck, T. Mast, R. Robertson, and G. D'Elia. 1980. Sports-related injuries in school-aged children. *American Journal of Sports Medicine*. 8(5): 318-324.

19. Hamill, B. 1994. Relative safety of weightlifting and weight training. *Journal of Strength and Conditioning Research*, 8(1): 53-57.

20. George, D., K. Stakiw, and C. Wright. 1989. Fatal accident with weightlifting equipment: Implications for safety standards. *Canadian Medical Association Journal*, 140(8): 925-926.

21. Faigenbaum, A.D., L.A. Miliken, and W.L. Westcott. 2003. Maximal strength testing in healthy children. *Journal of Strength and Conditioning Research*, 17(1): 162-166.

22. Conroy, B., W. Kraemer, C. Maresh, S. Fleck, M. Stone, A. Fry, P. Miller, and G. Dalsky. 1993. Bone mineral density in elite junior Olympic weightlifters. *Medicine and Science in Sports and Exercise*, 25(10): 1103-1109.

23. Fleck, S.J., P.M. Pattany, M.H. Stone, J.T. Kearney, W.J. Kraemer, J. Thrush, and K. Wong. 1993. Magnetic resonance imaging determination of left ventricular mass in elite junior Olympic weightlifters. *Medicine and Science in Sports and Exercise*, 25(4): 522-527.

24. Kraemer, W.J., A.C. Fry, B.J. Warren, M.H. Stone, S.J. Fleck, J.T. Kearney, B.P. Conroy, C.M. Maresh, C.A. Weseman, N.T. Triplett, and S.E. Gordon. 1992. Acute hormonal responses in elite junior weightlifters. *International Journal of Sports Medicine*, 13(2): 103-109.

25. Tharion, W.J., T.M. Rausch, E.A. Harman, and W.J. Kraemer. 1991. Effects of different resistance-exercise protocols on mood states. *Journal of Applied Sport Science Research*, 5(2): 60-65.

26. Kraemer, W., A. Fry, P. Frykman, B. Conroy, and J. Hoffman. 1989. Resistance training and youth. *Pediatric Exercise Science*, 1(4): 336-350.

27. Blimkie, C., J. Martin, D. Ramsay, D. Sale, and D. MacDougall. 1989. The effects of detraining and maintenance weight training on strength development in prepubertal boys. Abstract in *Canadian Journal of Sport Sciences*, 14: 104.

28. Blimkie, C.J. 1992. Resistance training during pre- and early puberty: Efficacy, trainability, mechanisms, and persistence. *Canadian Journal of Sport Sciences*, 17(4): 264-279.

29. Faigenbaum, A., W. Westcott, L. Micheli, A. Outerbridge, C. Long, R. LaRosa-Loud, and L. Zaichkowsky. 1996. The effects of strength training and detraining on children. *Journal of Strength and Conditioning Research*, 10(2): 109-114.

30. Ramsay, J.A., C.J.R. Blimkie, K. Smith, S. Gardner, J.D. MacDougall, and D.G. Sale. 1990. Strength training effects in prepubescent boys. *Medicine and Science in Sports and Exercise*, 22: 605-614.

31. Fukunga, T., K. Funato, and S. Ikegawa. 1992. The effects of resistance training on muscle area and strength in prepubescent age. *Annals of Physiological Anthropology*, 11(3): 357-364.

32. Mersch, F., and H. Stoboy. 1989. Strength training and muscle hypertrophy in children. In *Children and Exercise XIII*, ed. S. Oseid and K. Carlsen, 165-182. Champaign, IL: Human Kinetics.

CHAPTER 2

1. Suchomel, A. 2003. The biological age of prepubescent and pubescent children with low and high motor efficiency. *Anthropologischer Anzeiger*, 61(1): 67-77.

2. Loko, J., R. Aule, T. Sikkut, J. Ereline, and A. Viru. 2003. Age differences in growth and physical abilites in trained and untrained girls 10-17 years of age. *American Journal of Human Biology*, 15(1): 72-77.

3. Roemmich, J.N., R.J. Richmond, and A.D. Rogol. 2001. Consequences of sport training during puberty. *Journal of Endocrinological Investigations*, 24(9): 708-715.

4. Loucks, A.B. 1988. Osteoporosis prevention begins in childhood. In *Competitive Sports for Children and Youth: An Overview of Research and Issues*, ed. E.W. Brown and C.F. Bravta, 213-223. Champaign, IL: Human Kinetics.

5. Kontulainen, S.A., P.A. Kannus, M.E. Pasanen, H.T. Sievanen, A.O. Heinonen, P. Oja, and I. Vuori. 2002. Does previous participation in high-impact training result in residual bone gain in growing girls? One-year follow-up of a 9-month jumping intervention. *International Journal of Sports Medicine*, 23(8): 575-581.

6. Janz, K. 2002. Physical activity and bone development during childhood and adolescence: Implications for prevention of osteoporosis. *Minerva Pediatrics*, 54(2): 93-104.

7. MacKelvie, K.J., K.M. Khan, and H.A. McKay. 2002. Is there a critical period for bone response to weight-bearing exercise in children and adolescents? A systematic review. *British Journal of Sports Medicine*, 36: 250-257.

8. National Institutes of Health. 2000. Osteoporosis prevention, diagnosis, and therapy. *NIH Consensus Statement*, March 27-29, 17(1): 1-45.

9. Witzke, K.A., and C.M. Snow. 2000. Effects of plyometric jump training on bone mass in adolescent girls. *Medicine and Science in Sports and Exercise*, 32(6): 1051-1057.

10. Conroy, B.P., W.J. Kraemer, C.M. Maresh, and G.P. Dalsky. 1992. Adaptive responses of bone to physical activity. *Journal of Medicine, Exercise, Nutrition, and Health*, 1(2): 64-74.

11. Conroy, B., W. Kraemer, C. Maresh, S. Fleck, M. Stone, A. Fry, P. Miller, and G. Dalsky. 1993. Bone mineral density in elite junior Olympic weightlifters. *Medicine and Science in Sports and Exercise*, 25(10): 1103-1109.

12. Karlsson, M. 2002. Exercise increases bone mass in children but only insignificantly in adults. *Lakartidningen*, 99(32): 3400-3405.

13. Volek J.S., A.L. Gomez, T.P. Scheett, M.J. Sharman, D.N. French, M.R. Rubin, N.A. Ratamess, M.M. McGuigan, and W.J. Kraemer. 2003. Increasing fluid milk favorably affects bone mineral density responses to resistance training in adolescent boys. *Journal of the American Dietetic Association*, 103(10): 1353-1356.

14. Virvidakis, K., E. Georgiu, A. Korkotsidis, K. Ntalles, and C. Proukakis. 1990. Bone mineral content of junior competitive weightlifters. *International Journal of Sports Medicine*, 11: 244-246.

15. Boisseau, N., and P. Delamarche. 2000. Metabolic and hormonal responses to exercise in children and adolescents. *Sports Medicine*, 30(6): 405-422.

16. Bencke, J., R. Damsgaard, A. Saekmose, P. Jorgensen, K. Jorgensen, and K. Klausen. 2002. Anaerobic power and muscle strength characteristics of 11-year-old elite and non-elite boys and girls from gymnastics, team handball, tennis and swimming. *Scandinavian Journal of Medicine and Science in Sports*, 12(3): 171-178.

17. Poblano, A., S.J. Rothenberg, M.E. Fonseca, M.L. Cruz, T. Flores, and I. Zarco. Salivary testosterone and EEG spectra of 9- to 11-year-old male children. *Developmental Neuropsychology*, 23(3): 375-384.

18. Alway, S.E., J.D. MacDougall, D.G. Sale, J.R. Sutton, and A.J. McComas. 1988. Functional and structural adaptations in skeletal muscle of trained athletes. *Journal of Applied Physiology*, 64: 1114-1120.

19. Kraemer, W.J., S.A. Mazzetti, B.C. Nindl, L.A. Gotshalk, J.S. Volek, J.A. Bush, J.O. Marx, K. Dohi, A.L. Gómez, M. Miles, S.J. Fleck, R.U. Newton, and K. Häkkinen. 2001. Effect of resistance training on women's strength/power and occupational performances. *Medicine and Science in Sports and Exercise*, 33(6): 1011-1025.

20. Naughton, G., N.J. Farpour-Lambert, J. Carlson, M. Bradney, and E. Van Praagh. 2000. Physiological issues surrounding the performance of adolescent athletes. *Sports Medicine* 30(5): 309-325.

21. Mero, A., L. Jaakkola, and P.V. Komi. 1990. Serum hormones and physical performance capacity in young boy athletes during a 1-year training period. *European Journal of Applied Physiology*, 60(1): 32-37.

22. Hansen, L., J. Bangsbo, J. Twisk, and K. Klausen. 1999. Development of muscle strength in relation to training level and testosterone in young male soccer players. *Journal of Applied Physiology*, 87(3): 1141-1147.

23. Fahey, T.D., R. Rolph, P. Moungmee, J. Nagel, and S. Mortar. 1976. Serum testosterone, body composition, and strength of young adults. *Medicine and Science in Sports and Exercise*, 8: 31-34.

24. Kraemer, W.J., A.C. Fry, B.J. Warren, M.H. Stone, S.J. Fleck, J.T. Kearney, B.P. Conroy, C.M. Maresh, C.A. Weseman, N.T. Triplett, and S.E. Gordon. 1992. Acute hormonal responses in elite junior weightlifters. *International Journal of Sports Medicine*, 13(2): 103-109.

25. Kirkcaldy, B., R. Shephard, and R. Siefen. 2002. The relationship between physical activity and self-image and problem behaviour among adolescents. *Social Psychiatry and Psychiatric Epidemiology*, 37(11): 544-50.

26. Williams, P., and T. Cash. 2001. Effects of a circuit weight training program in the body images of college students. *International Journal of Eating Disorders*, 30(1): 75-82.

27. McCabe, M., and Ricciardelli, L. 2003. Body image and strategies to lose weight and increase muscle among boys and girls. *Health Psychology*, 22(1): 39-46.

28. Robbins, L., N. Pender, and A. Kazanis. 2003. Barriers to physical activity perceived by adolescent girls. *Journal of Midwifery and Women's Health*, 48(3): 206-12.

29. Prasad, S., and F. Cerny. 2002. Factors that influence adherence to exercise and their effectiveness: Application to cystic fibrosis. *Pediatric Pulmonology*, 34(1): 66-72.

30. Gordon-Larsen, P. 2001. Obesity-related knowledge, attitudes, and behaviors in obese and non-obese urban Philadelphia female adolescents. *Obesity Research*, 9(2): 112-118.

CHAPTER 3

1. Hogan, K.A., and R.H. Gross. 2003. Overuse injuries in pediatric athletes. *Orthopedic Clinics in North America*, 34(3): 405-15.

2. Jones, C.S., C. Christensen, and M. Young. 2000. Weight-training injury trends: A 20-year survey. *The Physician and Sportsmedicine*, 28(7): 1-9.

3. Reiff, G.G., W.R. Dixon, D. Jacoby, X.G. Ye, C.G. Spain, and P.A. Hunsicker. 1985. President's Council on Physical Fitness and Sports, *National School Population Fitness Survey* (Research Project 282-84-0086). Ann Arbor, MI: University of Michigan.

4. Fleck, S.J. 1999. Periodized strength training: A critical review. *Journal of Strength and Conditioning Research*, 13: 82-89.

5. Volek, J.S., A.L. Gomez, T.P. Scheett, M.J. Sharman, D.N. French, M.R. Rubin, N.A. Ratamess, M.M. McGuigan, W.J. Kraemer. 2003. Increasing fluid milk favorably affects bone mineral density responses to resistance training in adolescent boys. *Journal of the American Dietetic Association*, 103(10): 1353-1356.

6. Tharion, W.J., T.M. Rausch, E.A. Harman, and W.J. Kraemer. 1991. Effects of different resistance exercise protocols on mood states. *Journal of Applied Sport Science Research*, 5: 60-65.

7. Faigenbaum, A.D., L.A. Milliken, and W.L. Westcott. 2003. Maximal strength testing in healthy children. *Journal of Strength and Conditioning Research*, 17(1): 162-6.

8. Harman, E., J. Garhammer, and C. Pandorf. 2000. Administration, scoring, and interpretation of selected tests. In *Essentials of Strength and Conditioning*, ed. T.A. Baechle and R.W. Earle, 287-317. Champaign, IL: Human Kinetics.

9. Harman, E., and C. Pandorf. 2000. Principles of test selection and administration. In *Essentials of Strength and Conditioning*, ed. T.A. Baechle and R.W. Earle, 275-286. Champaign, IL: Human Kinetics.

CHAPTER 4

1. Yesalis, C.E., and V.S. Cowart. 1998. *The Steroids Game*. Champaign, IL: Human Kinetics.

2. Bahrke, M.S., and C.E. Yesalis, eds. 2002. *Performance-Enhancing Substances in Sport and Exercise*. Champaign, IL: Human Kinetics.

Index

About the Authors

William J. Kraemer's interest in strength training for young athletes started with his career as a junior high school teacher and coach in Wisconsin and Minnesota. Since 2001 he has served as a professor in the department of kinesiology working in the Human Performance Laboratory in the Neag School of Education at the University of Connecticut. He is also a professor in the department of physiology and neurobiology and a professor of medicine in the University of Connecticut's School of Medicine. He also holds an adjunct professorship at Edith Cowan University in Australia.

Dr. Kraemer was the John and Janice Fisher Endowed Chair in Exercise Physiology, Director of the Human Performance Laboratory, and a professor of physical education, biology, physiology, and health science at Ball State University in Muncie, Indiana. In addition, Dr. Kraemer is an adjunct professor at Indiana University Medical School. Prior to this appointment in 1998, he held the rank of professor of applied physiology at the Pennsylvania State University, where he had served since 1989 as director of the Laboratory for Sports Medicine in the department of kinesiology and was a member of the Noll Physiological Research Center. He also served as associate director for the Center for Cell Research at Penn State as well as the Director of Research in the Center for Sports Medicine.

Dr. Kraemer is a past president of the National Strength and Conditioning Association (NSCA) and was honored by the NSCA with their Outstanding Sports Scientist Award, Educator of the Year Award, and the NSCA's Lifetime Achievement Award. He is also a fellow in the American College of Sports Medicine. Dr. Kraemer is the current Editor-in-Chief of the *Journal of Strength and Conditioning Research*. He has authored and coauthored many articles and books on strength training athletes.

Steven J. Fleck is chair of the sport science department at Colorado College in Colorado Springs. Previously, he headed the physical conditioning program of the U.S. Olympic Committee; served as strength coach for the German Volleyball Association; and coached high school track, basketball, and football.

An internationally known expert on strength and anaerobic training, Fleck was a vice president of basic and applied research for the National Strength and Conditioning Association (NSCA). He is a fellow of the American College of Sports Medicine (ACSM). He was honored in 1991 as the NSCA Sport Scientist of the Year.

Fleck has authored many books and numerous articles on strength training and physical conditioning. He is also a columnist for *Muscular Development*.